QUICKEN® 2010
QuickSteps

About the Author

Bobbi Sandberg is an accountant and technical writer currently working in and enjoying the Pacific Northwest. A popular speaker and trainer, she has used and taught Quicken since its debut in the '80s. This is the latest in the series of several books she has co-authored with her colleagues at Matthews Technology, among them *Quicken 2007 QuickSteps* and *Microsoft Office Access 2007 QuickSteps*.

She is known as the person who can make computer software "understandable." One of her recent students said, "Now I can easily track my finances and before, I couldn't comfortably balance my checkbook." Bobbi combines her ability to explain complex concepts in plain language with her in-depth understanding of computers and accounting to make using financial software as easy as writing a check. She wishes for each reader a "smooth and successful" financial life!

About the Contributing Author

Marty Matthews is a principal in Matthews Technology, a firm dedicated to making technology easy through books, articles, websites, and consulting. Over the last 25 years Matthews Technology has produced over 100 computer-related books selling more than a million and a half copies. See its website at http://matthewstechnology.com.

About the Technical Editor

Mary Higgins is an electrical engineer by education and she works as a systems analyst in IT at a biotech company in the San Francisco Bay area. She writes extensively for work—business process documents, FAQs, functional and technical specifications, etc. She is a long-time Quicken user, having used each version since 1999. Mary enjoys pushing the limits of what the software is intended to do—click every button, navigate every menu path, read the Help files, etc. She reads and posts on the Quicken forums as it's always interesting to see how others are using Quicken and the different approaches to resolving issues.

QUICKEN® 2010
QuickSteps

BOBBI SANDBERG

MARTY MATTHEWS

New York Chicago San Francisco
Lisbon London Madrid Mexico City
Milan New Delhi San Juan
Seoul Singapore Sydney Toronto

The McGraw·Hill Companies

Cataloging-in-Publication Data is on file with the Library of Congress

McGraw-Hill books are available at special quantity discounts to use as premiums and sales promotions, or for use in corporate training programs. To contact a representative, please e-mail us at bulksales@mcgraw-hill.com.

QUICKEN® 2010 QUICKSTEPS

1234567890   CCI CCI   019

ISBN   978-0-07-163336-9
MHID   0-07-163336-7

SPONSORING EDITOR / Megg Morin

EDITORIAL SUPERVISOR / Janet Walden

PROJECT MANAGER / Madhu Bhardwaj, Glyph International

ACQUISITIONS COORDINATOR / Meghan Riley

TECHNICAL EDITOR / Mary Higgins

COPY EDITOR / Lisa McCoy

PROOFREADER / Claire Splan

INDEXER / Claire Splan

PRODUCTION SUPERVISOR / Jean Bodeaux

COMPOSITION / Glyph International

ILLUSTRATION / Glyph International

ART DIRECTOR, COVER / Jeff Weeks

COVER DESIGNER / Pattie Lee

SERIES CREATORS / Marty and Carole Matthews

SERIES DESIGN / Bailey Cunningham

To Marty with deep gratitude and humble appreciation for all of the encouragement, support, and laughter.
And to Megg (and Cooper) for reminding me of the joy of friendship and the excitement of growing up.
And, as always and forever, to Sandy.

Contents at a Glance

Chapter 1 **Stepping into Quicken** 1
Install Quicken, use the Setup tab, add accounts, import from
Microsoft Money, get help, understand Quicken terms, exit Quicken

Chapter 2 **Personalizing Quicken** 31
Modify views, manage accounts, set preferences, add cash flow
accounts, setup online services, work with categories, backup data

Chapter 3 **Adding More Accounts** 69
Track investments, add investment accounts, set up assets,
loan setup

Chapter 4 **Using Quicken Every Day** 99
Set preferences, enter and print checks, create a split transaction,
locate transactions, set up printer

Chapter 5 **Taking Control with Quicken** 125
Work with memorized payees, memorize and schedule
transactions, use the calendar, set report preferences, create a report

Chapter 6 **Tracking Your Assets and Liabilities** 153
Link assets and liabilities, adjust loan rates and asset values, set up
alerts, work with reports, use the calculators

Chapter 7 **Keeping Your Records Up to Date** 177
Reconcile banking accounts, manually and online; find and resolve
errors; update asset and liability accounts

Chapter 8 **Managing Your Investments** 201
Download quotes, work with investment alerts, analyze accounts,
allocate assets, use performance research tools

Chapter 9 **Making Plans for Your Future** 225
Create your own plan in Quicken with your income, tax rate,
savings, investments, and other assets and liabilities; create a budget

Chapter 10 **Getting Ready for Tax Time** 257
Set up the Tax Planner, enter income, interest; dividends, and
capital gains; set tax alerts; create tax reports; find deductions

Index 281

Contents

Acknowledgments..xiv

Introduction XV

Chapter 1 **Stepping into Quicken** 1
    Upgrading Quicken...2
    Meet Quicken..2
        Determine the Version for You.....................................2
    Install Quicken 2010..3
        Install Quicken..3
    Get Started with Quicken 5
        Start Quicken..5
    Creating a Quick Start Shortcut for Quicken...............................6
        Set Up Quicken for the First Time...............................6
        Use the Setup Tab...15
        Understand the Home Tab......................................16
        Add Accounts Manually..18
    Using the Ticker Symbol Lookup 22
    Using the Address Book 23
        Find Help 23
    Importing from Microsoft Money 25
        Exit Quicken...25
    Use Quicken and Windows Basics......................................26
        Recognize Quicken Terms 26
    Finding More Keyboard Shortcuts 29
        Use Windows Tools...29

Chapter 2 **Personalizing Quicken** 31
    Customize the Home Page 32
        Modify the Main View 33
        Change the Account Bar 34
        Amend Your Views..35
        Manage Accounts...37
    Using Classic Menus 40
        Edit an Account...41
    Using the Quicken Calendar 43
        Set Preferences...44
    Add and Change Accounts 47
        Add Cash Flow Accounts 47
    Use Quicken Online..50
        Understand Online Services....................................51
    Deciding to Use Online Banking Services.................................53
        Set Up Online Banking..53
        Activate One Step Update 57
        Manage Your Passwords.......................................57
        Use Quicken Bill Pay 61

Understand Categories 61
    Work with Categories..62
    Add a New Category 64
   🖉 Using Tax-Line Assignments..66
   🔍 Deleting Categories 67
Protect Your Quicken Data 67
    Back Up Your Data to External Media 68

Chapter 3   **Adding More Accounts** 69

Understand Financial Terminology 69
Use the Investing Tab..70
    Track Investments 71
    Set Up a Standard Brokerage or IRA Account......................72
   🖉 Understanding Placeholders in Investment Accounts...........76
    Enter Your Holdings...76
    Set Up One Step Update 81
    Add a 401(k) or 403(b) Account 84
   🔍 Creating a Single Mutual Fund Account.............................85
Use the Net Worth Tab...86
    Work with the Net Worth Tab 87
    Set Up a House Account with a Mortgage.............................87
    Add Other Net Worth Accounts 92
   🔍 Deleting and Hiding Accounts 93
    Add Other Debt Accounts 93
    Use EasyStep Loan Setup 94
   🔍 Printing an Amortization Schedule.....................................96

Chapter 4   **Using Quicken Every Day** 99

Understand Basic Transactions 99
Establish Preferences for Your Registers 100
    Set Register Preferences 101
    Determine QuickFill Preferences 103
    Set Notify Preferences..104
    Set Preferences for Writing Checks 104
   🔍 Setting Downloaded Transaction Preferences 105
Work with the Register..106
    Enter a Check...107
    Print Checks with Quicken...108
   🔍 Entering a Deposit 112
    Create a New Transaction Category 112
   🔍 Changing, Voiding, or Deleting a Transaction...................113
Perform Activities with Check Registers 113
    Create a Split Transaction 113
    Transfer Funds from One Account to Another 115
    Locate Transactions 116
    Filter Transactions for More Information..............................117
   🔍 Sorting Transactions 118
    Attach Digital Images to a Transaction 118
    Set Up Your Printer and Print a Register..............................120
   🔍 Using the Windows Clipboard 121
    Use Other Banking Tab Registers 122

Chapter 5 **Taking Control with Quicken** 125

Memorize Your Entries 125
    Create a Memorized Payee..126
    Change Memorized Payees..127
    Use Renaming Rules for Downloaded Transactions 128
    Create and Memorize a Split Transaction Using Percentages................130
    Locking a Memorized Payee...131
Create Bill Reminders and Scheduled Transactions...................132
    Understand Scheduled Transactions 132
    Schedule a Transaction..133
    Understanding Scheduled Transaction Methods................................139
    Create a Scheduled Transaction from a Register.................................139
    Work with Scheduled Transactions...142
    Use the Calendar...143
    Showing Transactions on Your Calendar 147
    Scheduling Repeating Online Payments 148
Use Reports and Graphs..148
    Set Report Preferences..148
    Create a Standard Report...150
    Creating a Mini-Report..151
    Create a Standard Graph..151

Chapter 6 **Tracking Your Assets and Liabilities** 153

Work with Asset and Liability Accounts 154
    Link an Asset to a Liability Account 155
    Linking Multiple Liability Accounts to One Asset Account...................156
    Adjust the Value of an Asset 156
    Understanding Depreciation...157
Work with Loans...158
    Adjust the Interest Rate on a Loan 158
    Handle Other Loan Functions 159
    Making Additional Principal Payments..161
Understand Alerts..165
    Deleting an Alert...166
    Set Up Alerts..166
Create Custom Reports..166
    Customize an Existing Report 166
    Save a Customized Report 170
    Manage Custom Folders for Saved Reports 171
    Recalling a Saved Report..172
    Add a Report to the Quicken Toolbar..172
    Create a Net Worth Report...173
    Use the Refinance and Loan Calculators..173

Chapter 7 **Keeping Your Records Up to Date**................. 177

Reconcile Checking and Savings Accounts...................................178
    Reconcile Quicken with Your Bank's Paper Statement...........................178
    Make Corrections in the Statement Summary Window.........................183
    Reconciling for the First Time 184
    Deal with Unrecorded Items..185
    Using a Quicken Adjustment..186
    Reconcile Credit Card Statements..186

5

6

7

Activating Automatic Reconciliation...188
Finding and Resolving Credit Card Errors...189
Reconcile Investment Accounts..189
Reconcile an Investment Account to a Paper Statement.........................189
Reconcile a Single Mutual Fund Account..190
Updating Prices Manually from a Paper Statement.....................................192
Update 401(k) Accounts...193
Understanding How Quicken Works with 401(k)/403(b) Accounts......195
Reconcile Property & Debt Accounts 196
Update an Asset or Liability Account..197
Use the Find And Replace Dialog Box..198
Watch for Escrow Discrepancies...199

Chapter 8 **Managing Your Investments** 201
Understand the Investing Tab..202
Download Current Quotes...203
Set Up Quicken.com...203
Customizing Your Quicken Toolbar..204
Use Quicken.com..204
Understanding Quicken.com Tools...206
Explore the Performance Subtab 206
Use the Growth Of $10,000 Utility..206
Customizing the Date Range..208
Filter the Average Annual Return Analysis 208
Allocate Your Assets...210
Scheduling One Step Updates...214
Work with the Portfolio Tab 214
Understand Portfolio Terms...214
Customize Your Portfolio View 214
Setting Options in Your Portfolio View 216
Work with Investing Tools..216
Use the Buy/Sell Preview Tool..217
Estimate Capital Gains..217
Use the Portfolio Analyzer 219
Open Online Research Tools 220
Manage Your Security List..222
Working with Your Watch List...223

Chapter 9 **Making Plans for Your Future** 225
Work with Assumptions...226
Understand How to Plan with Quicken..226
Enter Information About Yourself...227
Understanding Your Social Security Retirement Age 228
Enter Income Information and Your Tax Rate 228
Estimating Inflation for Your Plan..232
Consider Savings, Investments, and Rate of Return 233
Include Checking and Savings Accounts...233
Entering Your Expected Rate of Return..234
Include Investment Accounts...234
Work with Homes and Other Assets...234

Associating Income with an Asset in Your Plan.......................................237
Use the Loans and Debt Planner 238
Figure Your Living Expenses 239
Planning to Pay for College...241
Understand the Plan Results..241
Use the Planners...243
Use the Debt Reduction Planner...244
Using What If's 248
Work with the Spending Planner 249
Use the Calculators, Budgets, and Other Tools.....................................251
Get Quick Answers with Calculators..251
Create a Budget...251
Work with Your Budget 254

Chapter 10 **Getting Ready for Tax Time** 257

Use the Tax Planner..258
Enter the Tax Planner Options..259
Enter Income into the Tax Planner 261
Using the Tax Line in Categories..262
Enter Interest, Dividend, and Business Income 262
Enter Capital Gains...263
Determining the Type of Capital Gain..264
Work with Other Income or Losses...264
Work with Income Adjustments and Deductions....................................266
Deducting State Sales Tax..269
Update Your Federal Withholdings 269
Work with the Tax Center...271
Assign Tax-Related Expenses...272
See Your Taxable Income 273
Use Tax Tools 273
Creating Tax Reports 274
Use the Tax Category Audit 274
Use the Deduction Finder..275
Use the Itemized Deduction Estimator...276
Use the Tax Withholding Estimator 278

Index 281

Acknowledgments

The two names on the cover of this book are only part of the story. This project would not have been possible were it not for the efforts of an entire team.

- **Megg Morin**, acquisitions editor at McGraw-Hill, who is always encouraging, creative, helpful, and supportive.

- **Mary Higgins**, technical editor, who made the project better with each suggestion and creative idea.

- **Meghan Riley**, McGraw-Hill acquisitions coordinator, who supported and encouraged in every way.

- **Janet Walden**, McGraw-Hill editorial supervisor, for her quick eye, rapid response, and gracious attitude.

- **Madhu Bhardwaj** of Glyph International, who made deadlines, pressure, and time differences disappear with her encouragement and support.

- **Lisa McCoy**, copy editor, caught widely varied inconsistencies. Her suggested improvements to the text always added to its readability!

- Several banking people, who supplied information and support in so many ways. Special thanks to Kristen Haag and Dee Tarr of US Bank, and Anne Bobinac and Rob Mellish of Whidbey Island Bank.

- The entire Quicken 2010 beta team at Intuit, especially Eddy Wu and Dale Knievel who kept long hours and helped immeasurably. The team provided us with the great product from which this book stems.

—Bobbi Sandberg and Marty Matthews

Introduction

QuickSteps books are recipe books for computer users. They answer the question "How do I...?" by providing quick sets of steps to accomplish the most common tasks in a particular program. The sets of steps are the central focus of the book. QuickSteps sidebars show you how to quickly do many small functions or tasks that support the primary functions. Notes, Tips, and Cautions augment the steps, yet they are presented in such a manner as to not interrupt the flow of the steps. The brief introductions are minimal rather than narrative, and numerous illustrations and figures, many with callouts, support the steps.

QuickSteps books are organized by function and the tasks needed to perform that function. Each function is a chapter. Each task, or "How To," contains the steps needed for accomplishing the function along with relevant Notes, Tips, Cautions, and screenshots. Tasks will be easy to find through:

- The Table of Contents, which lists the functional areas (chapters) and tasks in the order they are presented

- A How To list of tasks on the opening page of each chapter

- The index with its alphabetical list of terms used in describing the functions and tasks

- Color-coded tabs for each chapter or functional area with an index to the tabs in the Contents at a Glance.

Conventions Used in This Book

QuickSteps uses several conventions designed to make the book easier for you to follow. Among these are

- A 🖋 in the Table of Contents or the How To list references a QuickFacts sidebar in a chapter.

- A 🔍 in the Table of Contents or the How To list references a QuickSteps sidebar in a chapter.

- **Bold type** is used for words on the screen that you are to do something with, such as click **Save As** or **Open**.

- *Italic* type is used for a word or phrase that is being defined or otherwise deserves special emphasis.

- <u>Underlined</u> type is used for text that you are to type from the keyboard. SMALL CAPITAL LETTERS are used for keys on the keyboard such as ENTER and SHIFT.

- When you are expected to enter a command, you are told to press the key(s). If you are to enter text or numbers, you are told to type them. Specific letters or numbers to be entered will be underlined.

How to...

- Determine the Version for You
- Upgrading Quicken
- Install Quicken
- Start Quicken
- Creating a Quick Start Shortcut for Quicken
- Set Up Quicken for the First Time
- Use the Setup Tab
- Understand the Home Tab
- Add Accounts Manually
- Using the Ticker Symbol Lookup
- Using the Address Book
- Find Help
- Importing from Microsoft Money
- Exit Quicken
- Recognize Quicken Terms
- Finding More Keyboard Shortcuts
- Use Windows Tools

Chapter 1
Stepping into Quicken

Welcome to Quicken 2010! As its name implies, Quicken is a personal financial tool—an easy way to account for all of your income, expenses, loan payments, assets, and liabilities. Much more than a digital check register or a financial organizer, Quicken can give you peace of mind and a way to control your money instead of letting your money control you. With Quicken, you can print checks; pay bills online; reconcile your bank, credit card, and investment account statements; track your expenses; and plan your financial future.

This chapter introduces you to the various versions of Quicken, shows you how to install it on your computer, explains some Quicken terms, reviews some Windows concepts, walks you through Quicken Setup, and shows you how to close the program when you have finished using it. Even if you are an experienced user of Quicken, it might be good to review this chapter to see some of the new features of Quicken 2010.

Meet Quicken

Quicken 2010 helps you set up your checking, savings, investment, and credit card accounts; enter transactions into those accounts; balance or reconcile the accounts to the institution's records; print checks; create reports; design and print graphs; manage your debt; and see tips to help save your hard-earned dollars. If you have an Internet connection, you can download information from your bank, investment house, and credit card company. Quicken also makes it quick and easy to transfer your data to TurboTax at year-end to make tax preparation less stressful.

Determine the Version for You

Quicken 2010 comes in several versions: the Starter edition, Deluxe, Premier, Home and Business, and Rental Property Manager. The version you select will depend on the tasks you want Quicken 2010 to perform.

- **Quicken 2010 Starter Edition** is often the best choice for new users. It lets you track your bank accounts, credit cards, investment accounts, and loans. With an Internet connection, you can work online with any of your accounts. It gives you links to insurance and mortgage information, as well as some handy budgeting tools.

- **Quicken 2010 Deluxe** gives you more power to make future financial decisions. It includes all of the features in the Starter edition and offers planning tools for taxes, college, and other major financial events. It features free investment information, debt reduction tips, and a Home Inventory and Emergency Records Organizer.

- **Quicken 2010 Premier** adds investment reports, comparisons, analyses, and a report generator for income tax Schedules A, B, and D.

- **Quicken 2010 Home & Business**, in addition to everything in the Premier edition, helps you run your small business and supplies business estimates, invoices, vehicle mileage tracking, and a host of other features. It prints business financial statements in the proper forms, creates customer and vendor lists, and helps you track specific projects and jobs.

You can upgrade any of the first three versions directly from your computer with an Internet connection. See the "Upgrading Quicken" QuickSteps.

UICKSTEPS

UPGRADING QUICKEN

If you purchase any version of Quicken 2010 and later want to upgrade, you can do so easily with your Internet connection.

1. Click **Help** on the Menu bar.

2. Depending on the Quicken version you have, you will see one or more of the following options for upgrading. Click the one that is correct for you:

   - **Which Quicken Is Best For You?** In either Quicken Starter or Deluxe edition, you can read about the other versions and decide if you want to upgrade.

Continued . . .

UICKSTEPS

UPGRADING QUICKEN (Continued)

- **Add More Investing & Tax Tools.** In either Quicken Starter or Deluxe edition, you can read about Quicken Premier and decide if you want to upgrade.

- **Add Business Tools Or Add Rental Property Tools.** In Quicken Starter, Deluxe, and Premier editions, you can read about additional editions for your home business or rental property and decide if you want to upgrade.

3. The window displayed by your choice in step 2 shows the features of the upgrades available to you. Select the upgrade you want. A Quicken web page opens where you can order your upgrade. Click **Products** to choose the upgraded product you want. Complete the order form, which will require a credit card for payment.

4. After your order has been accepted, Quicken will send you an e-mail to confirm your order with an *unlock code* to enter. The "unlock code" is the group of numbers or letters sent by Quicken when you add features to your Quicken version.

5. Click **Help** and then click **Unlock**.

6. You are prompted to either go online to unlock your file automatically or to enter the code from your confirmation e-mail.

Install Quicken 2010

Quicken 2010 can be installed on your computer for the first time, or it can update an earlier version. Either way, you need only follow the directions in a series of windows and dialog boxes to complete the task.

Install Quicken

To install Quicken:

1. Put the Quicken 2010 CD in a CD or DVD drive. Follow the installation instructions that appear on the screen. If you do not see the installation instructions, browse to the appropriate CD/DVD drive letter, and double-click the install.exe file. If you don't see the words "install.exe," you may see a CD icon with "install" or "install.exe" below it. In Microsoft Windows Vista or Windows 7, you may be asked if you want to allow this software to make changes to your computer. Given that you do, take the necessary actions to proceed.

2. Click **Next** to begin the installation. The InstallShield Wizard dialog box appears. Click **Next**.

3. The license agreement appears. Use the vertical scroll bar (see "Use Windows Tools" later in this chapter) to read through the license agreement, and click **I Agree To The**

Terms Of if you agree to its terms. If you do not accept the license agreement, you cannot go forward and Quicken 2010 will not be installed.

4. Clear the **Help Us Make Quicken Better** check box if you do not want Intuit to download statistical information about your use (it is done anonymously without revealing any of your personal information). If you aren't sure, click **Learn More** to read about what this means.

5. Click **Next**. If you want to install the program to its default location, click Next again. If you want to install the program in a location other than the default folder, click Change, and then:

   a. The Change Current Destination Folder dialog box appears. The default is a folder named "Quicken" in your Program Files folder, which displays at the bottom of the dialog box. Click the **Up One Level** icon to change the location of your Quicken folder. The Program Files folder appears in the Look In field.

   b. Click the **Up One Level** icon again to create a folder on another location. Click the New Folder icon to create a Quicken folder at your chosen location. Click **OK** when you have completed the task. You are returned to the Destination Folder dialog box. Click **Next**.

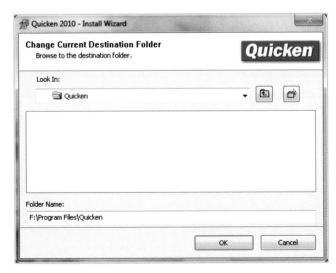

NOTE

Quicken 2010 does not allow more than one version of Quicken on your computer. You may install Deluxe or Premium edition, 2009 or 2010 version, but not more than one.

6. In all cases, the Ready To Install The Program dialog box appears. If you have a previous version of Quicken installed on your computer, it will be uninstalled before Quicken 2010 is installed.

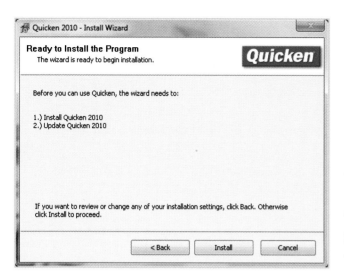

7. Quicken will install any current updates during the installation process.

8. If you want to make any changes before installation begins, click **Back**. Otherwise, click **Install** to continue.

Installation takes a few minutes, depending on the speed of your computer. A progress bar displays to let you know how it is proceeding.

9. When the installation and any updates are complete, the Installation Complete dialog box appears. Note the **Launch Quicken 2010** check box. To start Quicken now, click **Done**. The Quicken Home tab's Main View window appears.

10. If you clear the "Launch Quicken 2010" check box, and click **Done**, the wizard closes and you return to your desktop.

When the installation has finished, remove the CD from its drive and store it in a safe place. Should you ever need to reinstall the program, you will need the disk.

Get Started with Quicken

As part of the installation, Quicken places a number of icons on your desktop. With them, you can order a free credit report and check your credit score, apply for a credit card through Quicken, and get one month bill-paying for free. You also have a shortcut to start the program.

Start Quicken

You can start Quicken 2010 in several different ways:

- Double-click the **Quicken** icon on the Windows desktop.
- Click the **Start** button on the Windows taskbar, click **All Programs**, click **Quicken 2010**, and then click **Quicken 2010** again.
- Click the **Quicken 2010** icon on the taskbar (Windows 7) or on the Quick Launch toolbar (Windows Vista or XP) on the Windows taskbar, as explained in the "Creating a Quick Start Shortcut for Quicken" QuickSteps.

Whatever method you use, whether you click an icon or use the Start menu, Quicken 2010 opens.

QUICKSTEPS

CREATING A QUICK START SHORTCUT FOR QUICKEN

Depending on the version of Windows you have (7, Vista, or XP), you can create a quick way to start Quicken without opening the Start menu or locating its icon on the desktop.

WINDOWS 7

In Windows 7, you want to "pin" Quicken to the taskbar at the bottom of the window.

1. Start Quicken in any way described earlier.

2. Right-click the **Quicken** icon on the taskbar, and click **Pin This Program To Taskbar**.

When you close Quicken, the icon will stay on the taskbar; to start it again, you only need to click the icon.

WINDOWS VISTA AND WINDOWS XP

In Windows Vista or Windows XP, you want to add Quicken to the Quick Launch toolbar. The Quick Launch toolbar, located just to the right of the Start button on the Windows taskbar, allows you to cover your desktop with programs you are running and still quickly access your important programs with a single click. To create a shortcut on your Quick Launch toolbar:

1. Right-click a blank area of the Windows taskbar to display the taskbar menu.

2. Click **Toolbars**, and, if it is not already selected, click **Quick Launch** to activate the Quick Launch toolbar.

3. Ensure that **Lock The Taskbar** is unchecked. If the check mark appears, click **Lock the Taskbar** to turn off the check mark.

4. Drag the **Quicken** icon from the desktop to the Quick Launch toolbar. A small I-beam appears along with a shadow of the Quicken icon.

Continued . . .

Set Up Quicken for the First Time

If you have never used Quicken before, there are two ways to get started. The quickest way is to use the Main View Get Started button to enter your main checking account. However, if you use the Setup tab, Quicken will be able to give you a complete overview of your financial standing. Either way, the program is easy to start. If you choose the Main View option, start here:

1. After the installation is complete, the Welcome To Quicken 2010 dialog box appears. If you have not used Quicken before, click **I Am New To Quicken**, and click **Next**.

2. The Main View Quicken window under the Home tab appears, as seen in Figure 1-1. Click the **Get Started** button to begin.

Figure 1-1: Quicken's Home tab Main View helps you get started quickly.

QUICKSTEPS

CREATING A QUICK START SHORTCUT FOR QUICKEN *(Continued)*

5. Drag the I-beam to where you want the Quicken icon, and then release the mouse button. Your icon appears on the Quick Launch toolbar.

6. If you are using Windows 7, ensure the taskbar is unlocked and then simply drag the Quicken icon from the desktop to the taskbar.

Toolbars	▶
Cascade windows	
Show windows stacked	
Show windows side by side	
Show the desktop	
Start Task Manager	
Lock the taskbar	
Properties	

SET UP A BANK ACCOUNT WITH ONLINE SERVICES

The first step to quickly begin using Quicken is to set up your main checking account.

1. From the Home tab, click **Get Started** to open the Account Setup dialog box.

2. The Account Setup dialog box asks for the name of the bank where you have your main checking account, as seen in Figure 1-2. Quicken uses this information to determine whether your bank offers online services.

3. Enter the first few letters of your bank's name. A drop-down list appears. Choose your bank from the list, or, if your institution is not listed, look for another spelling or alternate name. For example, you might consider your bank's name to be Maintown Bank, while it is listed as Main Town Bank.

4. Click **Next**. Quicken attempts to obtain information about your bank online.

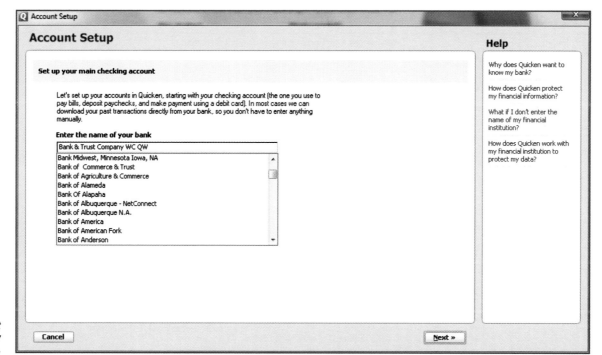

*Figure 1-2: **Quicken opens a list when you type the first few letters of your bank's name.***

5. After Quicken has gotten information about your financial institution, you are prompted to log in to your account by entering the user name and password issued to you by your bank, as seen in Figure 1-3. Fill out the information that identifies you to your bank to activate the account for downloading into Quicken, and click **Next**. Depending on your financial institution and your accounts, you may be asked for additional information here.

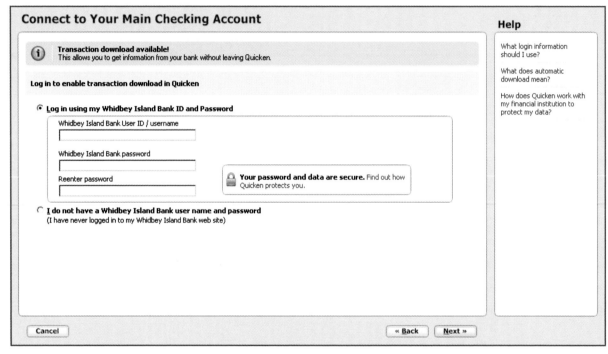

Figure 1-3: *Your bank issues you a user name and password so you can download transactions into Quicken to save time.*

6. If you do not yet have a user name and password, or if you do not want to download your transactions, click **I Don't Want To Download Transactions From (the name of your institution)**. Proceed to "Set Up a Bank Account Manually" next in this chapter.

7. Quicken connects to your financial institution and displays your accounts. By default, all of the accounts are selected to be added into Quicken. Clear the check box for any accounts you do not want to add. Click **Account Nickname** to type the name by which you identify this account. Click **Next**.

8. Quicken retrieves the data from your financial institution and enters transactions into a new Quicken account. The number of transactions that are downloaded depends on your bank. Some banks will download transactions for the last 60 days, while others download up to a year's worth of transactions. After the download is complete, you may add another bank or credit card account or start using Quicken. To start using Quicken, click **Done**.

SET UP A BANK ACCOUNT MANUALLY

You can set up accounts manually if your bank does not offer online services or you do not have an Internet connection. Follow steps 1 through 4 in "Set Up a Bank Account with Online Services" earlier in this chapter. Then:

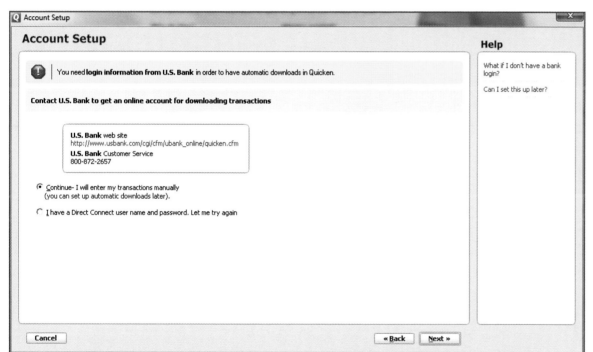

1. Click **Next**.

2. If your bank offers online services and you have not entered a user name and/or password, Quicken displays contact information about your institution. Otherwise, click **I Don't Want To Download Transactions From (the name of your institution)**, and click **Next**.

3. If you have a user name and password, click **I Have A Direct Connection User Name And Password. Let Me Try Again** to attempt to enter your information again, as shown in Figure 1-4. You are returned to the login dialog box.

4. Otherwise, click **Continue** to set up your account and add its transactions manually.

Figure 1-4: *You can choose to enter your account information manually even if your bank offers automatic downloads into Quicken.*

NOTE

If your bank is a large institution with many branches, you may see a dialog box indicating that Quicken needs to know the correct branch.

NOTE

Quicken protects your privacy by using secure Internet technology and encryption during any online transmission. For more information about Quicken's privacy policies, click **How Does Quicken Protect My Financial Information?**

NOTE

Some financial institutions have user names and passwords for online activity, such as online bill pay, that are different from the passwords required for Web access. Ensure that you have the correct user name and password for both activities. If you are unsure, check with your financial institution.

NOTE

Until some payments have been made, Quicken cannot create an accurate Estimate From Last n Payments figure.

5. Enter the name you would like to use for this account. By default, Quicken uses the type of account as the account name. For example, if you are setting up your first checking account, Quicken will call the account "Checking." Click **Next**.

6. Enter the date of your last bank statement and the ending balance shown on it. Click **Next**.

7. You may add another bank or credit card account or start using Quicken. To start using Quicken, click **Done**.

What Next?

Add another account	
You can add another account, like a checking account or credit card.	Add a credit card...
	Add a checking or savings...

| Or, you can start using Quicken now. (You can always add more accounts later.) | Start using Quicken |

ADD RECURRING BILLS

From the Home tab, click **Get Started** in the Stay On Top Of Monthly Bills section to enter the bills you pay every month. Quicken uses the downloaded transactions to display a set of suggested recurring bills and help you schedule your payments so you will never have another late fee. If you have not downloaded your transactions from your bank, you can still add your monthly bills.

1. Click **Add A Bill** to display the Add Bill Reminder dialog, as seen in Figure 1-5. Select from the drop-down list or enter the name of the payee in the Pay To field.

2. In the Amount field, keep the default **Fixed Amount** if the amount you pay every month is the same. Otherwise, click **Variable Amount** if the payment varies from month to month, such as your electric bill.

   a. If you choose Variable Amount, you can change the estimated amount. Click **Change** to open the Change Estimate dialog box.

   b. Choose **Do Not Estimate** if you want to enter the amount of the bill each month when you pay it.

   c. Choose **Estimated Amount** and enter an amount if you want to estimate on your own.

   d. Choose **Estimate From Last n Payments** if you want Quicken to enter an amount based on what you've paid the last few times. You can change the number of payments from which Quicken estimates by using the spinner or entering a number.

Add Bill Reminder

* Required fields **Help**

Who

Pay to* [Puget Sound Energy ⬥] [Address...]

Amount* ○ Fixed amount

○ Variable amount
Estimated amount: 135.00 (change)

How

Pay from account* [Checking ▾]

Payment method* [Manual Payment ▾]

You will pay this via check, cash, web site, etc.
(Payment will not be sent from Quicken) More...

Track Spending

Category [Utilities:Gas & Electric ⬥] [Split...]

Memo [   ]

When

Next due date* [8/10/2009 📅]

Remind me 3 days in advance (change)

How often?* [Monthly ▾]

● The 10th of every month

○ The [Second ▾] [Thursday ▾] of every month

○ The last day of every month

End on No end date (change)

Delivery method [Mail ▾]

Web site [Web site address] [Go]

[OK] [Cancel]

Help

What is a bill reminder?

What information do I need to enter?

What is the difference between a fixed and variable amount?

Why would I track a bill in Quicken?

Why should I select payment methods?

Why should I select delivery methods?

Why should I use categories?

Why should I use tags?

Can I change the reminder details later?

Will scheduling my bills duplicate my transactions in Quicken?

Can I see my reminders in Outlook?

Figure 1-5: The Add Bill Reminder dialog box helps you remember your monthly bills.

TIP

Categories are organizational tools to group similar information. For example, all payments to the phone company could be put into the Telephone category. Quicken supplies a number of categories with the program, but you can add new ones or delete those you don't want to use. Categories are handy for preparing taxes, budgeting, and analyzing where you are spending and receiving money.

e. Choose **Estimate From One Year Ago** if this is an annual payment and you want Quicken to find the amount from a year ago.

f. Click **OK** when you have completed the Change Estimate dialog box.

3. In the Pay From Account field, select the account from which you want to pay this bill.

4. Move to the **Payment Method** field. This field has a drop-down list from which you can make a selection. Click the down arrow to see the list, and use the vertical scrollbar to make your choice.

5. Enter the method by which this payment is to be delivered. Press the **DOWN ARROW** to see your options. Press **TAB** to type the payee's website if you choose. Otherwise, select or enter a category. Categories are discussed in depth in Chapter 2.

6. Enter any memo you want to appear when you pay this bill, such as your account number.

2 3 4 5 6 7 8 9 10

CAUTION

Some window envelopes allow memo information to be seen. If you mail checks in window envelopes, it is better not to put your account number in the memo line to ensure your privacy.

7. Enter the next date this bill is due. You can ask Quicken to remind you in advance in case you want to transfer money from one account to another to pay this bill. Click **Change** to open the Change Reminder Options dialog box.

   a. Enter the number of days in advance you want Quicken to remind you of this bill's due date in the Remind Me field. You may use the spinner or type in a number.

   b. Click **Automatically Enter The Transaction In Register** if the amount is taken from your account automatically. Insurance payments are often handled in this manner.

   c. Click **Use Only Business Days For Reminder Days** if you want Quicken to create a reminder using Monday through Friday only.

   d. Click **OK** to return to the Add Bill Reminder dialog box.

8. Click the down arrow in the How Often field to open the drop-down list to tell Quicken when this bill is due. Depending on which you choose, Quicken displays an estimated payment date, which you can adjust as necessary.

9. Tell Quicken when to end the series of payments. If there is an ending date, click **Change** to open the End Reminders dialog box.

   a. Click **End On** to enter the final payment date.

   b. Type a number or use the spinner to tell Quicken to stop reminding you after a certain number of reminders.

   c. Click **OK** to return to the Add Bill Reminder dialog box.

10. Click **OK** to return to the Stay On Top Of Monthly Bills dialog box.

11. Click **Add A Bill** to add another bill, or click **Next** to continue.

ADD INCOME

The Review Income dialog box reviews the income that was displayed when you downloaded your transactions. If you chose not to download, you can enter your paycheck or other income now.

1. Click **Add A Paycheck** to open the Set Up Paycheck dialog box, as seen in Figure 1-6.

2. Type the name of the company from whom you receive your paycheck. If you do not receive a paycheck, enter "Social Security" or some other name that represents this income source.

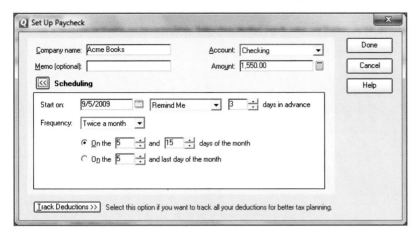

Figure 1-6: ***Use the Set Up Paycheck dialog box to enter your paychecks.***

3. Press **TAB** to move to the Memo field. Enter any additional information in this optional field.

4. Press **TAB** to move to the Account field. Enter the name of the bank account into which this income is deposited. Click the down arrow to see a drop-down list of your accounts.

5. Press **TAB** to move to the Amount field. Enter the amount of income you receive. If you do not receive the same amount each time, enter an average.

6. Press **TAB** to move to Scheduling, and then press **TAB** again to move to the Start On date. Type the date on which this income begins (usually your next pay date) in the Start On field. You may also click the small calendar icon to the right of the field and choose a date.

7. Press **TAB** to move to the Remind Me field. From the drop-down list, tell Quicken if you want to be reminded to enter this income amount or whether Quicken should enter it automatically on that date. If you choose Remind Me, enter the number of days in advance of the pay date you want to be reminded.

8. Press **TAB** to move to the Frequency field to tell Quicken how often you will be receiving this income. Click the down arrow to open a drop-down list from which to choose.

9. Click **Track Deductions** to open the Set Up Paycheck dialog box to track deductions from your paycheck.

ADD PAYCHECK INFORMATION

By using information from your regular paycheck, Quicken can create tax reports, help you plan for taxes, and export information to TurboTax for year-end tax reporting. If you have entered information in the Review Income section, it will appear in this dialog box, as seen in Figure 1-7. Otherwise, to set up a paycheck:

1. Type the name of your employer in the Company Name field if it isn't already there.

2. Press **TAB** to move to the optional Memo field. If you choose to leave this field empty, press **TAB** to move to the Account field. Type the name of the account, or press the down arrow to choose the account where this income is deposited if the current information is not correct.

Set Up Paycheck

Company name: Acme Books   Account: Checking
Memo (optional):

<< Scheduling

Start on: 8/26/2009   Remind Me   3 days in advance

Frequency: Twice a month

◉ On the 9 and 26 days of the month
○ On the 11 and last day of the month

Done
Cancel
Help

<< Track Net Only   Select this option if you only want to track net deposits from this paycheck.

Earnings

Name	Category	Amount		
Salary	Salary	1,550.00	Edit	Delete
Total		1,550.00		

Add Earning ▼

Pre-Tax Deductions

Name	Category/Account	Amount
Total		0.00

Add Pre-Tax Deduction ▼

Taxes

Name	Category	Amount		
Federal Tax	Tax:Fed	0.00	Edit	Delete
State Tax	Tax:State	0.00	Edit	Delete
Social Security (FICA)	Tax:Soc Sec	0.00	Edit	Delete
Medicare Tax	Tax:Medicare	0.00	Edit	Delete
Disability (SDI)	Tax:SDI	0.00	Edit	Delete
Total		0.00		

Add Tax Item ▼

After-Tax Deductions

Name	Category/Account	Amount
Total		0.00

Add After-Tax Deduction ▼

Deposit Accounts

Account	Memo	Amount
Checking	Primary Account	1,550.00

Add Deposit Account

Net Pay		1,550.00
W2 Gross		1,550.00

*Figure 1-7: **Quicken can track your salary, taxes, and other deductions when you enter your paycheck information.***

3. By default, the Scheduling section appears. Press the left-arrow box to close that section if you have already entered the information, or enter the dates and frequency in the appropriate fields.

4. Click **Track Net Only** if you do not want to keep track of your payroll deductions. However, if you want to simplify your tax preparation and track your tax withholdings, take the time to enter your deductions now.

5. Click **Edit** in the Earnings section to enter your gross salary if it is not currently there. Click **Add Earning** to choose another type of regular earnings from a drop-down list. For example, if you receive a regular commission each pay period, enter that as well.

6. Click each item on your paycheck to enter your salary, taxes, and other deductions. Click **Done** to close the window.

7. You may be prompted to enter year-to-date information. If you choose to enter that data, follow the prompts. Otherwise, click **I Do Not Want To Enter This Information**, and click **OK**. Click **Done** to close the dialog box and return to the Stay On Top Of Monthly Bills dialog box.

8. Click **Add Other Income** to add additional income items, or click **Done** to close the dialog box and return to the Home tab's Main View.

Enter Year-to-Date Information

Do you want to enter the year-to-date amounts for this paycheck? Quicken will use the year-to-date amounts in the Tax Planner to show your complete tax picture and help with tax planning.

○ I want to enter the year-to-date information
◉ I do not want to enter this information

OK   Help

SET GOALS

The next section helps you set goals for saving money. Click **Get Started** in the Set Spending Goals To Save Money section. The Review Your Spending Goals dialog box appears. Quicken suggests budgeting in several areas. To set monthly goals in each area:

1. Type your goal in the Suggested Monthly Goal field. Click **Apply** to set the amount.

2. Press **TAB** to move to the next category. You may choose 0 if you do not want to set a goal.

3. Click **Choose Categories To Watch** to open the Choose Categories dialog box.

4. Click each category for which you want to set a goal. Click **OK** when you have chosen all the categories to return to the Review Your Spending Goals dialog box.

5. Click **Done** to return to the Home tab's Main View window.

Use the Setup Tab

Quicken Setup walks you through the setup process. It takes a bit more time than using the Home tab's Get Started buttons, but you will have a more complete financial picture if you use this procedure. The Setup process walks you through a series of questions that will tailor the program to fit your needs.

1. Click the **Setup** tab to access the dialog box seen in Figure 1-8. You may also click **Tools** on the Menu bar and click **Go To Setup**. In either case, the Setup tab opens to the Quicken Setup window.

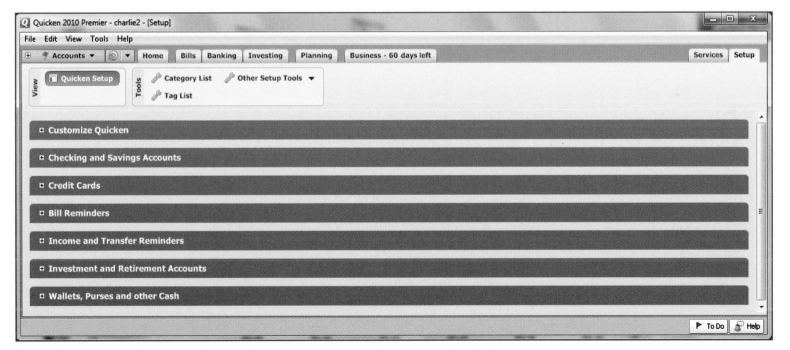

*Figure 1-8: **Use Quicken Setup to ensure that all of your financial information is entered into Quicken.***

2. In the Customize Quicken section, select your appropriate check boxes in the Tax Status area. Set any preferences that you need, and select which tab to display when Quicken starts. Additional information about customizing preferences is covered in Chapter 2.

3. In the Checking And Savings section, add any accounts that have not yet been added. Follow the directions as shown in "Set Up a Bank Account Manually" earlier in this chapter.

4. Add credit cards and bill reminders as necessary.

5. Enter any income items that you have not yet added.

6. Add any additional assets, loans, or other debt.

7. Add any investment or retirement accounts that you have not yet entered.

8. Add any cash accounts, such as money you keep in your wallet or purse.

Understand the Home Tab

The Quicken Home tab's Main View provides a summary of all the information you have entered into Quicken. Figure 1-9 shows the default display of the Home page. You will learn how to customize it in Chapter 2. The Quicken Home page has two major sections: the Account Bar on the left that shows the summary of your accounts, and the Main View on the right. In the Main View pane, you determine what information is displayed. By default, the view displays the spending, bills, and budgeting information that you entered when you began using Quicken. You can change the items that appear in this section of the window and add account registers, transaction lists, and several other items. You will learn how to customize and create additional views in Chapter 2. Around these panes are a number of objects that are common to other Windows programs and include:

- The **title bar**, which contains the name of the program or folder in the window, and is used to drag the window around the screen.

- The **Menu bar**, which contains the menus that are available in the window. Click a menu to open it, and then click one of its options.

- The **Minimize button**, which decreases the size of the window so that you see it only as a task on the taskbar.

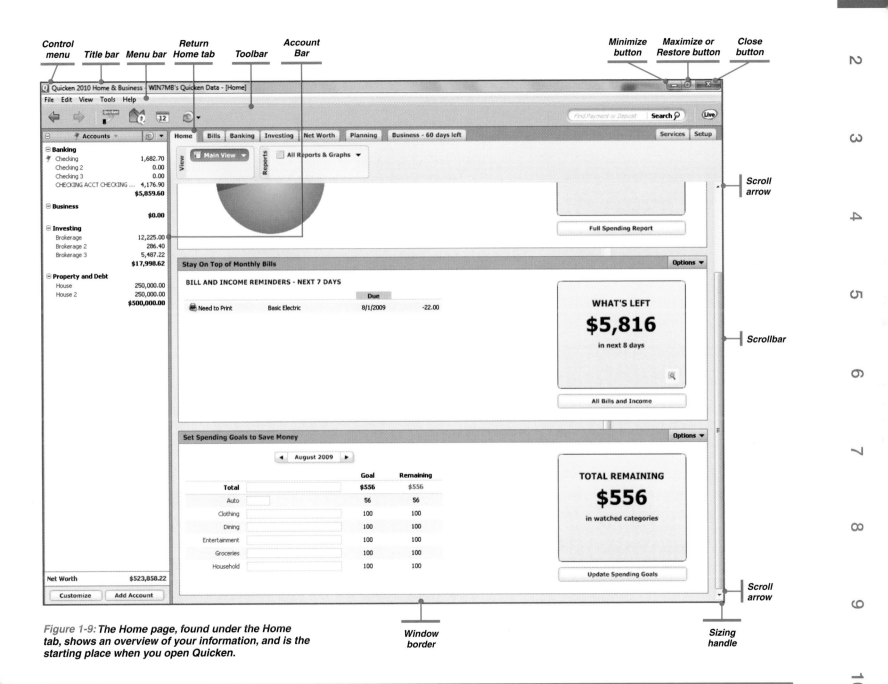

Figure 1-9: The Home page, found under the Home tab, shows an overview of your information, and is the starting place when you open Quicken.

- The **Maximize button**, which increases the size of the window so that it fills the screen. When the window is maximized, the Maximize button becomes a Restore button to return the window to the size it was before being maximized.

- The **Close button**, which closes the window and any program it contains.

- The **sizing handle**, which you can drag to size a window diagonally or to increase or decrease its height and width.

- The **window border**, which separates the window from the desktop and other windows, and can be used to size the window horizontally or vertically by dragging either the vertical or horizontal border.

Add Accounts Manually

Quicken 2010 separates your accounts into three specific centers on the Account Bar: Banking, Investments, and Property & Debt, as shown on the Account Bar at the left side of the Home tab in Figure 1-9. If you chose not to enter accounts as part of the See Where Your Money Goes section or by using the Setup tab, you can still add new accounts.

Add Account

1. Click **Add Account** at the bottom of the Quicken Account Bar.

2. The Account Setup dialog box appears. Select an account type from the list, and click **Next**. The most common accounts are checking, savings, credit card, and cash accounts. These accounts appear in the Banking center on the Account Bar.

3. If you have set up one or more accounts already, you will be asked if the new account is with one of your existing institutions. If so, click **Yes, I'll Select From The List Below**, and select the financial institution. If not, click **No, The Account Is At A Different Institution**. In either case, click **Next**.

4. Select the first letter of your account from the alphabet, or type the name of the bank where this account is held. Click **I Do Not Want To Enter My Financial Institution** if you choose not to download your transactions at this time. Click **Next** to continue.

5. If your bank offers download services, you have your password and PIN from that bank, and you wish to download your transactions, log in at the next dialog box. Click **Next** to connect with your bank and download your transactions.

6. If your bank doesn't offer download services or you don't want to use it, the Account Setup dialog box appears. Enter a name for this account, and click **Next**. The default

name for any new account is its type of account—for example, a savings account would be named "Savings."

a. Enter the date on the last statement you received. Quicken uses today's date by default.

b. Enter the ending balance shown on that statement. If you don't have the statement available, you can complete this information later.

c. Click **Next**. The Setup Complete dialog box displays. Click **Done**.

7. Using an account with download services, when the connection verification is complete, Quicken will display the accounts found at your bank, as seen in Figure 1-10. Choose the account you want to download, and indicate whether it is a new account to Quicken or if it already exists. If this is a new account in Quicken, give it a nickname. If you have already created the account, click **Exists In Quicken**, and choose the existing name from the drop-down list. Click **Next** to complete the download from your bank.

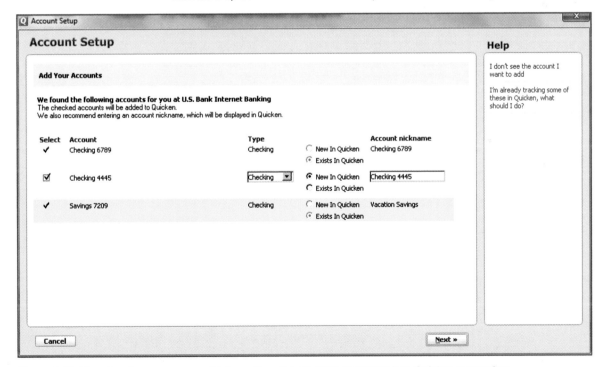

Figure 1-10: ***Downloading your account information directly from your bank into Quicken saves time.***

8. At the Setup Complete dialog box, note the connection type, the number of transactions that were downloaded, and any warnings that might appear. Click **Done**.

9. From the Account Bar, click the account into which you just downloaded to open the register, if necessary. Review each of the transactions. You may need to add new categories or change the payee name. Each financial institution has a slightly different format for downloaded transactions. See Chapter 2 for more information about online banking.

ADD INVESTMENT ACCOUNTS

To enter an account in the Investment center:

1. Click **Add Account**. At the Account Setup dialog box, choose Investing/Retirement. Note that a submenu appears asking the type of account, as seen in Figure 1-11.

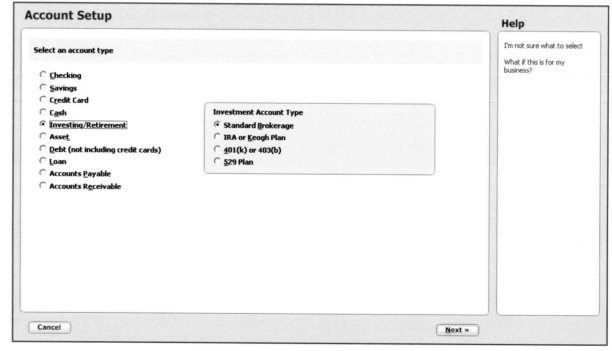

Figure 1-11: *Quicken lets you track several different types of investment accounts.*

2. Click the type of investment account you are adding. Click **Next**.

3. Enter the name of the financial institution, or click **I Do Not Want To Enter My Financial Institution**.

4. Click **Next** and enter an account name or nickname for this investment account. You can read more about investment accounts in Chapter 8.

5. Click **Next**. Depending on the type of investment account you chose, you may be asked if this is a tax-deferred account.

6. Click **Next** and enter the date of the last paper statement you received, or, if you are entering information from a brokerage website, the date the information was posted to the website. Enter the cash in the account and then the amount in a money market or sweep account.

Account Setup

Enter your cash balance and money market fund balance for Brokerage 3
Don't worry if you don't have your last statement- you can make changes to your account later.

Statement Ending Date [6/30/2009]

- If you are entering information **from a statement**, use the statement ending date.
- If you are entering information **from the brokerage web site**, use the date the information was posted (usually yesterday; sometimes today).

Cash [157.00]

Money Market [1,100.22]   Your financial institution may call this a "sweep" fund.

1,257.22   Total Cash Balance

Cancel   « Back   Next »

7. Click **Next** and enter the ticker symbol for securities (if any) in this account.

8. Click **Next** to download the current price.

9. Click **Next** to enter your current holdings information.

10. Enter the number of shares you own of each security.

11. Choose whether the security is a stock or mutual fund. If it is neither, click **Other**. You will have a chance to enter your cost information later in the process.

QUICKSTEPS

USING THE TICKER SYMBOL LOOKUP

When setting up your investment accounts, you may not know the ticker symbol for a particular security. You can use Ticker Symbol Lookup if you have an Internet connection. From the What Securities Are In This Account? dialog box:

1. Click **Ticker Symbol Lookup**. You are connected to the Internet, and the Quicken Symbol Lookup window will open.

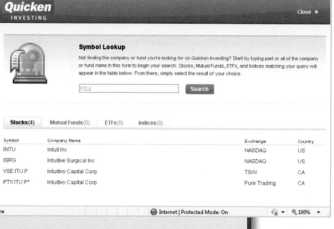

2. Type either the full name or part of the security name.

3. Click **Search**.

4. A list of choices will appear, with what Quicken considers to be the best match shown at the top of the list.

5. Highlight the symbol for your security.

Continued . . .

12. Click **Next**. The information you entered is displayed in a Summary window.

13. Click **Done** to close the Summary window, and then click **Done** again to close the Account Setup dialog box. The account is displayed in the Investing center and also shown on the Account Bar.

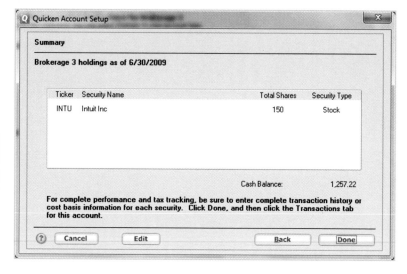

ADD PROPERTY & DEBT ACCOUNTS

You use accounts in the Property & Debt center to give Quicken information about your house, your car, or other major assets. (An asset is something you own that has significant value, like a rare painting or a stamp collection.)

1. Click **Add Account**. From the Account Setup dialog box, click the type of account you are adding. If you are adding your house, click **Asset** and a list of asset types will appear. Choose the type of asset, in this case "House," and click **Next**.

2. Give the account a name and, if it is asked, indicate if it is used for personal or business transactions.

3. Click **Next** and enter the date you acquired the house, its purchase price, and an approximate current value. You can enter approximate values and change them later.

USING THE TICKER SYMBOL LOOKUP *(Continued)*

6. Press **CTRL+C** to copy the symbol. You can also right-click to display a menu. Click **Copy** from the menu.

7. Close the Quicken Symbol Lookup window.

8. Return to Quicken and click the **Ticker** field.

9. Right-click and click **Paste** (or press **CTRL+V**) to copy the information into the Ticker field.

TIP

If you pay most of your bills with a check rather than paying them online, consider using checks you can print on your printer. You can order these checks directly from Quicken or from a number of other check printers you can easily find on the Internet.

UICKSTEPS

USING THE ADDRESS BOOK

You can use the Quicken Address Book to keep track of addresses for your payees, contact information, secondary address information (such as physical addresses), personal information (including the name of the payee's spouse and/or children), and up to three other types of miscellaneous information.

1. To access the Address Book, click **Tools** on the Menu bar, and then click **Address Book**.

Continued . . .

4. Click **Next**. Quicken asks if there is a mortgage on this house. If there is a mortgage, tell Quicken how you'd like to track the information. If you do not want to track the mortgage, choose that option and click **Next**. If you choose to track the mortgage, Quicken prompts you to set up the liability account and leads you through the steps. Chapter 6 has more detailed information about property and debt accounts.

5. Click **Next** to display the Setup Complete dialog box. Click Done to return to the Home page.

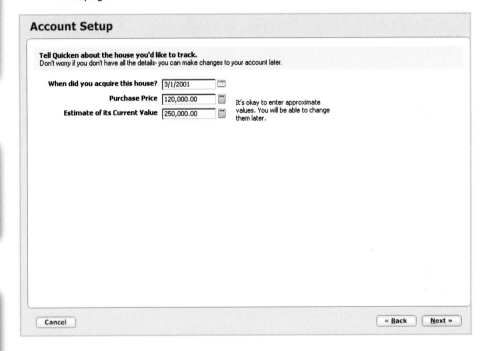

Find Help

The Quicken Help window, shown in Figure 1-12, provides a ready reference to answer your questions about Quicken and show you how to accomplish tasks. At any point in the program, pressing the **F1** key brings up the Help window with information about the current Quicken window. You also can click the **Help** menu and click **Quicken Help** to open the Help window for a broad range of information about Quicken.

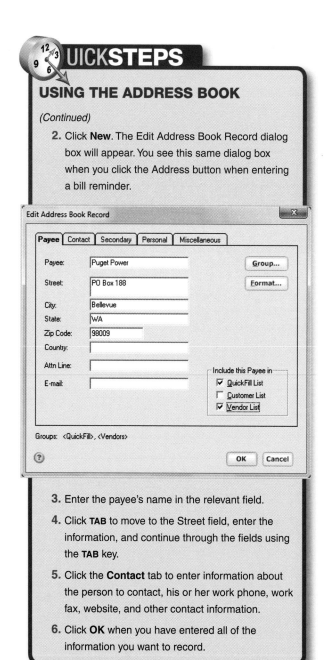

USING THE ADDRESS BOOK

(Continued)

2. Click **New**. The Edit Address Book Record dialog box will appear. You see this same dialog box when you click the Address button when entering a bill reminder.

3. Enter the payee's name in the relevant field.

4. Click **TAB** to move to the Street field, enter the information, and continue through the fields using the **TAB** key.

5. Click the **Contact** tab to enter information about the person to contact, his or her work phone, work fax, website, and other contact information.

6. Click **OK** when you have entered all of the information you want to record.

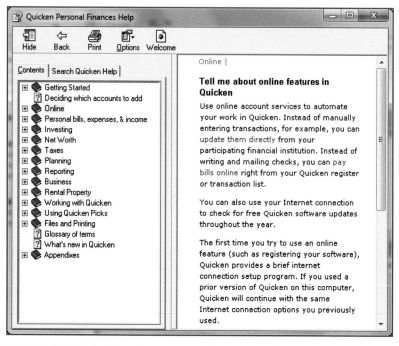

Figure 1-12: *Quicken Help gives answers to your questions.*

USE HELP

The Help window gives you two ways to find information:

- The **Contents** tab in the left pane of the Help window allows you to open a topic by clicking the plus sign on its left, open subtopics in the same way, and eventually click and view an article with the information you want.

- The **Search Quicken Help** tab allows you to enter a word or words in the text box at the top of the left pane and be given a list of articles, which you can click to display and read in the right pane.

USE OTHER HELP RESOURCES

The Help menu provides a number of other resources to assist you, which you can access by clicking one of the following options:

Help

Learn About Next Steps After Setup
Quicken Help
Current Window   F1
Product and Customer Support

Quicken Live Community
Quicken Support

Submit Feedback on Quicken
Join the Quicken Inner Circle

About Quicken
Privacy Statement

Unlock Again

Add Business Tools
Add Rental Property Tools

- **Learn About Next Steps After Setup**   This quick chart provides a timeline for entering your information into Quicken. The Setup tab is discussed earlier in this chapter.

- **Current Window**   This window displays information about the window with which you are presently working. You can also access help for the current window by pressing the F1 key.

- **Product And Customer Support**   This selection opens the Quicken Product And Customer Support options window, with troubleshooting tips, a link to frequently asked questions, and Quicken Technical Support on the Quicken.com website (you must have an Internet connection to view the site).

- **Quicken Live Community**   This is an online forum where Quicken users can exchange ideas, get answers to their questions, and participate in discussions.

- **Quicken Support**   This opens the support page on the Quicken website.

- **Submit Feedback On Quicken**   This selection allows you to give Intuit feedback on Quicken. This also requires an Internet connection. It is through feedback from users such as you that Quicken improves its products. Your input is important, and Quicken encourages you to contact them.

- **Join The Quicken Inner Circle**   The "Inner Circle" is a group of both new and veteran Quicken users who are willing to work with Intuit to ensure that Quicken stays viable in today's marketplace.

- **About Quicken**   This shows you which version of Quicken you are using, should you need to call customer support.

- **Privacy Statement**   This selection tells you how Quicken protects your personal information.

- **Unlock Again, Add Business Tools, and Add Rental Property Tools**   These selections appear in the Deluxe and Premier editions of Quicken, providing a fast way to upgrade your edition over the Internet.

Exit Quicken

When you have completed a Quicken session, you should exit the program. You will usually be encouraged to back up your work before you close it. That is always a good idea. Hard drive crashes, power outages, and computer malfunctions happen to all of us at one time or another. Backing up your files is discussed in more detail in Chapter 2.

QUICKSTEPS

IMPORTING FROM MICROSOFT MONEY

In June 2009, Microsoft announced that their financial software product, Microsoft Money, was being discontinued. If you are a former Microsoft Money user and are new to Quicken, you can quickly import up to 10,000 transactions into Quicken.

1. Back up your Microsoft Money file. After the backup, check the last few transactions in your checking account to ensure the file is up to date. Make a note of these transactions.

2. Create a new Quicken file. Do not enter any transactions.

Continued . . .

QUICKSTEPS

IMPORTING FROM MICROSOFT MONEY *(Continued)*

3. Click **File** on the Menu bar, and choose **File Import**.

> Web Connect File
> QIF File
> Addresses
> TurboTax File
> Microsoft Money® file

4. Click **Microsoft Money File**. Your .mny file appears in the Import From Microsoft Money File dialog box.

5. Select the file you want to import. Click **Open** and the transactions will be imported into your Quicken file.

6. Verify that your transactions have been imported by opening your checking account in Quicken and checking the last few transactions. They should be the same transactions you noted in step 1.

7. That's all there is to it. Welcome to Quicken!

You can exit Quicken in several ways:

- Click the Close button on the right side of the title bar.
- Click **File** on the Menu bar, and then click **Exit**.
- Hold down your **ALT** key and press the **F4** key.

Use Quicken and Windows Basics

If you are new to Quicken, take a few minutes to read this section. It discusses terms used with Quicken, as well as some that are used with all Windows-based programs. The dialog boxes and windows make more sense when you understand their contents.

Recognize Quicken Terms

Quicken is meant to be intuitive. You do most tasks with one or two clicks, and the design of each window is intended to be easy to use and understand. The terms defined here are used throughout Quicken and this book.

- **Accounts** in Quicken represent the separate checking, savings, credit card, and brokerage accounts you have, as well as your mortgage and car loans, as you can see in Figure 1-10. Each is considered an account by Quicken. The information about all of the accounts of any type that relate to you is kept within one Quicken data file. In Table 1-1, you can see the different account types used by Quicken, the location in which Quicken stores them, and some examples of each account type. There are standard accounts within each account type.

- **Data files** (or just "files") are how Quicken stores the information about your financial records. Just as a word-processing document is stored as a document file in a folder on your hard disk, Quicken stores your data file in a folder on your hard disk. A data file contains information about all of your accounts, assets, liabilities, financial goals, and tax plans. Each family's or person's information is stored in a separate file. For example, if you are taking care of Aunt Harriet's financial matters, her information is stored in a file separate from your personal data file.

- **Folders** are similar to the manila folders you store in a filing cabinet. Data files for your documents, spreadsheets, and Quicken files are stored in folders. Compare your hard drive to the filing cabinet in which you store paper files in folders to see the relationship with digital files and folders.

ACCOUNT TYPE/ LOCATION	EXAMPLES
Banking Accounts/ Banking Tab	These accounts track your checking, savings, and credit card accounts. You can even set up cash accounts for each member of your family to track allowances for the kids or cash kept in a cookie jar.
Investment Accounts/ Investing Tab	These track your investments. You can track your individual brokerage accounts, your IRAs, your mutual funds, or any other investment. If you have Quicken 2010 Deluxe, Premier, Business, or Rental Property edition, you can keep track of your 401(k) or 403(b) plans offered by your employer.
Property & Debt Accounts/Net Worth Tab	Here is where you keep track of your home mortgage and any other mortgages, your car and any loans on it, or any other property you own. You can track loans owed to you or by you. You can even record the value of your stamp collection or your son's baseball card collection. Assets and liability accounts are shown in the Net Worth tab.

Table 1-1: Types of Accounts in Quicken

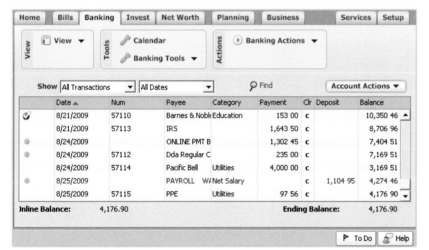

- **Registers** are similar to the paper check register used with a checking account, and show the checks you write and the deposits you make. Each noninvestment account in Quicken has its own register. You open a register by clicking the account in the Accounts list or in the Account Overview of the Banking, Investing, and Net Worth tabs. The menu items on the top of the register let you locate and delete transactions, write checks, and reconcile the account to a statement. The Overview tab shows the account attributes and status, as well as a graphic display of activity for a period of time you designate.

- **Transactions** are the checks you write, the payments you make, and all of the other individual financial events in your life. Quicken puts each event in either an account register or on an investment account transaction list.

- **Transaction lists** are used with investment accounts, such as a brokerage account or a 401(k) account, in place of a register. Quicken designed these lists to look like a brokerage statement, showing every transaction that has taken place.

- **Categories** are used to group similar transactions. Every time you enter a transaction into a Quicken register, you have the option of assigning it to a category.

- **Windows** are used to display related information on the screen. In addition to the basic Quicken window shown previously, there are several other types of windows used by Quicken to display various types of information.

  - The Internet window uses the built-in Quicken Web browser to display a Quicken web page.

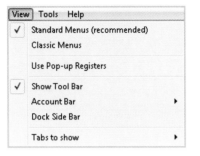

- List windows display information about related items, such as classes or categories.
- Report windows let you create customized reports from your accounts in a way you understand.

- **Menus** and the Menu bar are the tools Quicken and many other Windows-based programs use to give you access to the commands and features within the program. Click a menu name in the Menu bar to open the menu, and then click one of the options in the menu to select it. Some menu options have a right-pointing arrow on the right of the option. When you move the mouse pointer over that type of option, a submenu, or flyout menu, will open. When you right-click some objects within a window or dialog box, a context menu will open. Context menus show options specific to the item clicked.

- **Toolbars** are rows of buttons, frequently directly below the Menu bar. Click a button to perform its task, open a window, or display a dialog box. While the Quicken toolbar does not display by default, you can choose to display it. Click **View** and **Quicken Tool Bar** to show your Quicken toolbar.

- **Keyboard shortcuts** allow you to perform tasks from the keyboard rather than use the mouse and menus or toolbars. Table 1-2 lists the more frequently used keyboard shortcuts. If the shortcut is **CTRL+P**, for example, you are to hold down the **CTRL** key while pressing the **P** key on the keyboard. Then let go of both keys.

NOTE

Some of the more familiar Windows keyboard shortcuts may be used differently in some areas of Quicken. You can tell Quicken to use Windows shortcuts in the Setup section of Quicken Preferences.

ACTION (WINDOWS/QUICKEN)	KEYBOARD SHORTCUT
Copy to the Clipboard/Open the Category list	CTRL+C
Paste from the Clipboard/Void a transaction	CTRL+V
Print	CTRL+P
Open the Account List	CTRL+A
Create a backup file	CTRL+B
Open the Split Transaction dialog box	CTRL+S
Delete a transaction or a line in a split transaction	CTRL+D
Help	F1
Go to the next field or column	TAB

Table 1-2: *Keyboard Shortcuts in Quicken*

FINDING MORE KEYBOARD SHORTCUTS

To see additional keyboard shortcuts:

1. Click the **Help** menu, and then click **Quicken Help**.

2. Click the **Search Quicken Help** tab, type keyboard shortcuts, and then click **Ask**.

3. Click **Tell Me About Keyboard Shortcuts** in the Selected Topic list to see the upper part of the list of shortcuts, shown in Figure 1-13.

4. Click the scrollbar on the right side of the window to see the remainder of the shortcuts list.

5. When you are done, click **Close** in the title bar to close the Quicken Personal Finance Help window.

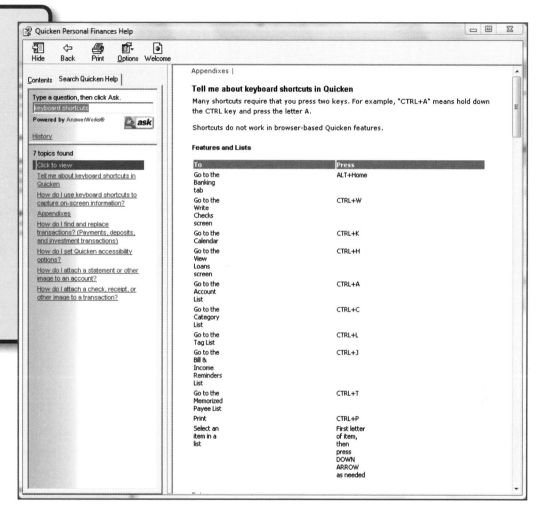

Figure 1-13: **Keyboard shortcuts help you get around Quicken without removing your hands from the keyboard.**

Use Windows Tools

Quicken 2010 has a familiar feel if you are used to working with other Windows-based programs. For example, the Minimize, Maximize, and Close buttons appear in the title bar on the upper-right corner of every window.

As with all Windows programs, if you have more than one window (or program) open at the same time, the *active window* is the one with the brightest title bar.

- **Windows** are areas of the screen in which you can see a program that is running and provide primary control of that program. When Quicken starts, it opens in its own window. Windows generally have menus and can be sized.

- **Dialog boxes** are used by Quicken and other Windows programs to communicate with you, the user, and for you to communicate with the program. They can be message boxes that require no action other than clicking OK, or smaller areas of the screen with check boxes, options, drop-down lists, text boxes, and other controls that let you add information and control what is happening in a program, as you can see in Figure 1-14. The primary parts of dialog boxes are:

  - The **title bar** contains the name of the dialog box, and is used to drag the box around the desktop.

  - A **drop-down list box** opens a list from which you can choose one item that will be displayed when the list is closed.

  - A **list box** (not shown) lets you select one or more items from a list; it may include a scrollbar.

  - A **check box** lets you turn features on or off.

  - A **text box** lets you enter and edit text.

  - **Command buttons** perform functions such as closing the dialog box and accepting the changes (the OK button) or closing the dialog box and ignoring the changes (the Cancel button).

  - **Tabs** let you select from among several pages in a dialog box.

  - **Option buttons**, also called *radio buttons*, let you select one among mutually exclusive options.

  - A **spinner** lets you select from a sequential series of numbers.

  - A **slider** lets you select from several values.

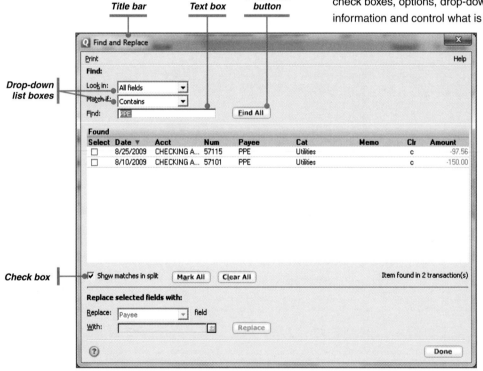

Figure 1-14: *Dialog boxes provide the primary means of controlling what is happening in a program.*

How to...

- Modify the Main View
- Change the Account Bar
- Amend Your Views
- Manage Accounts
- *Using Classic Menus*
- Edit an Account
- *Using the Quicken Calendar*
- Set Preferences
- Add Cash Flow Accounts
- Understand Online Services
- *Deciding to Use Online Banking Services*
- Set Up Online Banking
- Activate One Step Update
- Manage Your Passwords
- Use Quicken Bill Pay
- Work with Categories
- Add a New Category
- *Using Tax-Line Assignments*
- *Deleting Categories*
- Back Up Your Data to External Media

Chapter 2
Personalizing Quicken

In Chapter 1 you saw how to install Quicken and how to establish your initial accounts. When you were finished, however, the look and feel of Quicken is the default style built into the product. For many people, this is fine, and their whole experience with Quicken is with the default style. However, Quicken provides a number of ways that you can customize it—both in how it looks and how it operates—allowing you to tailor the program to meet your specific needs. Quicken most likely will become an important program that you use often. As a result, it should reflect what you want. In this chapter you will see how to customize the Home tab so that it reflects you, how to add and change accounts, how to set up online banking, and how to add and delete categories so that they provide the level of organization you want for your finances.

Customize the Home Page

After you have completed Quicken's installation, the default Quicken Home page is displayed, as shown in Figure 2-1. You can customize the Home page by modifying the Main View, showing or hiding the Quicken Tool Bar, changing the location of the Account Bar, creating additional views, and setting your preferences for the way various elements on the page are used.

Figure 2-1: The Quicken Home page can be customized to meet your needs.

Modify the Main View

In the Home tab, the Main View button appears on the Action Bar. This view can be customized to display any of the more than 40 available options. To customize the main view:

NOTE

By default, the Available Items list displays only a few commands. Use the scrollbar to display the more than 40 available items.

1. Click the down arrow on the **Main View** button to see the menu.

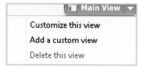

2. Click **Customize This View** to change what shows on your Home page. The Customize View dialog is displayed, as seen in Figure 2-2.

3. To add an item to the Main View, select the item in the **Available Items** list on the left, and then click **Add**.

4. To remove an item, select the item in the **Chosen Items** list on the right, and then click **Remove**.

5. To change the order in which items are displayed on the page, select the item in the **Chosen Items** list on the right, and click either the **Move Up** or **Move Down** button. One click moves the item up or down one place.

6. If you want to stop the process, click **Cancel**.

7. When finished, click **OK** to set the changes and close the dialog box.

ADD A CUSTOM VIEW

To create your own view, click the **Main View** down arrow, and click **Add A Custom View** from the menu. From the Customize View dialog that appears, follow steps 3 through 7 in the previous section.

DELETE A VIEW

After you have created at least one customized view, you may delete a view. To delete a view, click the down arrow of the view you want to delete to open the menu. Click **Delete This View**. A message box opens asking if you are sure you want to delete this view. If you are, click **Yes**.

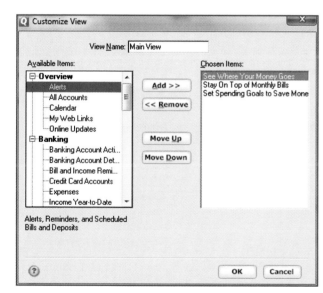

Figure 2-2: **The Customize View dialog box allows you to personalize your Quicken Home page.**

Display Account Bar | One Step Update

🗕 ⚑ Accounts	🔄 Update
🗖 **Banking**	**$153,525.43**
⚑ Checking	22,747.74
Money Market	29,589.67
Brokerage (Cash)	1,707.01
Checking 6789	139.12
My Wallet	45.00
Cash Account	0.00
Checking 2	0.00
Savings	73,852.08
Vacation Savings	25,444.81
Credit Card - Seattle	0.00
Credit Card - Island	0.00
🗖 **Investing**	**$32,283.92**
🗖 **Property & Debt**	**$658,400.40**
Rental House	195,000.00
House	250,000.00
Dodge Caravan	19,350.00
Horses and Equipment	11,124.76
Home Inventory	29,377.00
Second House	250,000.00
Rental House Loan	-28,112.84
House Loan	-48,294.68
Dodge Caravan Loan	-13,695.00
Horses & Equipment	-6,348.84
Net Worth	**$844,209.75**
Add Account	⚙

Figure 2-3: You can see each of your accounts and its balance in the Account Bar.

Change the Account Bar

The Account Bar is, by default, docked on the left side of the Home page. It displays your accounts in the various activity centers, as seen in Figure 2-3.

At the top of the Account Bar you see a small minus sign to the left of the word "Accounts." When you click the minus sign, the Account Bar closes. When the Account Bar is closed, the small minus sign turns into a plus sign. To permanently (until you click the minus sign) open the Account Bar, click the plus sign.

The Account Bar can be changed in the following ways:

- Right-click anywhere within the Account Bar to view the Account Bar context menu. With this menu you can:

  - Click **Collapse All Accounts** to show only the totals in each center.

  - Click **Expand All Accounts** to show the amounts in each separate account within each center.

  - Click **Show Amounts** to show the balance in each account. Click **Hide Amounts** to show the account name only.

  - Click **Show Cents In Amounts** to display the cents in each balance.

  - Click **Show Current Balance In Bar** to display the balance in each account as of today's date. Click **Show Ending Balance In Bar** to display the balance after any future transactions have been entered.

  - Click **Show Account Bar On Left** to display the Account Bar on the left side of your Activity Center. Click **Show Account Bar On Right** to display it on the right side.

  - Click **Minimize Account Bar** to show only the top part of the Account Bar.

  - Click **Add New Account** to display the Quicken Account Setup dialog box.

  - Click **Add/Remove Accounts From Bar**, **Rearrange Accounts**, or **Delete/Hide Accounts In Quicken** to open the Account List dialog box.

Context menu:

	Collapse all accounts
✓	Expand all accounts
✓	Show amounts
	Hide amounts
✓	Show cents in amounts
✓	Show Current Balance in bar
	Show Ending Balance in bar
✓	Show Account Bar on left
	Show Account Bar on right
	Minimize Account Bar
	Add new account
	Add/remove accounts from bar
	Rearrange accounts
	Delete/hide accounts in Quicken

Accounts	Update
⊞ Banking	$3,337.67
⊞ Investing	$0.00
⊞ Property	$307,169.84
Net Worth	$310,507.51
Add Account	⚙

- A plus sign to the left of each activity center name indicates that there are accounts within that center. A minus sign indicates that there are no accounts set up in that center or that all accounts are displayed. Click the plus sign to display individual accounts.

- Click the up or down arrows at the top or bottom of the Account Bar to scroll if not all of your accounts are displayed at one time, as shown here.

Accounts	Update
⬆	
⊞ Banking	$3,337.67
⬇	
Net Worth	$310,507.51
Add Account	⚙

- Click **Customize** (the small gear icon) at the bottom of the Account Bar to display the Account List. See "Manage Accounts" later in this chapter.

Add Account ⚙ | Customize

- Click **Add Account** to set up a new account as described in Chapter 1.

Amend Your Views

When Quicken opens, the Menu bar appears above the Account Bar and the tabs. Click each Menu bar item to see the options or commands on the menu. You can change from the recommended Standard menus to Classic menus and add other items with the View menu. From the View menu, you can also choose to use pop-up registers, show or hide the Quicken Tool Bar, set the location of the Account Bar and Side Bar, and tell Quicken which tabs to display.

View   Tools   Help
✓ Standard Menus (recommended)
   Classic Menus

   Use Pop-up Registers

   Show Tool Bar
   Account Bar   ▶
   Dock Side Bar

   Tabs to show   ▶

1. From the Menu bar, click **View**. Click **Classic Menus** to display additional menus. See the "Using Classic Menus" QuickFacts elsewhere in this chapter for more information about Classic menus.

2. Again open the **View** menu, and click **Use Pop-Up Registers** to make pop-up registers available. Normally, when you choose an account from the Account Bar, the register opens within its center, as shown in Figure 2-4. Pop-up registers appear in a new window on top of the Quicken window, as shown in Figure 2-5. These register windows can be moved around and placed anywhere on the screen that you choose. Click Close (the red X) on the pop-up register window title bar to close the register.

NOTE

The additional menus available when you choose the Classic Menus option under View are similar to the choices available under each of the tabs.

Figure 2-4: This account register displays transactions within the Banking tab.

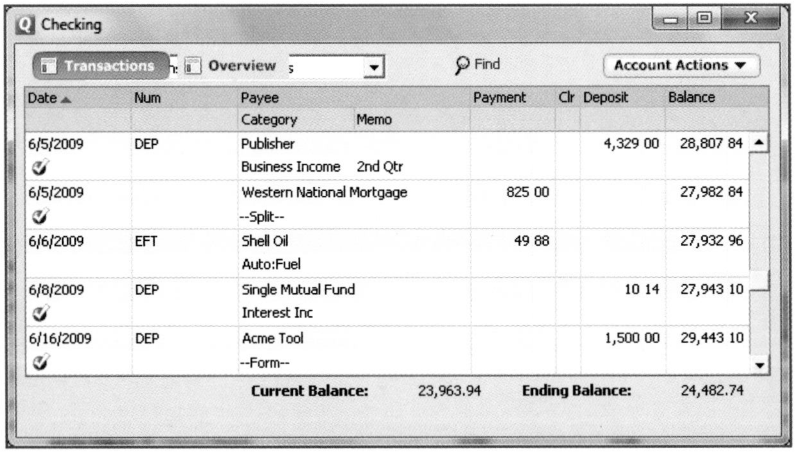

Figure 2-5: Pop-up registers can be moved around the window by dragging the title bar.

3. From the View menu, click **Show Tool Bar** to display the Quicken Tool Bar, which provides the following features:

- Use the left-pointing arrow to go back to a previous page in Quicken. Use the right-pointing arrow to go to the next page. These arrows are not available until you have gone to several pages within the Quicken program.

- Click the Quicken Services icon—the Quicken logo with the hand holding it up—to open the Quicken Products And Services page with your Internet connection.

- Click the Quicken.com icon to open the Quicken website in its own window in Quicken, or with pop-up registers turned on, in a separate window.

- Click the Calendar icon to open the Quicken Calendar. The Calendar is covered later in this chapter.

- Click the One-Step Update icon to update your accounts directly from their financial institution. See more about online banking later in this chapter.

4. In the View menu, click **Account Bar** to tell Quicken how you want the Account Bar to be displayed. Your options are

- Docked on the left or right side of your screen

- Minimized or hidden

5. The View menu's Dock Side Bar option is available for those with monitors wider than 1400 × 1124. You may choose to dock the Side Bar (which is rarely used in Quicken 2010) to keep it visible, or clear that option to move the Side Bar around your screen.

6. Click **Tabs To Show** to open the list of six tabs. You may choose the tabs to display by clicking the check box before their name. However, if you have entered transactions in any of the centers, the tab for that center will display by default.

7. If you opened Classic menus, pop-up registers, the Tool Bar, and the Side Bar and don't want them permanently displayed, open the View menu and deselect these items.

Manage Accounts

You manage your accounts and determine how they are displayed using the Account List dialog box, which appears when you click **Customize** (the small gear icon) at the bottom of the Account Bar. The Account List dialog, shown in Figure 2-6, allows you to review and manage your accounts in more detail.

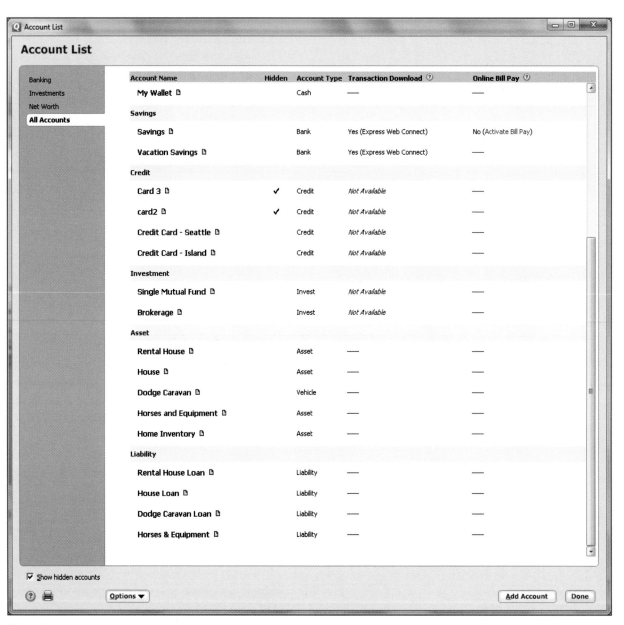

Account Name	Hidden	Account Type	Transaction Download ⑦	Online Bill Pay ⑦
My Wallet ▯		Cash	—	—
Savings				
Savings ▯		Bank	Yes (Express Web Connect)	No (Activate Bill Pay)
Vacation Savings ▯		Bank	Yes (Express Web Connect)	—
Credit				
Card 3 ▯	✔	Credit	*Not Available*	—
card2 ▯	✔	Credit	*Not Available*	—
Credit Card - Seattle ▯		Credit	*Not Available*	—
Credit Card - Island ▯		Credit	*Not Available*	—
Investment				
Single Mutual Fund ▯		Invest	*Not Available*	—
Brokerage ▯		Invest	*Not Available*	—
Asset				
Rental House ▯		Asset	—	—
House ▯		Asset	—	—
Dodge Caravan ▯		Vehicle	—	—
Horses and Equipment ▯		Asset	—	—
Home Inventory ▯		Asset	—	—
Liability				
Rental House Loan ▯		Liability	—	—
House Loan ▯		Liability	—	—
Dodge Caravan Loan ▯		Liability	—	—
Horses & Equipment ▯		Liability	—	—

Banking · Investments · Net Worth · **All Accounts**

☑ Show hidden accounts

Options ▼   Add Account   Done

Figure 2-6: You can manage your various accounts from the Account List dialog.

To show all of your accounts, click **All Accounts** on the left side of the dialog. To see only the accounts in each activity center, choose that center. For example, to see all of your Investment accounts, click **Investments** on the left side of the Account List dialog.

By default, there are five columns in the Account List:

- Account Name shows the name of each account. Click the name of the account with which you want to work.

- The Hidden column displays any accounts you want to hide from Quicken's totals. The Hidden column doesn't appear until you hide one of your accounts.

- The Account Type column indicates the type of account, for example, bank, investment account, asset, or liability.

- The Transaction Download column indicates what type of online connection is associated with this account. See "Use Quicken Online" later in this chapter for more information about online connections.

- Online Bill Pay indicates whether or not this account has been set up to pay bills online through the financial institution where this account is held.

Click the name of an account to open a dialog area within the window that allows you to manage that account, as seen in Figure 2-7.

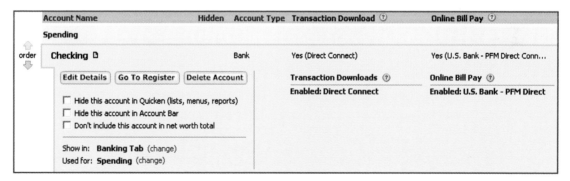

Figure 2-7: *You can edit, hide, or delete an account from the dialog area found in the Account List.*

- Click the **Order** arrow on the left of the accounts to change where the account appears in the Account Bar.

QUICKFACTS

USING CLASSIC MENUS

While most of us use the recommended Standard menus, Classic menus offer familiar choices for those who have used earlier versions of Quicken. To use Classic menus:

1. From the Quicken Menu bar, click **View**s and then click **Classic Menus**.

2. Additional menus appear. You see Home, Bills, Banking, Investing, Planning, Services, and Reports menus added to the Menu bar.

3. If you click **View** again, you will see a different menu from what was displayed with Standard menus.

4. By default, the Show Tabs And Action Bar command is chosen. However, you can change that option by clicking either **Show Action Bar Only** or **No Tabs Or Action Bar**.

5. Each Classic menu item has its own commands.

   - Click the **Home** menu to see links to the Home tab's Main View and any custom views you have created on the Home tab.

   - The Bills menu opens when you click **Bills** on the Classic menu. From this menu you can display:

     - The Upcoming-Timeline and Upcoming-Lists, which display your scheduled transactions in either a list or graphic format.

Continued . . .

- Click **Edit Details** within the dialog area to open the Account Details dialog, as seen in Figure 2-8. See "Edit an Account" elsewhere in this chapter. Click **OK** to close Account Details dialog.

- In the Account List dialog area, click the **Go To Register** button to open the register for the selected account.

- Click **Delete Account** to open the Delete Account dialog. To delete an account:

  - Click **Delete Account** to open a message box.

  - If you want to delete this account, you must type <u>Yes</u> to confirm the deletion. Then, click **OK**.

    - Click **Cancel** to close the dialog if you choose not to delete the account. A message will appear telling you the account was not deleted.

    - Click **Help** to open the Quicken Help window.

- In the Account List dialog area, click **Hide This Account In Quicken** to remove the account and its balance from lists, menus, and reports.

  - Click **Hide This Account In Account Bar** to hide the name of the account but include the total in a section called "Other Accounts."

- Click **Don't Include This Account In Net Worth Total** to tell Quicken not to add this account's balance into the total net worth shown on the Account Bar.

- Click **Change** in the Show In or Used For field to open the Change Account Tab dialog. This dialog allows you to organize your accounts within Quicken. You can change the tab location of an account as well as what it is used for.

- If Online Bill Payment is available for the selected account and you have not enabled it, click **Activate Bill Payment** to open the Account Setup dialog. See "Use Quicken Online" later in this chapter.

- If any accounts are hidden, click the **Show Hidden Accounts** check box at the lower-left corner of the Account List window to display all of your Quicken accounts. This is not displayed if you haven't hidden an account.

- Click the question mark icon to open Quicken Help; click the printer icon to print the Account List.

- Click **Options** to see display options for your accounts.

- Click **Add Account** to open the Account Setup dialog.

- Click **Done** when you have completed your changes.

Edit an Account

You can edit information about each account from the Account List dialog box. Select the account you want to edit, and click the **Edit Details** button to display the Account Details dialog box, as seen in Figure 2-8. Use the TAB key to move between the fields in this dialog.

1. Click in the **Account Name** text box to change the name of the account, or click in the **Description** text box to add or change the account description.

2. Click the **Yes** radio button in the Tax-Deferred field if the account is tax-deferred. **No** is chosen by default.

3. Enter any interest rate in the Interest Rate field.

USING CLASSIC MENUS (Continued)

- From the Planning menu, you have the same options that are available from the Spending Planner, Cash Flow, Lifetime Planner, and Tax Center subtabs under the Planning tab.

- The Services menu shows links to the More From Quicken tab, which offers Quicken Services and Quicken Picks.

- The Reports menu gives you links to the many available Quicken reports. These reports are also available on the Action Bar in each tab.

As you can see, each menu item in the Classic menus takes you to the same locations as the links in each center's tab. These menus simply offer a more familiar way of navigation for previous users of Quicken.

To return to the Standard view, which is what is used throughout this book, open the **View** menu and choose **Standard Menus**.

4. Enter any minimum or maximum balances in the Set Up Alerts fields.

5. When you enable online services, the account location, financial institution, account and routing numbers, and customer ID will fill in automatically. In the remaining text boxes, type any additional information about the account, such as a contact name, the institution's phone number, and so on.

6. Click the **Online Services** tab to amend the online banking information. See "Use Quicken Online" later in this chapter for more information about online banking.

7. Click the **Delete Account** button at the bottom to open the Delete dialog box.

8. Click **Tax Schedule Info** to select the tax schedules for transfers in and/or out of this account. Click the relevant down arrow to display a drop-down list of tax schedules from which you can choose.

9. Click **OK** or **Cancel** to close the Account Details dialog.

Figure 2-8: The Account Details dialog box gives you a chance to edit, delete, and add information about an account.

UICKSTEPS

USING THE QUICKEN CALENDAR

From the Quicken calendar, you see in a glance the bills and income items for each day of a month. To open the Quicken Calendar:

1. Click **Tools** and then click **Calendar**. You can also use the keyboard shortcut **CTRL+K**. Either action will open the Quicken Calendar shown in Figure 2-9.

2. Enter the date in the Go To Date field to focus on that date.

3. Use the arrows to the right and left of the current month to see earlier or future months.

4. Click **Add Note** to open the Add Note dialog. You can quickly add a note to any date on the calendar. A small note icon will appear next to the numeric date on your calendar. Click the icon to open it.

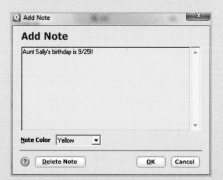

5. Click **Options** to open a menu from which you can determine what is shown on the calendar.

   • Choose the Show options to show transactions, reminders, and balances in each day's box on the calendar, as seen in Figure 2-9.

Continued ...

Figure 2-9: *The Quicken calendar gives you a visual picture of when you will receive income and have to pay bills.*

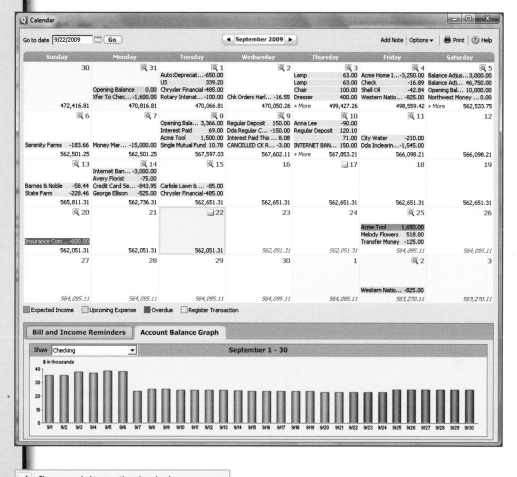

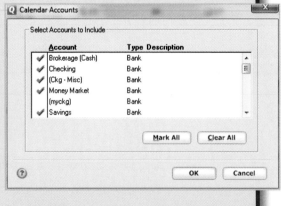

QUICKSTEPS

USING THE QUICKEN CALENDAR

(Continued)

- Click **Show Snapshots Below Calendar** to display the Bill and Income Reminders and Account Balance Graph tabs below the calendar. If you do not want these tabs available, clear the check mark.

- Click **Show Memorized Payee List** to display the list of your memorized payees at the right of the calendar.

- Click **Edit Memorized Payee List** to open the list and make changes. See Chapter 5 for more information about memorized payees.

- Click **Select Calendar Accounts** to choose which accounts to include in your calendar.

6. Click **Print** to open the Print dialog and print the calendar.

7. Click **Help** to open the Quicken Help window.

8. If you have chosen to display the "snapshots" below the calendar, you can manage your reminders from the Bill And Income Reminders tab.

Continued . . .

Set Preferences

Preferences are the ways in which you make Quicken behave the way you want. For example, when you start Quicken, instead of displaying the Home tab, you can choose to display the Banking tab. This is a startup preference. Other types of preferences in Quicken include backup preferences, register preferences, and report preferences. This section will discuss startup and setup preferences. The remaining preferences will be discussed elsewhere in this book. To change the startup and setup preferences:

1. Click the **Edit** menu, click **Preferences**, and click **Quicken Preferences**. The Quicken Preferences dialog box appears with the startup preferences displayed, as shown in Figure 2-10.

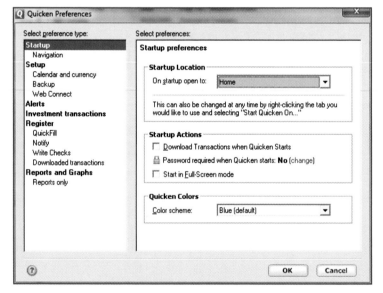

Figure 2-10: **You can control many of the nuances of Quicken through the Quicken Preferences dialog box.**

2. In the Startup Preferences section on the right side of the dialog box:

- Click the **On Startup Open To** down arrow, and choose what you want to appear when you start Quicken.

- Click **Download Transactions When Quicken Starts** to automatically download all of the transactions in your online accounts.

USING THE QUICKEN CALENDAR

(Continued)

See Chapter 5 for information on working with reminders.

9. The Account Balance Graph tab displays a graph showing account balances for one or multiple accounts.

Transactions on each day of the month are color-coded per the legend on the bottom of the calendar. Close the calendar to return to the Quicken Home page and the current month's information.

NOTE

You can display the Quicken calendar from any Manage Reminders window by double-clicking the small calendar at the bottom of the window.

- In the Password Required When Quicken Starts section, click **Change** to change your Quicken passwords. See "Manage Your Passwords" later in this chapter.

- Click **Start In Full-Screen Mode** to open the Quicken window with only the Menu bar displayed.

- Click the **Color Scheme** down arrow to choose another color scheme for Quicken.

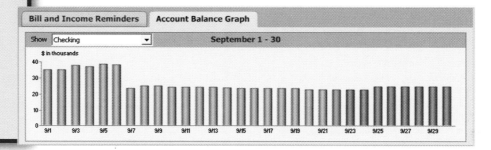

3. Click **Navigation** to tell Quicken how you want to move around within the program.

- Click **Use Classic Menus** in the Main Navigation section to use Classic menus. Classic menus are discussed elsewhere in this chapter.

- In the Optional Navigation section, choose how your Account Bar, the Quicken Tool Bar, and the Side Bar display in Quicken.

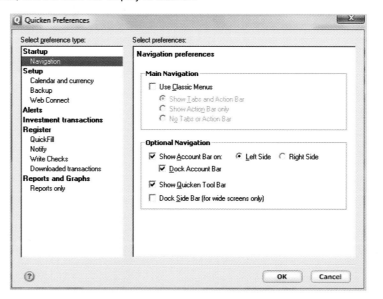

4. Click **Setup** in the left column. The setup preferences are displayed.

SHORTCUT KEYS	WINDOWS	QUICKEN
CTRL+C	Copy	Open the Category list
CTRL+V	Paste	Void a transaction
CTRL+X	Cut	Show the matching entry, for example, in a liability register
CTRL+Z	Undo	Display more detail about a report amount

*Table 2-1: **Alternative Mappings of Shortcut Keys in Windows and Quicken***

NOTE

Most people keep the Windows standard for the **CTRL+C**, **CTRL+V**, **CTRL+X**, and **CTRL+Z** shortcut keys because the Windows commands are heavily used in many Windows programs, while the Quicken commands are infrequently used.

- Choose whether to map keyboard shortcuts to Quicken or Windows standards. See Table 2-1 for what these shortcuts do in each case. The Windows standard is the default (see Chapter 1 for more information).

- Choose whether to turn off the Quicken sounds—for example, the "ka-chung" sound that plays every time you enter a transaction—by clicking that option to deselect it.

- Chose to turn off animation within the program by clearing that check box.

- Choose whether to automatically minimize pop-up windows by clicking that option.

5. Click **Calendar And Currency** to open those preferences.

- Choose how you want your calendar displayed. You may choose either a calendar year or a fiscal year.

- If you choose to display your calendar as a fiscal year, choose the month the fiscal year begins.

- Click **Multicurrency Support** if you use more than one currency in Quicken.

6. Click **Backup** to open the backup preferences. Choose **Automatic Backups** or **Manual Backup Reminder**, or both. See "Protect Your Quicken Data" later in this chapter.

7. Click **Web Connect** to set how you want Quicken to manage Web Connect data.

8. **OK** to close the dialog box when you are finished.

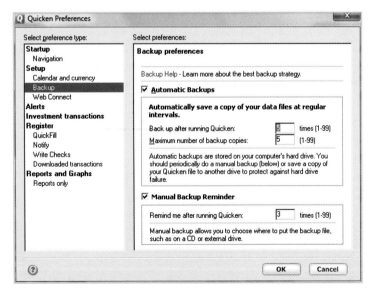

Add and Change Accounts

Accounts are central to Quicken's operation, whether they are checking, investment, or property and debt accounts. In Chapter 1 you saw how to get started setting up accounts with Quicken New User Setup. As you use Quicken, it is likely that you will want to add accounts and modify the accounts you already have. This section will look at adding and modifying checking and savings accounts. In later chapters you'll see how to add and modify accounts in other centers.

Add Cash Flow Accounts

If you did not use Quicken Setup to create all the checking, savings, and credit card accounts you want, you can do it here.

1. Click **Add Account** in the Account Bar.

   –Or–

   From the Banking tab Account Overview view, click **Options** and click **Add An Account**.

   –Or–

   From the Setup tab, in the Checking And Savings Accounts section, click **Add Checking Account** or **Add Savings Account**. From the Credit Cards section, click **Add Credit Card**, or, from the Wallets, Purses And Other Cash section, click **Add Cash Account**.

   All methods open a Quicken Account Setup dialog box. What message you see first will depend on how you opened the dialog.

   - When you open the dialog from the Add Account button at the bottom of the Account Bar, you are prompted to select an account type from all the account types available in Quicken.

   - From the Banking tab, click **Options**, and click **Add An Account**. You can choose a checking, a savings, or a cash account.

   - From the Setup tab, you have already chosen which account type to enter (Checking, Savings, etc.).

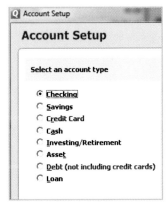

2. You are asked to tell Quicken the institution at which this account is held. If you have already added accounts, you are shown a list of your current financial institutions along with the User ID associated with that account/institution. If the name is not on the list, click **No, The Account Is At A Different Institution Or Has A Different Login**. Click **Next** to continue.

3. If you are adding an account with a new institution, type the name of your financial institution. Often, you can begin typing the first few letters of the name of your institution to display a list, and then click yours. To set up an account without online banking services, click **I Do Not Want To Enter My Financial Institution.** You can set up online banking later when your institution offers it. Click **Next** to continue. If you are setting up an institution without online banking, go to step 8.

4. If you have entered the name of your financial institution, a connection window opens and moves to a login dialog, as seen in Figure 2-11.

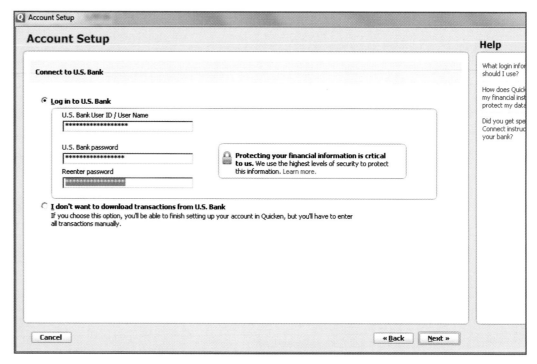

Figure 2-11: **Log in to your financial institution to enable transaction downloads to Quicken.**

NOTE

Some financial institutions ask for additional information as you are signing in. If so, simply enter that information during the connection process.

TIP

For the account name, you can use any combination of letters, numbers, and spaces, except the following characters: right and left brackets ([ ]), the forward slash (/), colon (:), caret (^), and vertical bar (|). If you do not type a name, Quicken uses the type of account as the default name.

5. If you have chosen an institution with which you have a user name, enter that. You are then prompted for the password or PIN provided by or used with your bank. If you do not have your User ID, password, or PIN and wish to use your bank's online services, click the relevant options on the right of the dialog box. Reenter your password to connect to your bank with your Internet connection.

6. If you have chosen a new institution, you are prompted for the user name and password provided by the institution. Enter them and click **Next** to connect with your Internet connection.

7. When the download is complete, check the accounts you want to add to Quicken.

8. Enter an account name, and click **Next**.

9. If you have downloaded transactions, the Setup Complete dialog appears, as seen in Figure 2-12.

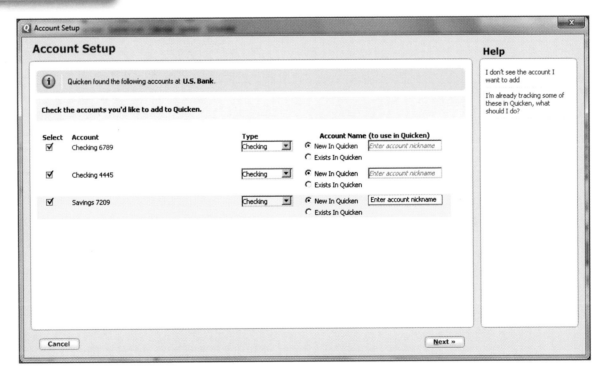

Figure 2-12: A summary of downloaded account information is displayed when the download is complete.

TIP

Many Quicken users find that using the 10-key pad on their computer keyboard is the easiest way to enter numbers.

CAUTION

You can enter dates into Quicken 2010 in any format *except* formats that use dashes, such as 10-8-09.

TIP

When you use a cash account, make sure you include ATM withdrawals and deposits to and from your cash account. You could even set up a cash account just for ATM withdrawals.

TIP

Recording each credit card charge helps you prevent errors and credit card fraud. If a charge appears that you have not made, you can notify your credit card company at once. If your credit card company offers a Quicken download service, you can download the information directly into your Quicken register.

10. If you have not downloaded, you are prompted for the date of the last bank statement and its ending balance.

11. Click **Done**.

ADD A CASH ACCOUNT

Cash accounts are useful for tracking where your money goes. You can set up cash accounts for each member of the family. To set up a cash account:

1. From the Setup tab in the Wallet, Purses And Other Cash section, click **Add Cash Account**.

2. Type a name for the account, such as Nick's Allowance, and click **Next**.

3. If you want to start keeping track of your cash spending as of today, leave the default of today's date. If you want to use another date, enter the one you want.

4. Press **TAB**, enter the amount of cash you are starting with, and click **Next**. The Setup Complete dialog appears.

5. Click **Done** to close the dialog. Your new cash account appears on the Account Bar in the Banking center.

Tracking your spending with cash accounts allows each member of the family to see exactly where his or her money goes. It can be a valuable tool for anyone, but especially for young people as they learn to handle money.

Use Quicken Online

Most banks and credit unions, as well as brokerages, mortgage lenders, and insurance companies, give you the option of connecting to them online and potentially interfacing with Quicken. With banks and credit unions, at least two services are usually offered: online account access and online bill paying. With the online account access service, you use an Internet connection to connect to your financial institution's computer to see what checks have cleared, what deposits have been posted, and what service charges or other *automatically recurring* transactions have been posted to your account. (Automatically recurring transactions are transactions that you have agreed to be automatically deducted from or added to your account on a regular basis, such as property tax, car loan payments, or Social Security checks.) Online banking also allows you to transfer between accounts—from checking to savings, for example, or from your savings account to your credit card account to pay your credit card bill.

The online bill-paying service lets you pay bills electronically rather than by writing a check. You tell the bank the name of the payee, the address, and the amount to pay, and the bank facilitates the payment, either electronically or by writing the check. You can usually set up regularly scheduled payments, such as insurance or mortgage payments, so that those payments are never late.

Quicken also offers bill-paying services through Quicken Bill Pay. Available for any U.S. checking account, the service stores payee information for you, so whenever you make a new payment, account numbers and payee information appear automatically. You just fill in the correct amount to pay. As with some banks, but not all, there is a charge for this service.

Understand Online Services

Today, most financial institutions offer some type of online financial service. This saves them money and offers consumers a valuable tool. All such online services require an Internet connection. Some institutions charge a fee for these services, although many do not. Over time, your costs may be less than working with paper statements, paying bills by check, mailing payments, and buying stamps. Check with your institution to determine its costs for the services they provide. Table 2-2 explains these services.

Working online can save you time and money, and as more financial institutions are going online, their security procedures are becoming more stringent. Many institutions discuss these procedures on their websites, and others provide brochures about maintaining security online. You can help by ensuring you keep your User ID, password, and/or PIN in a secure place; by keeping your antivirus program up-to-date; and by using a good firewall. When using any online service, remember that with any benefit comes some risk.

SERVICE	DESCRIPTION
Online Account Access	This service allows you to look at your account through the financial institution's website. You can see which checks or deposits have been posted and any fees charged to your account. Some institutions allow you to transfer money between accounts. Some also allow you to transfer funds from your banking account to your credit card account to pay your bill. This type of access is now available through many types of companies. Firms as diverse as insurance, utility, telephone, and even gasoline companies are beginning to offer forms of online account access.
Online Bill Payment	With this service, your bank or credit union pays your bills from your existing account. Working with information you give them, the institution will either electronically transfer money from your account to your payee's account or actually prepare a check they send to your payee. While not all institutions support this service, you can get the same service by subscribing to Quicken Bill Pay.
Transaction Download	With this service, you can *download* (copy from the bank's computer to Quicken) all of your account activity. There are three ways to download transactions. Which type you use will depend on your financial institution. ● **Web Connect** This service requires that you log on to the institution's website, enter your identifying information, and indicate which items you want downloaded to Quicken. With this method, you can usually specify a date range for the download. ● **Express Web Connect** With this method, you can access all of the institution's services directly from within Quicken and there is no need to log onto the institution's website. One Step Update uses this method, and Quicken remembers your login information from session to session. ● **Direct Connect** If your institution offers this service, you can create two-way communication with your financial institution instead of the one-way communication available with Express Web Connect. You can transfer from account to account from within Quicken and use the institution's online bill paying services if they are available. Unlike the other two methods, some institutions charge a fee for some services when using the Direct Connect method.

Table 2-2: *Online Services Offered by Many Financial Institutions*

TIP

In many, if not most, instances, if you have an existing Internet connection that you use for e-mail and web browsing, your Quicken Internet connection is automatically set up when you install Quicken, and you need to do nothing further to use Quicken's online features.

UNDERSTAND INTERNET SECURITY

As the Internet has gained popularity, so have the risks in using it. Viruses, worms, spyware, and adware have become part of our vocabulary. As you start to work online, take a moment to understand what each problem is and how to guard your computer and data, as described in Table 2-3.

Before you start your online financial transactions, understand the online security issues and take steps to protect your computer. Your financial institution is working to protect your information on its end, but you need to do your part as well.

DECIDING TO USE ONLINE BANKING SERVICES

In making the decision whether to use online banking services, consider the following points:

- While electronic banking is becoming more common, not all financial institutions make it available through Quicken—or even offer it at all. Ensure your bank or credit union has the service available.

- You need an Internet connection to use these services.

- To ensure security, carefully protect your User ID, password, and/or PIN for your financial institution. Most financial institutions transmit using *encrypted* data. That means anyone intercepting the transmission would see only gibberish. Quicken uses the same method to send information to your financial institution.

- Your records should be up-to-date and your last paper statement reconciled before you start the service.

- You should understand how to use Quicken to record a check, create a deposit, reconcile your accounts, and transfer between accounts before you use the electronic services.

- Financial institutions may charge a fee for some of their online services. Compute the cost of doing it yourself (postage, gas to go to the post office, envelopes, and your time). Compare those costs to the fees charged by Quicken or your financial institution.

PROBLEM	DEFINITION	SOLUTION
Virus	A program that attaches itself to other files on your computer. There are many forms of viruses, each performing different, usually malevolent, functions on your computer.	Install an antivirus program with a subscription for automatic updates, and make sure it is continually running.
Worm	A type of virus that replicates itself repeatedly through a computer network or security breach in your computer. Because it keeps copying itself, a worm can fill up a hard drive and cause your network to malfunction.	
Trojan horse	A computer program that claims to do one thing, such as a game, music, or a story, but has hidden parts that can erase files or even your entire hard drive.	
Adware	The banners and pop-up ads that come with programs you download from the Internet. Often these programs are free, and to support them, the program owner sells space for ads to display on your computer every time you use the program.	Install an anti-adware program.
Spyware	A computer program that downloads with another program from the Internet. Spyware can monitor what you do, keep track of your keystrokes, discern credit card and other personally identifying numbers, and pass that information back to its author.	Install an antispyware program.

Table 2-3: **Security Issues Associated with the Internet and How to Control Them**

Set Up Online Banking

Before you can use online banking services, you must have a working Internet connection. You get such a connection through an *Internet service provider,* or ISP. Ask your friends and neighbors, check your phone book, or call your local telephone company or cable TV company to find an ISP in your area.

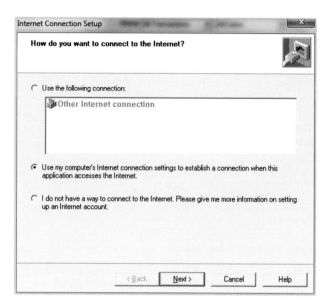

The ISP will give you the information you need to get an Internet connection and set it up in Windows. To set up your Internet connection in Quicken:

1. Click the **Edit** menu, click **Preferences**, and then click **Internet Connection Setup**. The Internet Connection Setup dialog box appears.

2. Choose one of the following three options:

   - Click **Use The Following Connection** to use a listed connection that is different from what your computer normally uses. For example, if your ISP or financial institution requires that you run a program before connecting, or if you are unsure of or unable to use your Windows Internet connection, select this method.

   - Click **Use My Computer's Internet Connection Settings To Establish A Connection When This Application Accesses The Internet**, which is the default, whereby Quicken can detect an Internet connection in Windows.

   - Click **I Do Not Have A Way To Connect To The Internet. Please Give Me More Information On Setting Up An Internet Account** for information that may help you connect to the Internet.

3. Click **Next**. The Connection Settings dialog box appears and confirms the way you are to connect to the Internet. Click **Done** if you're satisfied with this connection. Otherwise, click **Back** to return to the previous dialog box and make another selection.

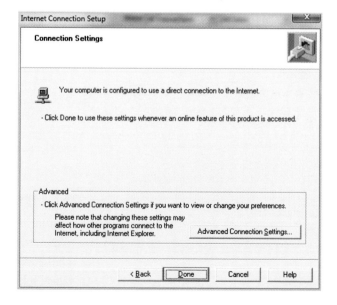

CAUTION

Unless you are an expert with Internet settings, do not make a change through the Advanced Connection Settings dialog box. Any change you make in that Windows system dialog box may affect how other programs connect to the Internet.

Once you have established your Internet connection, you are prepared to contact your bank to sign up for their online services. Many financial institutions allow you to sign up on their website, while others require that you call your local branch. Either way, most institutions need you to fill out an application, send a voided check or complete other paperwork, and agree to their fees. Then, you may need to wait a few days to get your identification number, password, or PIN sent to you by regular mail.

CONNECTION METHODS

There are several methods by which Quicken can update your transactions and balances. Depending on your financial institution, Quicken chooses the best method. Table 2-4 explains the differences. An X under a connection service indicates that the feature applies to that service.

Table 2-4: The Three Ways Quicken Can Update from Your Financial Institution

FEATURE	DIRECT CONNECT	EXPRESS WEB CONNECT	WEB CONNECT
You must set up this service in Quicken even if you already log on to your financial institution's website.	X	X	
Quicken can remember your logon information for you. This can include Customer ID, password, and, in some cases, supplemental information.	X	X	
Two-way communication with your financial institution is possible. You can access account information, transfer money from one account to another, pay bills, and so forth.	X		
All services are available from within Quicken. You don't need to log on to your financial institution's website.	X	X	
You can use One Step Update to update multiple accounts during one session on the Internet.	X	X	
You can usually specify a date range for transactions you want to download.			X
Downloaded transactions are automatically matched with existing transactions, and new transactions are entered into your register.	X	X	X
Your financial institution may require a monthly fee for this service.	X	X	

TIP

While you are waiting for the bank to send you your information to use online banking, ensure that all of your transactions are entered into Quicken and your latest paper statement has been reconciled.

IMPLEMENT ONLINE BANKING

For an account that is not already online, once you have received the login information from the financial institution, you have several ways to implement the online service.

1. For an existing account, click its name in the Account Bar to see its register in the Banking tab.

2. Click **Account Actions** and click **Set Up Online** to open the Account Setup dialog.

3. If you have already set up some accounts for online services, the Account Setup dialog box will display a list of those accounts and the corresponding user identification. If the account you want to set up for online services is at one of the institutions on the list, choose that institution and the User ID by clicking the appropriate radio button, as seen in Figure 2-13.

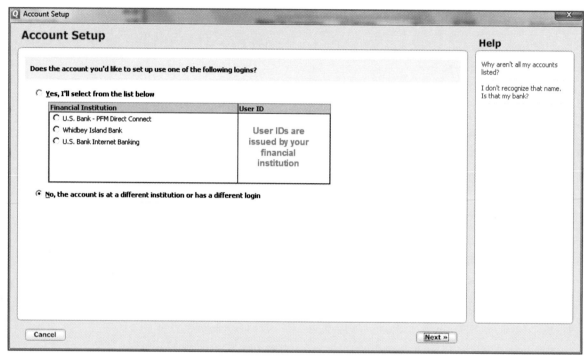

Figure 2-13: *User identification names and numbers are issued by your financial institution.*

4. Click **Next** to enter the password associated with that account. Enter the password and reenter it to ensure you've entered it correctly. Click **Next**, and go to step 7.

5. If the account you are currently setting up for online services is at a different location or has a different user name, click **No, The Account Is At A Different Institution Or Has A Different Login**, and click **Next**.

6. At the next dialog box, type the name of the institution and your login information. Click **Next**.

7. Some institutions may display a dialog box that asks for more information. Fill in the information as needed, and then click **Next**. A dialog box appears, notifying you that you have successfully set up the account.

8. Click **Next** to download your first set of transactions. When you are notified that you have successfully completed the download, click **Done**.

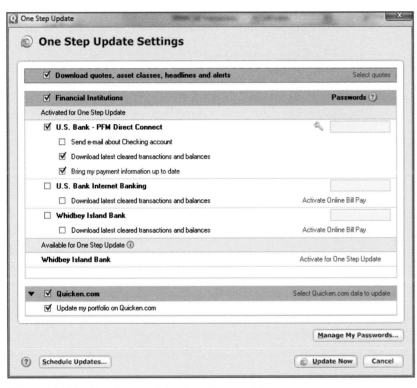

Figure 2-14: *The One Step Update dialog lets you tailor your download to meet your requirements.*

Activate One Step Update

Once you have set up your accounts for online services, you can update all of your transactions and balances at once with One Step Update.

1. Click the **One Step Update** symbol ⓒ Update on the upper-right corner of the Account Bar. The One Step Update Settings dialog appears, as seen in Figure 2-14.

2. Select the institution and information you want to download, and click **Update Now**. Your balances will be updated and transactions downloaded for the accounts you chose.

   - While the information is being downloaded, you can continue to work in other parts of Quicken.

   - Should you need to cancel the update, click **Cancel**.

3. If you want to change how Quicken manages your passwords, click **Manage My Passwords**. For further information, see "Manage Your Passwords."

4. When the update is completed, you are returned to the page from which you started the update.

Manage Your Passwords

Two types of passwords are available for use within Quicken. You can set a password for your Quicken data file so that others cannot access the file without the password. You can also set a password that is required if transactions are modified. This type of password is especially useful after you have filed your income tax and other financial reports for a specific year and want to ensure changes are not made to the data.

To set a password for your Quicken data file:

1. Click **File** and click **Set Password For This Data File**. The Quicken File Password dialog appears.

- In the New Password field, type the password you choose to use.
- In the Confirm Password field, retype the same password.
- Click **OK** to close the dialog.

2. To create a password so that existing transactions cannot be modified without the password:

a. Click **File** and click **Set Password To Modify Transactions**.

b. In the Password To Modify Existing Transactions dialog box that appears, type and confirm the password.

c. Enter the date through which the password is required. For example, if you are done with financial reporting through 12/31/2008, enter 12/31/2008.

d. Click **OK** to close the dialog.

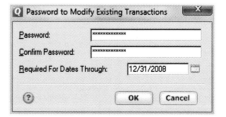

In addition, most financial institutions require passwords to access your information. There are two methods of managing your passwords. The first is the least convenient—entering each password individually. The most secure and convenient method is to store your passwords in the Quicken Password Vault. To do so:

1. Click **Manage My Passwords** from the One Step Update dialog, or click **Tools** from the Quicken Menu bar and choose **Password Vault** and then click **Set Up New Password Vault**.

[**Manage My Passwords...**]

2. Either way will open the Password Vault Setup wizard, as seen in Figure 2-15. Click **Next** to begin.

Figure 2-15: *You can save time by storing your passwords in the Quicken Password Vault.*

3. Select the financial institution from the drop-down list. Click **Next**. If you have several accounts with different User IDs for this financial institution, select the relevant User ID for the password you want to store.

   ● Enter the password you use for this account. The fields may not be left blank.

   ● Enter the password again for confirmation. Click **Next**.

4. If you have multiple accounts with different financial institutions or multiple accounts with the same institution but with different User IDs, you are asked if you want to enter additional passwords. If so, click **Yes** to repeat the process.

If you are finished storing passwords, click **No** and then click **Next**.

5. Enter a master password. The master password protects your Password Vault. It must contain at least six characters with both numbers and letters.

Enter the master password again to confirm it.

6. The password summary displays, showing the passwords that have been stored for each of your accounts.

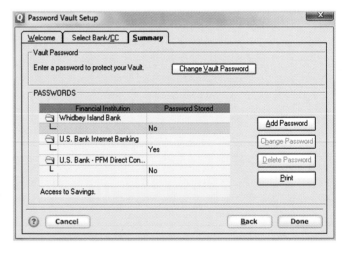

CHANGE YOUR MASTER PASSWORD

It is a good idea to change your master password every six months or so. To change it:

1. Click **Tools** and then click **Password Vault** from the Quicken Menu bar.

2. Click **Add Or Edit Passwords** to open the Edit Password Vault dialog box.

3. Click **Change Vault Password**, enter and confirm a new password, and click **Add** to change the Vault password.

4. Click **Change Password**, enter and confirm a new password, and click **Change** to change the password for your individual accounts.

5. Click **Done** to complete the changes.

CAUTION

Deleting the Password Vault removes all stored passwords and erases the current Password Vault master password.

TIP

When you create a password, make it a *strong* password. A strong password is at least eight characters long and contains *all* of the following: uppercase and lowercase letters, numbers, and one or two special characters, like !, @, #, $, %, ^, &, or *. A strong password should not be recognizable as any kind of name, an address, a date, a telephone number, or a word in any language. Also, it is important to change passwords at least two to four times a year.

DELETE A PASSWORD VAULT

If you have changed banks or want to start over, you can do so. To completely reset the Password Vault, delete the existing Password Vault and set it up again. To delete the current Password Vault:

1. Click **Tools** and click **Password Vault**.

2. Click **Delete Vault And All Saved Passwords**.

3. You are asked if you are sure you want to delete the Password Vault. If so, click **Yes**.

Use Quicken Bill Pay

If your financial institution does not supply online bill-paying services, or if you choose not to use them, Quicken offers a similar service. Quicken Bill Pay is available for all U.S. customers with an Internet connection, who can use it to pay bills to any United States vendor from anywhere in the world.

1. Click **Tools** and click **Quicken Bill Pay** from the Quicken Menu bar.

2. Click **Learn About Quicken Bill Pay** to read a complete description of this service. This service is especially useful if you have a small business or travel extensively. The service allows you to choose the account from which to pay, how much to pay, when to pay, and to schedule recurring payments. The cost for this online service may be offset by postage, time in check preparation, and ease in handling this task.

Understand Categories

A *category* is a description or label for an expense or a source of income. For example, payments to your telephone company might use the Telephone category. You can create subcategories for each category. For example, your trash pickup service might be a subcategory of Utilities. There are two types of categories: Income and Expense. As you set up your accounts and prepare to enter transactions, it is a good idea to set up categories at the same time.

Quicken supplies a number of preset categories for you to use. It also remembers the category you assign for each payee. Quicken customizes your list of categories in response to your answers in Quicken New User Setup. You can add new categories and delete any of the preset categories that do not apply to you.

Work with Categories

To view the preset Category List and add and remove categories:

1. Click the **Tools** menu, and then click **Category List**. Your Category List is displayed, as shown in Figure 2-16. The list shows all of the Income and Expense categories in alphabetical order.

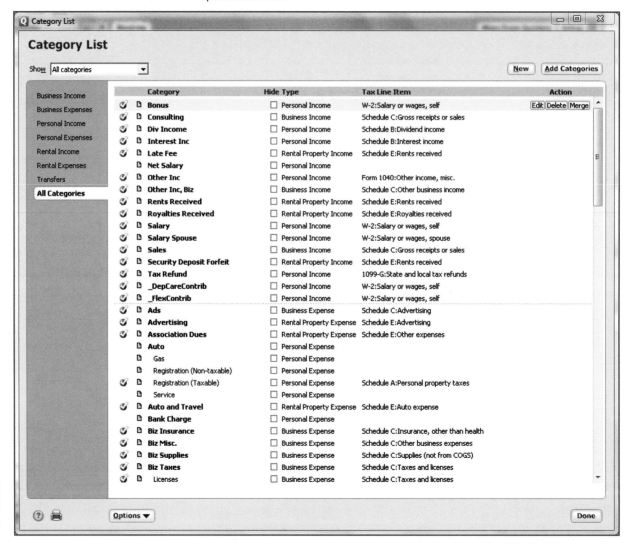

Figure 2-16: The Category List displays the categories you can use to organize your finances.

NOTE

The seven Quicken sets of available categories are Standard, Married, Homeowner, Business, Children, Investment, and Rentals & Royalties.

2. Click the **Show** field drop-down list to choose the categories you want to display, or click a name from the list on the left side of the window.

3. Click **New** to add a new category. See "Add a New Category" later in this chapter.

4. Click **Add Categories** on the right side of the Category List to choose what categories to make available. Quicken supplies a long list of categories for each of its seven preset lists of available categories. This option allows you to add categories to each set of available categories. For example, you might want to choose the Standard set and add a Bonus Personal Income category to that set.

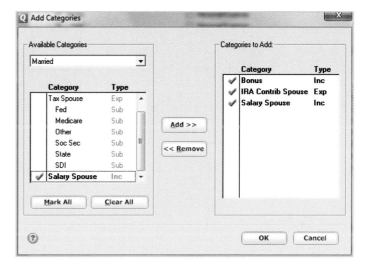

- Choose a type of category from the Available Categories drop-down list.
- Click a category from the Category And Type list.
- Click **Add** to add it to available categories in this group.
- If you want to remove a category, click **Remove**.
- If you want to make all categories available for each group, click **Mark All**.
- Click **Clear All** to start over.
- Click **OK** when you've added all the categories you want to use on a regular basis.

5. From the bottom-left area of the Category List, click the **Help** icon to open the Quicken Help dialog; click the **Print** icon to print the list.

TIP

You can also open the Category List by pressing **CTRL+SHIFT+C**.

TIP

When selecting categories in the Add Categories dialog box, you can select multiple contiguous categories (categories that are next to each other) by holding down the **SHIFT** key while clicking the first and last categories.

6. Click **Options** at the bottom of the Category List to tell Quicken how to display your list.

- **Show Descriptions** displays the description entered for each category.
- **Show Category Group** displays the group into which you've put this category. See "Assign Category Groups" later in this chapter.
- **Show Type** tells Quicken to include the type of category each item is. For example, Bonus is usually a Personal Income item.
- **Show Tax Line Item** includes the tax information you've entered about the category.

Add a New Category

To add a new category:

1. Click the **Tools** menu, click **Category List**, and click **New** in the upper-right corner of the list. The Setup Category dialog box appears.

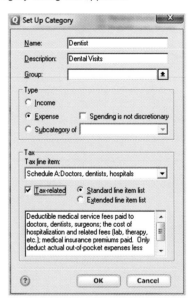

2. Type a name for your new category. Press **TAB** or click in the **Description** field.

3. Type any description necessary, such as <u>Part-time job</u> or <u>Annual homeowner dues</u>.

4. Press **TAB** or click in the **Group** field. You have the option to assign this category to a group. Quicken predefines three groups: Discretionary, Income, and Mandatory Expenses. You can add new groups or choose not to use groups.

TIP

Do not combine alimony payments you receive with child support payments you receive. Instead, create a separate category for each item. Check with your tax professional for further information.

TIP

Assigning tax-line items to categories makes it easier to create tax reports and plan for tax time.

5. Click either **Income** or **Expense** to properly designate this category.

6. If this category is a subcategory, select the primary category (see "Insert an Expense Category with Subcategories" later in this chapter).

7. If this category is tax-related, click **Tax-Related**. Then choose the tax-line item to which it applies:

   a. Click the **Tax Line Item** down arrow to display a list of possible tax lines from which to choose.

   b. Click the relevant line, or you may choose to leave this field blank. A small explanation appears in the box below when a tax-line item is chosen.

8. Click **OK** to finish adding the category and close the dialog.

ASSIGN CATEGORY GROUPS

From the Options menu on the Category List, click **Assign Category Groups**. The Assign Category Group dialog box appears.

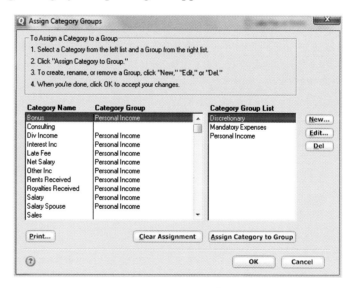

1. Click a category from the Category Name list.

2. Click a category group from the Category Group list.

3. Click **Assign Category To Group**. Repeat the process for all the assignments you want to make.

4. Click **OK** to close the dialog when you are done.

1
3
4
5
6
7
8
9
10

USING TAX-LINE ASSIGNMENTS

While Quicken does not require that you include tax information in categories, entering this information can save a lot of time when preparing your taxes. By using them, Quicken can:

- Display up-to-date tax information in the Tax Center window. By knowing your tax position, you can talk to your tax professional about options well before year-end.

- Prepare tax reports by tax schedule or form. These reports will assist your tax professional and perhaps save you money in tax-preparation fees.

- Create reports that describe taxable and nontaxable dividends, interest, and other items separately.

- Help you use the Tax Planner within Quicken (see Chapter 10).

- Export your data directly into Intuit's TurboTax to help you prepare your income tax return.

The time you spend assigning tax-line items to your categories can save a lot of time and money at the end of the year.

TIP

Just because Quicken uses a specific category or subcategory does not mean you have to use it in the same way. For example, if you want all of your insurance expenses to be one category, delete the subcategories.

RENAME A CATEGORY

You can rename a category to make it more meaningful.

1. In the Category List window, right-click the name of the category, and click **Edit**. The Edit Category dialog box appears.

> New
> Edit
> Delete
> Merge

2. The Name field should already be selected. If not, click in it to select it, and type a new name.

3. If this category is tax-related, review the tax-line item to ensure it is still correct.

4. Click **OK** to close the Edit Category dialog box.

INSERT AN EXPENSE CATEGORY WITH SUBCATEGORIES

Expense categories are the best way to find out just where you are spending your money. You can use any of the predefined categories or add your own. You can also create subcategories to show more detail. When you categorize each item, you can create reports and graphs that show spending patterns and habits. You can even create budgets for categories or groups of categories.

1. Follow the instructions in "Add a New Category" earlier in this chapter to add a category to which you want to add subcategories.

2. To add a subcategory to your new category, right-click the parent category in the Category List, and click **New** from the context menu. The Set Up Category dialog box appears.

3. Type the name of your subcategory. Press **TAB** to move to the Description field, and type a description if you want.

4. Leave the **Group** field blank, or click the **Group** down arrow, and make a selection from the drop-down list.

5. Click the **Subcategory Of** option. Type the name of the parent category, or choose it from the drop-down list.

6. If this expense has tax implications, click **Tax-Related** and choose the tax-line item from the drop-down list. Otherwise, leave the **Tax** field empty.

7. Click **OK** to close the dialog box.

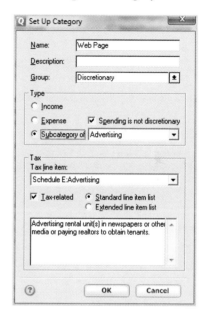

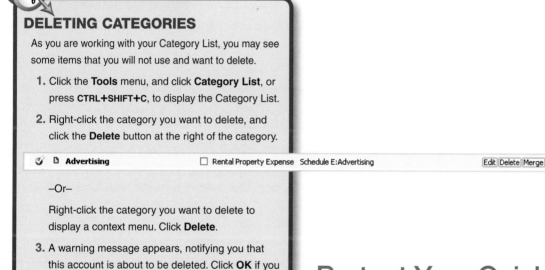

TIP

You can choose to hide a category by clicking the **Hide** check box. Hidden categories do not appear on the Category List, but are still included in the Quicken data file.

QUICKSTEPS

DELETING CATEGORIES

As you are working with your Category List, you may see some items that you will not use and want to delete.

1. Click the **Tools** menu, and click **Category List**, or press **CTRL+SHIFT+C**, to display the Category List.

2. Right-click the category you want to delete, and click the **Delete** button at the right of the category.

–Or–

Right-click the category you want to delete to display a context menu. Click **Delete**.

3. A warning message appears, notifying you that this account is about to be deleted. Click **OK** if you want to delete the account, or click **Cancel** if this was an error.

4. If you click **OK**, the category disappears from the Category List.

5. Click **OK** to close the Category List.

You will see the new category as a subcategory on the Category List. The Category List displays the categories in alphabetical order. Subcategories are displayed in alphabetical order indented underneath the parent category.

Protect Your Quicken Data

Computers have been a great asset to many of us. However, like any machine, they are prone to failures of many kinds. Once you have started using Quicken regularly, it becomes important to protect your information and store it in another location should your hard drive fail or something else happen to your computer.

Quicken offers an easy solution to this problem called Quicken Backup. *Backup* (or back up—the verb form) is a computer term that means storing a copy of your information in a location other than on your computer.

You can back up your information to a floppy disk, a CD, another drive that is connected to your computer (such as a flash or thumb drive), or to a hard drive on another computer. You might choose to alternate your backup to two different flash drives each time you use the program, and then back up all of your data to a recordable CD and store it in your bank safety deposit box a couple of times a year.

Back Up Your Data to External Media

To create a backup data file to a disk on your computer:

1. Click **File** on the Quicken Menu bar, and then click **Backup And Restore**.

2. Click **Back Up Quicken File** to display the Quicken Backup dialog box.

   –Or–

   Press **CTRL+B**.

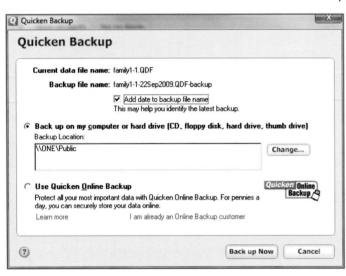

*Figure 2-17: **Quicken Backup protects your data.***

3. The Quicken Backup dialog appears, as seen in Figure 2-17.

4. The current data file information and the default backup file name assigned by Quicken are displayed.

5. Clear the **Add Date To File Name** check box if you do not want to add the date to your backup file name.

6. Click **Back Up On My Computer Or Hard Drive (CD, Floppy Disk, Hard Drive, Thumb Drive)**.

7. The location to which this data file will be backed up appears in the Backup Location field. Click **Change** to back up your information to another location.

8. If you have signed up for the fee-based Quicken backup service, click **Use Quicken Online Backup** instead of the Back Up On My Computer option.

9. Click **Back Up Now**.

10. When the backup is complete, a message box appears telling you that your data file has been successfully backed up.

11. Click **OK** to close the message box.

How to...

- *Track Investments*
- *Set Up a Standard Brokerage or IRA Account*
- *Enter Your Holdings*
- *Understanding Placeholders in Investment Accounts*
- *Set Up One Step Update*
- *Add a 401(k) or 403(b) Account*
- *Creating a Single Mutual Fund Account*
- *Work with the Net Worth Tab*
- *Set Up a House Account with a Mortgage*
- *Add Other Net Worth Accounts*
- *Deleting and Hiding Accounts*
- *Add Other Debt Accounts*
- *Use EasyStep Loan Setup*
- *Printing an Amortization Schedule*

Chapter 3
Adding More Accounts

In the first two chapters, the focus was on setting up the checking, savings, and credit card accounts. In this chapter you'll look at the Investing and the Net Worth tabs, learn how to set up their accounts, and examine some of the Quicken tools that are available in those areas. Both areas are optional, depending on how much detail you want to maintain in Quicken.

Understand Financial Terminology

Before you begin working with the Investing and Net Worth accounts, review the terms that are used in these areas, as explained in Table 3-1.

TERM	DEFINITION
Asset	Something you own that you expect to increase in value
Brokerage	A company that buys and sells stocks and bonds for a fee on behalf of their clients
Default	A setting or other value used by a computer program. Quicken names an account "Asset" by default if you do not choose another name.
Depreciation	A decrease or loss in value due to age, wear, or market conditions
Equity	The market value of an asset, less any debt owed on that asset
Interest	Rent or payment on borrowed money
Interest rate	The percentage of a debt charged for borrowing money
Investment	Something you expect to increase in value or to generate income
Market value	The amount for which an asset can be sold today
Mutual fund	An investment portfolio that contains the securities of other companies and sells shares of the portfolio
Performance	How a specific investment behaves over time—for example, how much money it earns
Portfolio	A set of investments
Principal	The original amount of a debt or investment on which interest is calculated
Real property	Assets that consist of land and/or buildings
Securities	Documents that show ownership, such as a stock certificate or a bond
Stock	Capital raised by selling portions (*shares*) of the ownership of a corporation. Stockholders receive a share of profits called *dividends* based on the number of shares they own.

Table 3-1: Definitions Pertaining to the Investment and Net Worth Accounts in Quicken

TIP

You can look up financial terms with which you are not familiar by typing them in at Google.com.

Use the Investing Tab

The Investing center can contain four types of investment accounts:

- **Standard brokerage accounts** allow you to track stocks, bonds, mutual funds, and annuities. You can download information directly from your brokerage company or enter items manually to keep track of your capital gains or losses, cash balances, market values, performance, and shares for one or more securities.

- **IRA or Keogh accounts** track your retirement plans.

- **401(k) and 403(b) accounts** track your pre-tax contribution investment accounts for your retirement. It is important to set up a separate account for each plan.

- **529 Plan** tracks this educational savings plan to ensure your children's college tuition.

Table 3-2 describes which type of account to use for a particular type of investment.

INVESTMENT	USE THIS ACCOUNT TYPE
401(k) and 401(b)	401(k) or 403(b)
Annuities	Standard brokerage account
Brokerage account	Standard brokerage account
CD or money market account	Standard brokerage account (Note: You can also set these up as standard savings accounts in the Cash Flow center.)
Dividend reinvestment program	Standard brokerage account
Employee stock options or employee stock purchase plans (ESPP)	Standard brokerage account
IRA (any type)	IRA or Keogh account
Real estate investment trusts (REIT)	Standard brokerage account
Real property	Asset account
529 Educational Plan (can be an IRA in some states)	529 Plan
Stocks and bonds (certificates that you hold, including U.S. savings bonds)	Standard brokerage account
Treasury bills	Standard brokerage account

Table 3-2: *Types of Quicken Investment Accounts to Use with Various Investments*

TIP

If you hold bonds or stock certificates in a safe deposit box or other secure location, you can still track your information in a standard brokerage account.

TIP

Review your portfolio each year at the same time you receive your Personal Earnings and Benefit Estimate Statement from the Social Security Administration.

Track Investments

Using Quicken to track your investments allows you to consolidate all of your investment information so that you can easily see the value of your total portfolio at any time. Understanding the performance history of several different types of investments and being able to calculate capital gains quickly can be extremely helpful throughout the year, as well as at year-end for tax purposes.

You open the Investing center by clicking the **Investing** tab. You can also right-click **Investing** from the Account Bar and click **Go To Investing**. Figure 3-1 shows the Investing center before you have set up any investing accounts.

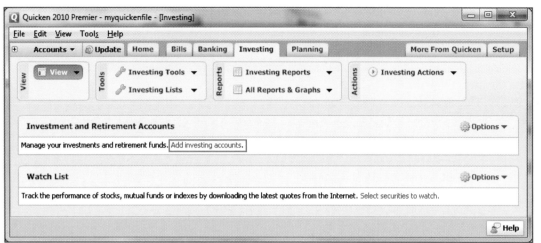

Figure 3-1: **You can add new accounts and manage all of your investing activities with tools found by clicking the Investing tab.**

Set Up a Standard Brokerage or IRA Account

Setting up an account in the Investing center is similar to setting up an account in the Banking center. To set up your first investing account:

1. Select the **Investing** tab, and click **Add Investing Accounts**, as seen in Figure 3-1. This view appears only when you have not yet entered any investment accounts.

If you have already entered an account in this center, from the Investing tab, click **Investing Actions,** click **Investing Accounts**, and click **Add Account**.

–Or–

Select the **Setup** tab, and from the Investment And Retirement Accounts section, click **Add Investment Account** to open the same dialog box.

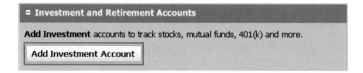

–Or–

In the Investing center, click **Options** and click **Add An Account**.

–Or–

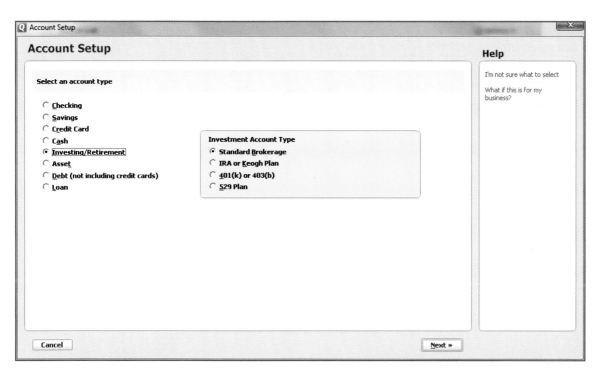

Figure 3-2: *You can choose from four types of investment accounts in Quicken.*

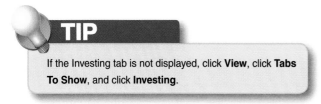

TIP

If the Investing tab is not displayed, click **View**, click **Tabs To Show**, and click **Investing**.

Right-click anywhere in the Account Bar, and from the context menu that appears, click **Add New Account**.

–Or–

Click **Add Account** at the bottom of the Account Bar.

2. In all cases, the Account Setup dialog box appears, as shown in Figure 3-2. Depending on which option you chose to set up the new account, you may only see the Investment Account Type list from which to choose.

3. Choose the type of account you want to set up, and click **Next**. If you have entered Standard Brokerage, IRA or Keogh Plan, or 401(k) or 403(b), you have the following two choices:

● **The Account Is Held At The Following Institution.** For this default option, type the first few letters of the name of your brokerage. A drop-down list appears as Quicken tries to match the name you are typing. Select the name of your brokerage from the list.

● **I Do Not Want To Enter My Financial Institution.** Use this option if you do not want to download from your broker, or if your institution does not offer download services.

4. After you have chosen one of the two options, click **Next** to continue. If you have entered the name of your brokerage and are connected to the Internet, a brief message appears that Quicken is connecting to the brokerage. If your institution has download services available, you are prompted to enter your user name and password information, as seen in Figure 3-3.

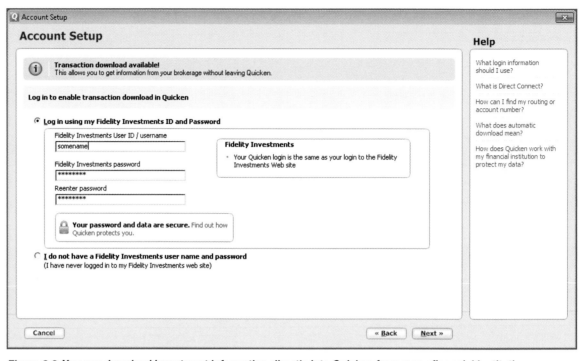

Figure 3-3: *You can download investment information directly into Quicken from many financial institutions.*

NOTE

Most financial institutions require that you sign up for their download service prior to using the Quicken download. Most institutions require an account number or ID and a password or PIN that they assign.

5. Depending on the type of investment and your institution, you may also see a message similar to the one shown in Figure 3-4.

6. You are prompted to enter a name that you will use for this account in Quicken. If you are entering a 529 Plan, this is the first dialog box you will see.

7. Depending on the type of investment account you are setting up, you may also be prompted for information about your holdings. See "Enter Your Holdings" later in this chapter for more information.

8. If you do not choose online setup, or if your institution does not support online setup, the next dialog box asks you to name the account you are adding. Type a name for this account. You can type any name that identifies the account for you. You might consider using the name of the brokerage firm or other institution. If this account is an IRA or Keogh account, you are asked if this is for you or your spouse. You are also asked to choose the type of IRA from a drop-down list. Choose one and click **Next** to continue.

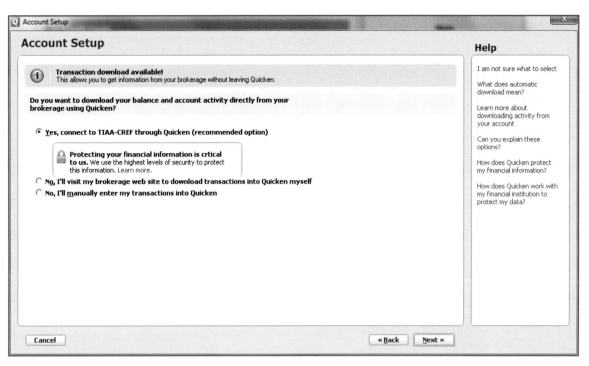

Figure 3-4: *Either tell Quicken to download your transactions at the same time you are creating your account or that you will download them at a later time.*

9. Using either your last statement or your account on the firm's website, enter the last statement date (or the "as of" date), the ending cash balance in the account, and any money-market fund balances in the account, and then click **Next**.

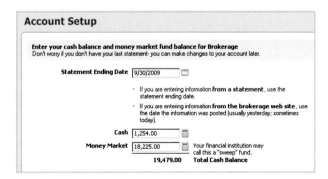

TIP

Some firms call the cash amounts not invested on a given date a *sweep account*.

QUICK**FACTS**

UNDERSTANDING PLACEHOLDERS IN INVESTMENT ACCOUNTS

You may see a note in an investment account that says "Placeholder entries for missing data are used in these calculations." Quicken uses these entries when you have not entered either the purchase date or purchase price of a security. Placeholder entries simply record the name and number of shares in an investment account transaction. When you enter all of the information about a security, including purchase date and price, Quicken can track the performance of these securities.

If you want to let Quicken correctly reflect the data, either download the information from your financial institution, if it is available, or enter the information directly from the original purchase information statement. As you enter each transaction, Quicken subtracts what you enter from the placeholder entry until all of the current shares have been entered.

10. You may be prompted for additional information, such as the securities that are in the account. If you want Quicken to download current information about each security, type its symbol. If you do not have an Internet connection, you can just type the name of the security. You can add more information later (see "Enter Your Holdings" later in this chapter). Click **Next** to continue.

11. After you have entered all the information about this new investing account, click **Done** to complete the account setup.

Refer to Table 3-2 for some suggestions as to which Quicken investment account you should use for each of your investments.

Enter Your Holdings

As you create your new investment account, at some point you may be prompted to enter information about each of the securities that are held in the account. The point at which this prompt appears will vary by the type of account you are creating. With your Internet connection, Quicken can help you find the ticker symbols for your securities.

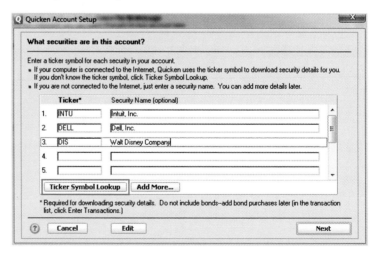

1. In the Quicken Account Setup: What Securities Are In This Account dialog box, select the first text box to enter the ticker symbol for the first security. If you do not know the symbol and have an Internet connection, click **Ticker Symbol Lookup** to open the Quicken Investing Symbol Lookup page, as seen in Figure 3-5.

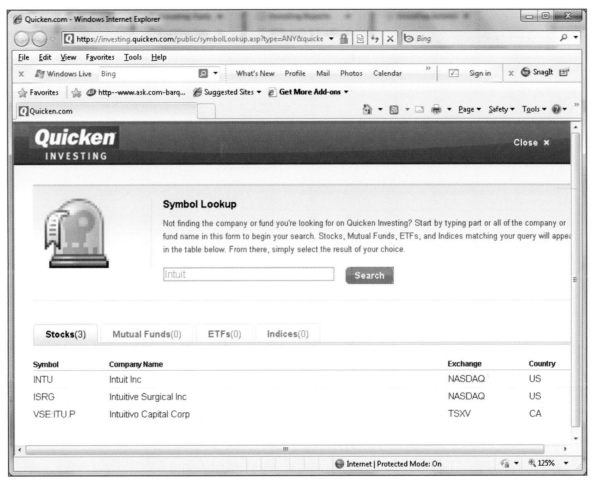

Figure 3-5: *You can use the Quicken Symbol Lookup to find the ticker symbol for many of your securities.*

2. Use your TAB key to move through the text boxes, entering each of the securities in the account. If you need to add more than five, click the **Add More** button.

3. After you have entered all of the securities in this account, click **Next**.

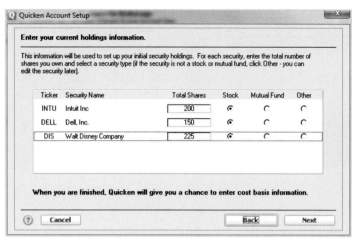

4. You are prompted to enter the total shares you hold for each security. Click in the **Total Shares** text box, and type the number of shares. Click the radio buttons to indicate if the security is a stock, a mutual fund, or another type of security. Use TAB to move between fields. Click **Next** to continue.

5. A summary window shows all of the information you have entered about your securities. If there is a cash balance, that displays as well. Click **Done** to continue.

6. Quicken may ask if this is a single mutual-fund account. If so, click **Yes** and then click **Next**. See the "Creating a Single Mutual Fund Account" QuickSteps later in this chapter. If this account is not a single mutual fund account, click **No** and then click **Next**.

7. The Setup Complete dialog box appears. Click **Done** to return to the Investing center.

Your new account information appears in the Investing center, as seen in Figure 3-6. With your Internet connection, Quicken downloaded the current prices for your securities. However, Quicken cannot calculate the gain or loss on each investment without knowing what you paid for your securities.

Figure 3-6: Quicken automatically updates the current price of your securities if you're online; if you enter the cost, Quicken can calculate your gain or loss.

The amount you paid is called your *cost basis*. Quicken displays an asterisk in the Gain/Loss columns, called a *placeholder entry*, until you complete the information. You may enter this information now or later.

ENTER COSTS FOR SECURITIES

To enter the cost for your security:

1. Select the **Investing** tab, and choose the account with which you want to work. When that account is displayed, click the **Transactions subtab** if it is not already selected, as seen in Figure 3-7.

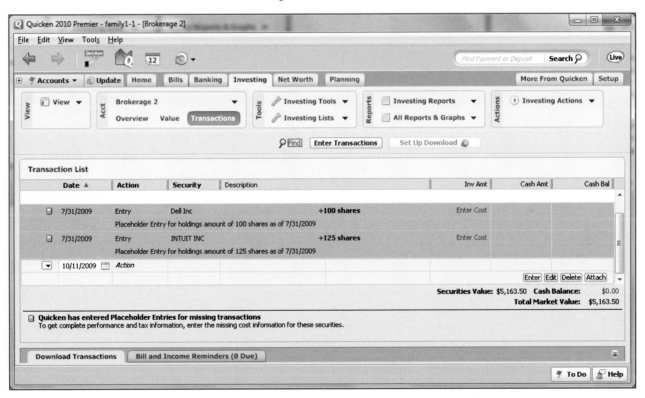

Figure 3-7: Placeholder entries show the number of shares you own, but not what you paid for those shares.

If your placeholder entries don't show, you may need to set the preferences to view hidden investment transactions. Click **Edit** and click **Preferences**. Then click **Quicken Preferences**, click **Investment Transactions**, and click **Show Hidden Transactions**. For a more complete display in the account register, choose **Two Line** in the List Display text box.

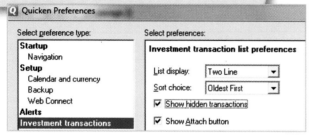

2. Click **Enter Cost** in the Inv Amt column for a security for which you want to enter the cost. The Enter Missing Transactions dialog box appears.

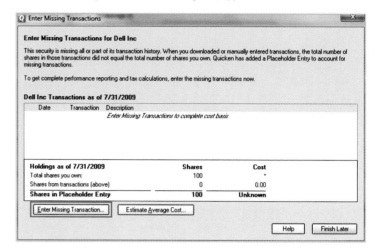

3. Click **Enter Missing Transaction**. The Buy-Shares Bought dialog box appears.

● Enter the transaction date, number of shares, the price per share that you paid on that date, and the commission you paid. Quicken will calculate a total cost. Click **Enter/Done** when finished.

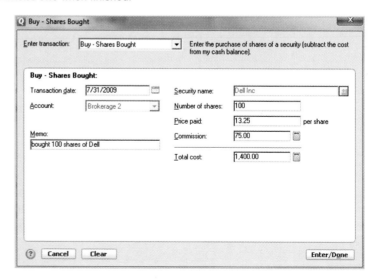

–Or–

- If you purchased the shares over time, click **Estimate Average Cost**. Enter values in either the **Total Cost** or the **Share Price** fields, and click **OK**. This option is not as accurate as entering each batch of shares you purchased, but it is quicker and may be enough if you don't need all the detail. You can come back and enter the individual transactions at a later date.

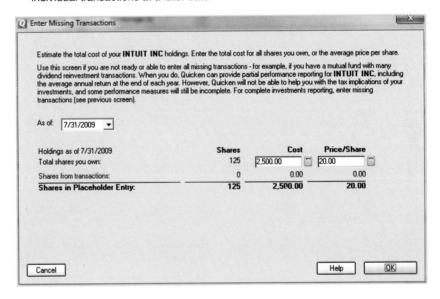

4. Repeat steps 1 through 3 for each security you own.

Set Up One Step Update

Quicken 2010 allows you to update all of your financial information in one step. You can download transactions from your bank, credit union, brokerage firm, or credit card company. This single-access feature allows you to schedule downloads at your convenience or whenever you use Quicken. To set up One Step Update:

1. Click **Update** at the top of the Account Bar to display the One Step Update Settings dialog box. You can also access this dialog box from the Quicken menu. Click **Tools** and click **One Step Update**.

2. Depending on how you have managed the passwords for each of your financial institutions, you may be prompted for individual passwords or for your Password Vault password.

3. Click **Download Quotes, Asset Classes, Headlines And Alerts** to obtain information about the holdings you have entered. Click **Select Quotes** to open the Customize Online Updates dialog box, and choose the relevant holdings.

USE THE QUOTES TAB

In the Customize Online Updates dialog box:

1. Click the **Quotes** tab, and click **Mark All** to mark all securities for which you want current quotes. Click **Clear All** if you want to choose only a few.

2. To exclude any one item, click the check mark in front of the security name to clear it. To add a new security, click **New Security**. Enter the information for this new security. If necessary, use the Look Up button to find its ticker symbol. Click **Next**. Quicken uses your Internet connection to download information about this security. Click **Done** to add the security to your list.

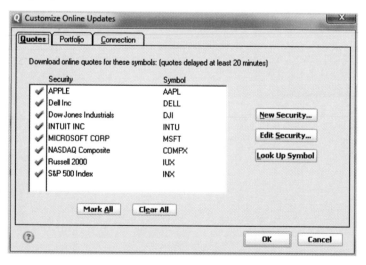

3. Select any security on the list, and click **Edit Security** to view information about that security and make any changes to its details. When you are done making any changes, click **OK**.

USE THE PORTFOLIO TAB

The Portfolio tab lets you set up accounts on Quicken.com so that you can track your investment accounts and Watch List from any Internet connection throughout the world. If you have created your Quicken.com account during registration, you can access it by going to www.quicken.com/investments and signing in.

To make changes in the Portfolio tab:

1. Click **Mark All** or **Clear All** as described earlier in this section.
2. Click **Track My Watch List On Quicken.com** to receive information about holdings on your Watch List.
3. Click **Send My Shares** to track the value of your securities.
4. Click **Send Only My Symbols** to track only the current market-share prices of your portfolio.

USE THE CONNECTION TAB

The Connection tab has several options:

- Click **Send Anonymous Product Usage Data During One Step Update** to help improve Quicken. No personal or financial information is collected—only information on how you, the Quicken user, utilize the items available to you.
- Click **Run One Step Update When Starting Quicken** to automatically update selected account balances, quotes, and your Watch List, and to obtain current stock prices. This feature requires an Internet connection.
- Click **Quicken.com Login** if you want to change your Quicken.com member ID and/or password at the same time you run One Step Update.

When you have selected the accounts to update and chosen your other settings, click **OK** to close the Customize Online Updates dialog box. You are returned to the One Step Update Settings dialog box. From here, you can click **Quicken.com** to update your information that you have selected previously. Click **Manage My Passwords** to work with the Password Vault. If you want to schedule updates, click **Schedule Updates** to establish what you want updated and how often.

Click **Update Now** to run the update, or click **Cancel** to close the One Step Update Settings dialog box.

Add a 401(k) or 403(b) Account

Entering a 401(k) or 403(b) account is similar to setting up an investment account, as described in "Set Up a Standard Brokerage or IRA Account" earlier in this chapter. Use steps 1 through 6 in that section, choosing **401(k)** or **403(b)** as the type of account. Then, in the **Tell Us About This Account** dialog box:

1. Enter the date of your last paper statement (optional), enter your employer's name, select whether this account is from your current employer or a previous employer, and designate whether this account is your account or that of your spouse.

2. If your statement shows how many shares you own, click **Yes**. If not, click **No**. Click **Next** to continue.

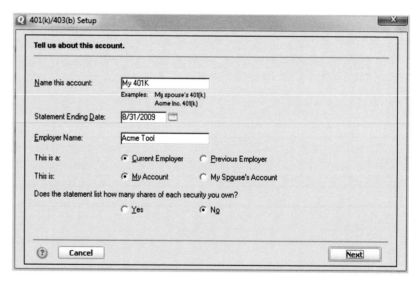

3. When asked if you would like to track loans against this account, click **No** if there are no loans. If there are loans against this account, click **Yes** and enter the number of loans. Click **Next** to continue.

CAUTION

While some 401(k) plans allow you to take loans against the funds in the plan, it may not be a good idea. The interest payments on these loans are not tax-deductible, and you lose the growth you would have gotten on the amount of the loan. See your tax professional for more information.

QUICKSTEPS

CREATING A SINGLE MUTUAL FUND ACCOUNT

A single mutual fund account is an account that you buy directly from a mutual fund company. Many new investors start with this type of account, as it often requires a smaller initial investment, and one can contribute regular, small amounts. This type of fund has no cash or money market balance, as all contributions are used to purchase more shares in the fund. When you first buy a single mutual fund from a mutual fund company (or if you already own one), you can use a single mutual fund account to track it. To add this type of account, follow the first six steps in setting up an investment account as described in "Set Up a Standard Brokerage or IRA Account" earlier in this chapter, selecting the appropriate account type (Standard Brokerage, IRA, etc).

1. When asked to enter the securities in the new account, click **Next**. A message box appears asking if you are sure you want to create an account with no security holdings. Click **Yes**. At the resulting dialog box, click **Done**.

2. A dialog box appears asking if this is a single mutual fund account, as seen in Figure 3-8.

Continued . . .

4. If you clicked **Yes** in step 3, you are asked for a description of this loan and its current balance. Click **Set Up An Account To Track The Remaining Balance Of This Loan**, type the original loan amount, and click **Next**.

5. You are asked about the securities in this account. Type the ticker symbol if you know it, or type the name of the security. You can enter all the details later if you want. Click **Next** to continue.

6. Enter the total shares you own and the total market value of the shares shown on your statement. Click **Next**.

Figure 3-8: *Single mutual fund accounts have no cash balance or securities.*

3. At the Are You Setting Up This Type Of Account? dialog box click **Yes**. Click **Next** to continue.

4. The Summary dialog box appears. Review your account and, when you are ready, click **Done** to complete the setup.

This account tracks only the one mutual fund. The register displays share balances and the market value of these shares, but does not track interest, miscellaneous income, or expenses, as all dividends from the shares are usually reinvested. If your single mutual fund holder offers online services, you may download information directly into your account register. If you are unable to download transactions, or if you choose not to download, you can update this type of account from your paper statement, as described in "Enter Costs for Securities" earlier in this chapter.

7. Review the summary of what you have entered. If you have chosen to enter the information from your paper statement, the summary should match the total shown on that statement. Click **Done** to finish setting up this account. You are returned to the Setup Complete dialog box. Click **Done**.

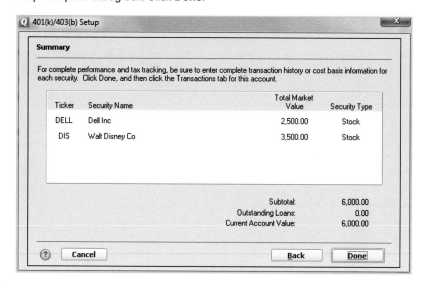

Use the Net Worth Tab

The Net Worth tab contains accounts that provide a way to integrate all your other financial information into Quicken so that you can see your total financial position at any given moment. The Property and Debt accounts in this tab include:

- **House** accounts are used for your main residence, vacation home, rental properties, or other real estate. You can create a liability account for each property at the same time you create the asset account.

- **Vehicle** accounts are used for all types of vehicles, including cars, trucks, motorcycles, boats, motor homes, and campers. You can create liability accounts for the loans on each vehicle at the same time you create the asset accounts.

- **Asset** accounts are used for assets other than real property, vehicles, or investments. Examples include sterling silver, antiques, baseball card collections, first-edition and rare books, and business equipment.

- **Liability** accounts are used for personal debts other than credit cards. Credit cards are, by default, included with the Banking accounts. Examples of liability accounts include personal loans and promissory notes you owe banks, loan companies, and individuals, as well as student loans. You can also link a liability with an asset, such as a home equity loan or line of credit. For more information on linking asset and liability accounts, see Chapter 6.

Work with the Net Worth Tab

You use the Net Worth tab to:

- Record your major assets and debts to better understand your overall financial standing.

- Allow Quicken to calculate the amount due on your mortgage and other obligations.

- Track the amount of interest you are paying on any specific debt and in total.

Not all Quicken users need to enter information in the Net Worth tab, but if you have a mortgage, make car payments, or have other assets and liabilities, you might want to consider adding the information to Quicken so that you can see your true financial picture.

Set Up a House Account with a Mortgage

For most people, their biggest asset is their home. There are several methods by which you can enter this asset and any associated liability.

1. Right-click the Account Bar, and from the context menu, click **Add New Account**, or use any of the alternative ways to add an account described earlier in "Set Up a Standard Brokerage or IRA Account."

Depending on the method you choose, the Account Setup dialog box appears.

NOTE

If the Net Worth tab is not displayed, from the Quicken menu, click **View**, click **Tabs To Show**, and click **Net Worth**.

2. If necessary, click **Asset** and **House** as shown in Figure 3-9, and click **Next**.

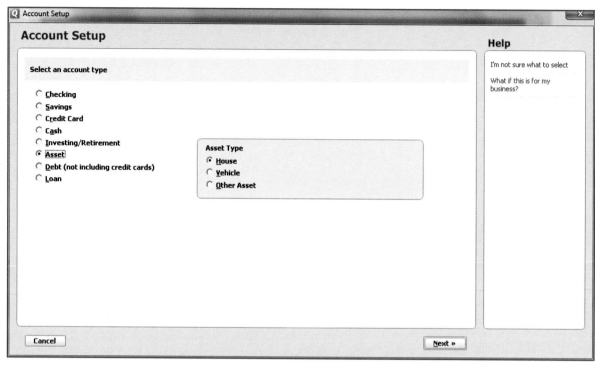

Figure 3-9: Use the Account Setup dialog box to create a Quicken asset account for your home.

3. Type a name for the account. Quicken uses "House" as the default. If you have more than one house account, Quicken uses "House 2," "House 3," and so forth, unless you type another name. Click **Next**.

4. Enter or select the date you acquired the property. You can use the small calendar icon to the right of the date of acquisition field to select the date. Press **TAB** to move to the next field.

5. Enter the purchase price, and again press **TAB**. Estimate the value of your home today. Quicken requires that you enter an amount, so use your best guess. You can change the value later. Click **Next**.

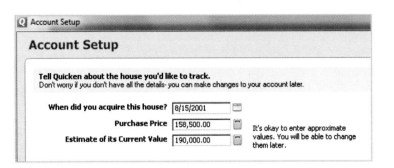

6. Choose if and how you want the liability account set up for the house:

- Click **Yes** and **I'd Like To Track The Mortgage In Quicken** if you have not already created a liability account for the mortgage.

- Click **Yes** and **I'm Already Tracking The Mortgage In Quicken** if you have entered the liability account. Choose which account is associated with this asset in the **Select Existing Account** drop-down box.

- Click **Yes** and **I Do Not Want To Track The Mortgage In Quicken** if that is your choice.

- Click **No** if you have no mortgage.

7. Click Next to continue.

SET UP A MORTGAGE IN QUICKEN

If you chose to track the mortgage in Quicken and you have not already set up the mortgage liability account, the EasyStep Loan Setup Wizard appears.

1. Click **Next** to continue setting up the loan.

2. Click **Borrow Money** and click **Next**.

3. By default, Quicken will create an account and show it as "House Loan" in the existing account text box. If you want to change the account, click **New Account** and type a name you want to use for this mortgage in the text box. Click **Next**.

4. At the next dialog box, tell Quicken if any payments have been made on this loan. Click **Yes** if payments have been made, and **No** if they have not. Click **Next** to continue.

5. Continue through the wizard, entering the original balance and length of the loan, how it is compounded, and how often you make payments, pressing TAB to move from field to field. Use the small calculator icon to the right of the **Original Balance** field if you want. Click **Next** to continue.

TIP

Try using the 10-key pad on your keyboard to enter numbers (make sure the NUMLOCK light on the keyboard is lit; press the NUMLOCK key if it isn't). Using the 10-key pad is similar to using a calculator.

The compounding period reflects how your lending institution computes the interest charged on the loan. The more often the institution calculates the interest, the more interest you pay. Most institutions compound interest daily.

6. If you are unsure of the payment amount, enter the interest rate, and click **Calculate**. Quicken will compute the amount of principal and interest for each payment. Click **Done**. A message appears advising you that Quicken has calculated the next loan payment. You are instructed to click **OK** to return to the Loan Setup dialog box. You see the estimate of the current balance, the next payment amount, and the date on which it is due. You can change this later if you want.

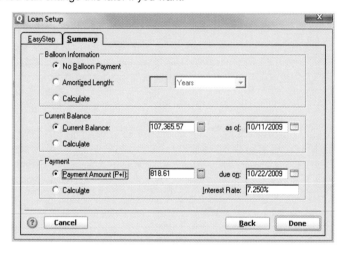

7. Click **Done**. The Edit Loan Payment dialog box appears. If you want, change the interest rate and/or adjust the principal and interest payment.

8. Click **Edit** to include other amounts you pay with your mortgage payment, such as real estate taxes and homeowners' insurance. In the **Split Transaction** dialog box, enter the category for each portion and the amount for each category, and then click **OK**.

9. Click in the **Payee** field to enter the name of your mortgage lender. Adjust the next payment date, and, if desired, change the interest category. By default, Quicken uses "Interest Exp" as the category.

10. If you will be printing the check from Quicken, click **Print Check** in the Type drop-down list.

11. Click **Payment Method** to select how the payment will be entered into Quicken.

- Choose **Scheduled Bill** to tell Quicken how to enter the payment, from which account it is to be paid, and how many days in advance the payment should be entered.

- Click **Memorized Payee** to simply memorize the payee and not schedule the payment.

- If you have enabled this mortgage payment as a recurring online payment, click **Repeating Online Payment**.

- Click **OK** to close the Select Payment Method dialog box.

12. Enter any memo, such as the account number, that should be included on the printed check.

13. Click **Address** to create an address for the payee's name you entered. This option is available only if you choose Print Check as the transaction type.

14. Click **Pay Now** to set up a payment. Click **OK** to close the dialog box.

15. After you have completed editing the loan, click **OK**.

16. At the dialog box to which you are returned, click **Done**.

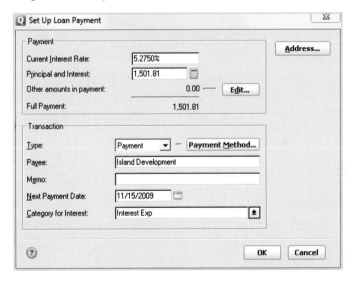

NOTE

Some variable-rate or adjustable-rate loans change the interest rate with the next payment that is due. Others change the interest rate for all future payments.

Your new asset account and its related liability account appear in both the Net Worth page (see Figure 3-10) and the Account Bar.

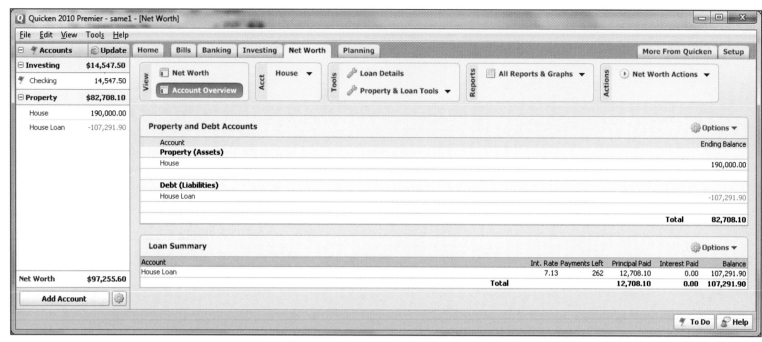

Figure 3-10: *You see both your property and your debts when opening the Net Worth tab.*

Add Other Net Worth Accounts

You can create other accounts within the Net Worth tab. As you work with the dialog boxes, you will see similarities between the various accounts. To add a vehicle, for example:

1. Click **Add Account** from the Account Bar, or use any of the other methods to add an account described earlier in this chapter.

2. Click **Asset**, if necessary, and click **Vehicle**. Click **Next**.

NOTE

If one of your vehicles is a motor home, consult your tax professional to see if you should consider this your primary home or a second home.

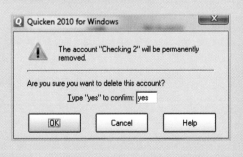

QUICKSTEPS

DELETING AND HIDING ACCOUNTS

If you want to remove an account from view in Quicken, you can *delete* it, which means the account and all its related transactions are permanently removed from Quicken. Or you can *hide* it so that it is not seen in the Account Bar and not included in the totals. If you hide an account, you still have access to all of its related transactions.

DELETE AN ACCOUNT

1. Click the **Tools** menu, and click **Account List**, or press **CTRL+A**, to display the Account List.

   –Or–

   Right-click the account in the Account Bar, and click **Delete/Hide Accounts In Quicken**.

2. Click the account you want to delete, and click **Delete** in the options and information displayed beneath the account name. A dialog box appears, prompting you to confirm that you want to delete this account.

3. Type <u>yes</u> to verify that you want to delete the account (it does not matter if you use uppercase or lowercase letters).

4. Click **OK** to delete this account.

Continued . . .

3. Enter the name of the vehicle, and identify its make, model, and year, pressing **TAB** to move from field to field. Enter the date you acquired the vehicle, its purchase price, and its estimated current value, and then click **Next**.

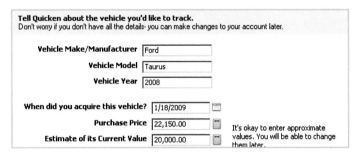

4. Choose if and how you want the liability account set up for the vehicle.

   - Click **Yes** and **I'd Like To Track This Loan In Quicken** if you have not already created a liability account for the vehicle.

   - Click **Yes** and **I'm Already Tracking The Loan In Quicken** if you have entered the liability account. Choose which account is associated with this asset in the **Select Existing Account** drop-down box.

   - Click **Yes** and **I Do Not Want To Track The Loan In Quicken** if that is your choice.

   - Click **No** if there is no loan on this car. Click **Next** to continue.

5. If you indicated that you wanted to create a loan, the Loan Setup Wizard appears. Follow the instructions as shown in "Use EasyStep Loan Setup" later in this chapter. Otherwise, if you chose not to track the loan, click **Done** at the next window.

Add Other Debt Accounts

Other debt accounts are used for loans other than for your house or vehicle. These types of loans can be promissory notes, student loans, loans against insurance policies, loans for medical expenses, or any other liability.

1. Click **Add Account** in the Account Bar, or use any of the other methods described to add an account.

2. Click **Debt** and click **Next**. Type a name for the debt, and click **Next**.

DELETING AND HIDING ACCOUNTS

(Continued)

HIDE AN ACCOUNT

1. Click the **Tools** menu and click **Account List**, or press **CTRL+A** to display the Account List.

   –Or–

   Right-click the account in the Account Bar, and click **Delete/Hide Accounts In Quicken**.

2. Select the account you want to hide, and click the **Hide This Account In Quicken (Lists, Menus, Reports)** check box to hide this account everywhere in Quicken. By default, the next two options are also selected.

3. Click the **Hide This Account In Account Bar** check box to keep the account from displaying in the Quicken Account Bar. The total of all balances in accounts that you have hidden in this manner will appear on the Account Bar as a total in "Other Accounts."

4. Click **Don't Include This Account In Net Worth Total** to keep the account's balance from being included in the totals. The account will still show in the Account Bar, but its balance will not be included in the totals.

5. Click **Done** to close the Account List dialog box.

| Edit Details | Go To Register | Delete Account |

☐ Hide this account in Quicken (lists, menus, reports)
☑ Hide this account in Account Bar
☐ Don't include this account in net worth total

Show in: **Banking Tab** (change)
Used for: **Spending** (change)

---

3. Enter the starting date of the loan or the date on which you want to start keeping track of this loan. Then enter the value of the loan—that is, what you owed on that date.

4. If the debt has tax implications, click **Tax**. Consult your tax professional for information on tax implications, and, if needed, enter the recommended information. Click **Done**.

Account Setup

Enter the ending date from your latest statement (or the date you want to start tracking this liability) and the balance of the liability

Date to start tracking | 9/1/2009 |

Liability Amount | 11,000.00 | This becomes the opening balance of your Quicken Account.

Enter Optional tax information | Tax... |

5. A dialog box appears asking if you want to set up an amortized loan to be associated with this account. This provides a payment schedule. If so, click **Yes**, and the EasyStep Loan Wizard will start (see "Use EasyStep Loan Setup"). If not, click **Next** and then click **Done**.

Use EasyStep Loan Setup

Quicken provides EasyStep Loan Setup to help you set up an amortized loan. This feature can be opened automatically, as described in the previous section, or you can open it directly.

1. From the bottom of the Account Bar, click **Add Account** and choose **Loan**.

   –Or–

   From the Net Worth tab's Loan Summary section, click **Options** and click **Add A New Loan**.

   Either way, the EasyStep Loan Setup Wizard appears. Click **Next** to begin the wizard.

2. Choose between borrowing money and loaning money. Borrowing is the default. Click **Next**.

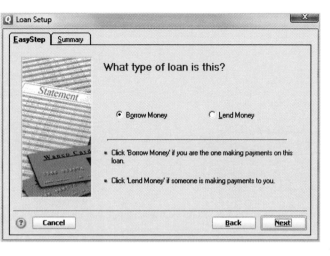

3. Enter the name of a new account, or link this loan to an existing account, and click **Next**.

4. If you have made payments on this loan, click **Yes**; otherwise, click **No**. Then click **Next**. You are asked for the initial loan information.

5. If this is a new account, you are required to provide the opening date and original balance of the loan. If this is an existing account, Quicken provides the information for you. Click **Next** to continue.

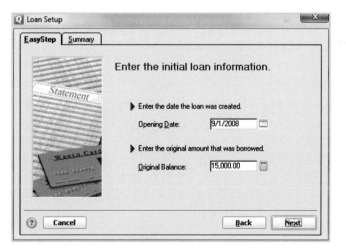

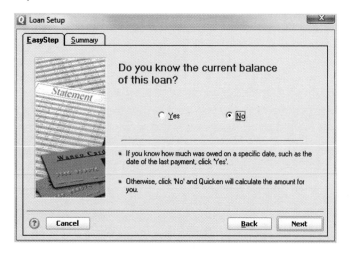

NOTE

By default, the EasyStep Loan Setup compounds interest monthly, but many lending institutions compound it daily.

QUICKSTEPS

PRINTING AN AMORTIZATION SCHEDULE

As you continue to work with loans in Quicken, you may want to print a payment schedule. To print this payment schedule (often called an *amortization schedule*):

1. Click **Tools** on the Quicken Menu bar, and click **Loan Details** to display the View Loans dialog box. (You can also use **CTRL + H** keyboard shortcut.) Click **Choose Loan** to see a drop-down list of all your loans, and click the loan for which you want to print the schedule.

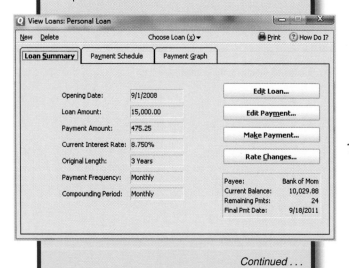

Continued . . .

6. If there is a balloon payment, click **Yes**; otherwise, click **No** and then click **Next**. Enter the original length of the loan, and click **Next**. Select how you pay the loan (the default is monthly), and click **Next** again. Enter how often interest is compounded, and click **Next**.

7. If you said you made a payment amount in step 5, you are asked if you know the current balance. If you haven't made a payment, skip to step 11. If you know the current balance, click **Yes**, click **Next**, enter the date and amount of the current balance, and click **Next** again. Otherwise, click **No** to have Quicken calculate the amount for you.

8. Click **Next**. Enter the date on which the next payment is due, and click **Next**. If you know the amount of the next payment, click **Yes** and click **Next**. Enter the payment and click **Next** again. If you don't know the amount of the next payment, click **No** to have Quicken calculate it for you. Click **Next** to continue.

9. Enter the interest rate for this loan, and click **Next**.

10. If you didn't know the payment, a summary screen appears showing you the basis upon which Quicken will calculate the amount for you. Click **Next**. Another summary screen appears showing the opening date, original balance and length of the loan, and the payment period. Click **Next**. A third summary screen appears with information that Quicken will use to calculate both the current balance and the next payment amount. Click **Done**.

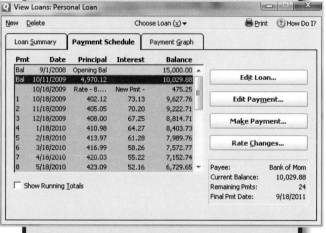

PRINTING AN AMORTIZATION
SCHEDULE *(Continued)*

2. Click **Payment Schedule** and click **Print** on the
   Menu bar.

3. Close the View Loans dialog box.

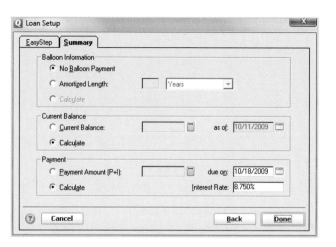

11. You are told that Quicken has calculated the next loan payment. Click **OK** and, if all is
in order, click **Done** again.

12. Review the loan payment information, and enter the name of the payee. The default
is the standard Interest Exp category, but you can change it to another category or
create a new category. If all appears to be correct, click **OK**.

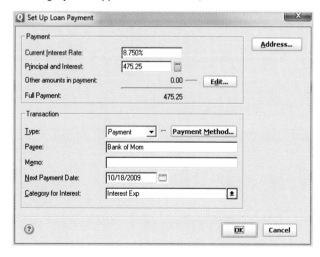

TIP

If you pay additional principal payments on your home
mortgage or on another loan, you can reduce the total
amount of interest you have to pay.

13. If there is an associated asset with this loan and you want to enter it, click **Yes** to
create the asset account; enter the asset name, acquisition date, and current value;
and then click **Done**. Otherwise, click **No** to finish creating the liability account and
return to the Loan Summary section of the Net Worth tab.

How to...

- Set Register Preferences
- Determine QuickFill Preferences
- Set Notify Preferences
- Set Preferences for Writing Checks
- Setting Downloaded Transaction Preferences
- Enter a Check
- Print Checks with Quicken
- Entering a Deposit
- Create a New Transaction Category
- Changing, Voiding, or Deleting a Transaction
- Create a Split Transaction
- Transfer Funds from One Account to Another
- Locate Transactions
- Filter Transactions for More Information
- Sorting Transactions
- Attach Digital Images to a Transaction
- Set Up Your Printer and Print a Register
- Using the Windows Clipboard
- Use Other Banking Tab Registers

Chapter 4
Using Quicken Every Day

In earlier chapters you learned how to install Quicken and set up your Quicken accounts. In this chapter you will learn how to use Quicken every day to record your checks, deposits, and other transactions. You'll learn to use the check register and credit card registers, with both manual and online transactions. But first, you'll be introduced to some definitions that are used throughout this chapter.

Understand Basic Transactions

A *transaction* in Quicken is something that affects the balance in an account. You enter a transaction into the *register* of the account. A register looks like a checkbook register, where you enter the activity, or transactions, regarding your accounts. Table 4-1 explains some of the terms used when talking about transactions. When using these terms, it is important to distinguish between:

- **Checking or savings accounts** in which you deposit your money and write checks or make withdrawals against your own funds. In essence, the bank owes you your money.

- **Credit card accounts** in which the bank extends you a line of credit, you make charges against that line, and then make payments to it. In essence, you owe the bank their money.

TERM	DEFINITION
Charge or debit	A transaction that increases the balance in a credit card account or decreases the balance in a checking account. A charge can also be something you purchased with a credit card or a fee from a financial institution.
Credit	A transaction that decreases the balance in a credit card, like a payment, or increases the balance in a checking account, like a deposit.
Deposit	A transaction that increases the balance in a checking or savings account.
Field	An area where you can make an entry, such as the date *field* or the amount *field*.
Payee	The company or person to whom you make a payment; for a deposit, it is the person from whom you get money you are depositing.
Payment	A transaction that lowers the balance in a credit card account.
Reconcile	To make what you have entered into a Quicken account agree with the statement you receive from your financial institution.
Transaction	An action that changes the balance in an account.
Transfer	To move funds from one account to another.

Table 4-1: Terms Used with Quicken Transactions

You create a transaction when you write a check, make a deposit, enter a credit card charge, or make a payment on your credit card. To keep your account register up to date, you need to enter the transaction into the account register, either manually or by downloading the information from the financial institution. You also need to reconcile your accounts on a regular basis against your financial institution's records. Quicken offers an Automatic Reconciliation feature. Chapter 7 discusses that and other methods of reconciling your accounts in more detail.

Establish Preferences for Your Registers

CAUTION

The settings used for investment accounts are slightly different because they use transaction lists rather than registers.

Before you use a register for the first time, you may want to set your preferences. Preferences are the ways in which you tell Quicken how to display and process your information.

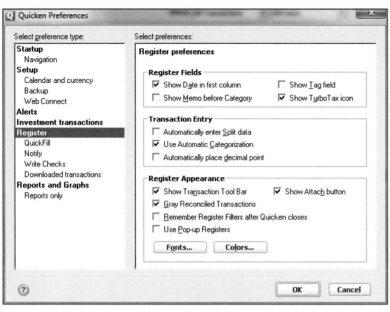

Figure 4-1: Quicken gives you a number of ways to customize the register to meet your needs.

Set Register Preferences

To set your preferences for an account:

1. Click the **Edit** menu, click **Preferences**, and then click **Quicken Preferences**.

2. Click **Register**. The Quicken Register Preferences dialog box appears, as shown in Figure 4-1. Select the order in which you want the register fields displayed.

- **Show Date In First Column**, which is selected by default, can be deselected to show the check number as the first field and the date as the second field.

- **Show Memo Before Category**, which is not selected by default, can be selected to display the Memo field first in your register, instead of showing the Category field first.

- **Show Tag Field** can be selected if you opt to use Tags to organize your transactions.

- **Show TurboTax Icon**, selected by default, indicates that a transaction has tax implications.

3. In the Transaction Entry area, click the relevant check boxes.

- **Automatically Enter Split Data** changes the way you enter a split transaction (see "Create a Split Transaction" later in this chapter). This check box is not selected by default.

- **Use Automatic Categorization** lets Quicken choose the category for a transaction based on an internal database or on the category you used before for this payee. This check box is selected by default.

- **Automatically Place Decimal Point** sets the decimal point to two places. By default, Quicken enters zero cents when you enter a number. For example, if you type the number 23 in the Amount field, Quicken displays it as $23.00. If you choose to set the decimal point automatically, the number 23 becomes .23, or 23 cents. This check box is not selected by default.

4. In the Register Appearance area, select how you want the register to look.

- **Show Transaction Toolbar** allows you to display the transaction toolbar on the right side of your transaction entry field. It has Enter, Edit, Split, and Attach buttons displayed by default. The Attach button is a paper clip icon.

- Clear the **Show Attach Button** check box if you do not want to see the Attach paper clip icon. The Attach button allows you to add notes, images, or flags to a transaction.

- **Gray Reconciled Transactions**, which is selected by default, displays all reconciled transactions in gray rather than in black. This feature allows you to quickly scan your register and find transactions that have not yet cleared the bank.

- Clicking **Remember Register Filters After Quicken Closes** saves the settings you set in the filter fields shown at the top of your register.

- Use **Pop-up Registers** allows your register to display in a separate, moveable window, not attached to its tab center.

5. Click the **Fonts** button to see a menu of available fonts for the register. You can choose from several different fonts and sizes. Click the font and size to see in the preview box how characters in the register would look using this font. When finished, click **OK**.

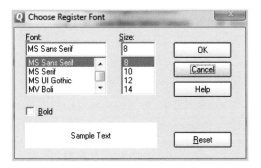

If you choose too large a font, Quicken displays a warning message. Click **OK** to close the dialog box.

NOTE

Some fonts display better than others. Look at how your choice appears in the register. If you can't read it easily, choose another font and/or size.

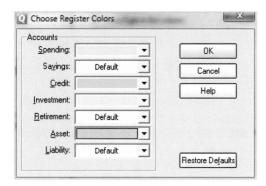

6. Click the **Colors** button to display the available colors for each register. Click the down arrow to the right of each account name to see the available choices. You can choose from seven different colors, including the default color. Click **OK** to close the dialog box.

7. Click **OK** to close the dialog box when you have selected your register preferences.

Determine QuickFill Preferences

Quicken saves you time during data entry with what Intuit calls *QuickFill* features. For example, Quicken provides drop-down lists from which you can choose categories and payees. You can choose to have a field automatically completed after typing only a few letters using Quicken's memorization of payees, transactions, and categories. You can determine how these features work in the QuickFill Preferences dialog box, shown in Figure 4-2.

1. Click the **Edit** menu, click **Preferences**, click **Quicken Preferences**, and then click **QuickFill**. The QuickFill Preferences dialog box appears. In the Data Entry area:

   a. Choose whether to use the **ENTER** key in addition to the **TAB** key to move between fields in your registers. By default, the **ENTER** key is used only to complete a transaction.

   b. Choose whether to automatically complete each field using the entry previously made for this payee. If you choose this option, which is selected by default, you can also choose whether to have Quicken recall your memorized payees.

   c. Choose whether to have Quicken display a drop-down list for the number, payee, and category fields (this is selected by default).

   d. Choose whether you want the leading character in the payee and category names capitalized.

   e. Choose whether you want Quicken to display the buttons on QuickFill fields. If you choose to clear this check box, the buttons, which open the lists, will not display.

Figure 4-2: Use QuickFill preferences to configure your registers according to the way you want to enter and view your data.

Automatic List Updating

☑ Automatically memorize new payees
☑ Automatically memorize to the Calendar list
☑ Add Address Book QuickFill group items to Memorized Payee List
☑ Remove memorized payees not used in last [9] months

Notify preferences

Notify

☑ When entering out-of-date transactions
☑ Before changing existing transactions
☑ When entering uncategorized transactions
☑ To run a reconcile report after reconcile
☑ Warn if a check number is re-used

NOTE

If you choose a two-digit year, the on-screen image still shows four digits, but when you print the check, only the rightmost two digits are printed.

2. In the Automatic List Updating area:

   a. Choose to automatically memorize new payees and memorize transactions to the Calendar List.

   b. Choose to automatically add any Address Book QuickFill group items to the Memorized Payee List.

   c. Click **Remove Memorized Payees Not Used In Last *nn* Months** to remove seldom-used payees. If you select this option, enter the number of months after which the payees should be removed.

3. Click **OK** when finished.

Set Notify Preferences

Notify preferences tell Quicken the circumstances in which you want to receive warning messages. By default, all warnings are activated.

1. Click the **Edit** menu, click **Preferences**, click **Quicken Preferences**, and then click **Notify**. The Notify Preferences dialog box appears.

2. Choose whether to get a warning message when:

   ● Entering transactions that are not in the current year

   ● Changing an existing transaction

   ● Entering a transaction without a category

   ● Not running a reconciliation report after you complete a reconciliation

   ● Using a check number more than once

3. Click **OK** when finished.

Set Preferences for Writing Checks

Quicken gives you six options from which to choose when using the program to write checks, as shown in Figure 4-3. To set those options:

1. Click the **Edit** menu, click **Preferences**, click **Quicken Preferences**, and then click **Write Checks**. The Write Checks Preferences dialog box appears.

2. Choose whether you want a four-digit year, such as 4/5/2010, or a two-digit year, such as 4/5/10, to be printed on your checks.

QUICKSTEPS

SETTING DOWNLOADED TRANSACTION PREFERENCES

You can set preferences for transactions you download from financial institutions.

1. Automatic Transaction Entry automatically records all downloaded transactions in the register to which they belong. If you turn off this automatic-entry capability, you must review and approve each downloaded transaction.

Downloaded transactions preferences

Automatic Transaction Entry

☑ Automatically add downloaded transactions to registers

If you do not use this option, all downloaded transactions must be manually reviewed and accepted before they are added to your register. Unaccepted transactions will not display in reports, graphs and other product features.

Renaming Rules

☑ Apply renaming rules to downloaded transactions
　☑ Automatically create rules when manually renaming
　Renaming Rules...

☑ Capitalize first letter only in downloaded payee names

2. Choose whether to apply renaming rules to downloaded transactions. Renaming rules change the name of a payee on a downloaded transaction—for example, "Grocery 198775" becomes "Corner Grocery" in your register. Renaming rules are discussed further in Chapter 5.

   - Click **Automatically Create Rules When Manually Renaming** to clear the check box. This option will create a renaming rule when you manually change the name of a payee.

   - Click **Renaming Rules** to see any existing rules and to add, change, or delete renaming rules.

3. Choose whether to capitalize only the first letters in the payee names you are downloading.

4. Click **OK** to close the dialog box.

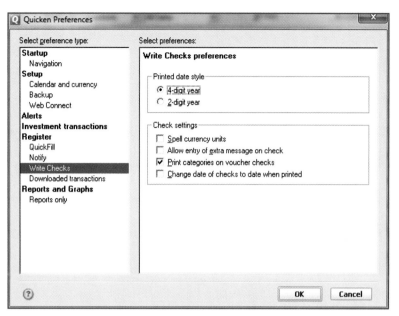

Figure 4-3: Quicken's check-writing options allow you to format checks the way you want.

3. Click the **Spell Currency Units** check box to have Quicken print the currency amount on your check with the currency unit displayed, for example, "Twenty Dollars and 37 Cents" rather than "Twenty and 37/100."

4. Click the **Allow Entry Of Extra Message On Check** check box if you want to include information for the payee's records, such as your account number or the invoice number you are paying with this check.

5. Click the **Print Categories On Voucher Checks** check box if you want to include that information. A voucher check has a perforated portion that can include additional information.

6. Click the **Change Date Of Checks To Date When Printed** check box if you enter data over time and print all your checks at once.

7. Click **OK** to close the dialog box.

Work with the Register

The register in Quicken looks a lot like the paper check register you may have used in the past. It displays in the color choices you selected in your preferences setup. You can open a register in two ways:

- Click the name of the register's account on the Account Bar on the left of your Quicken page.

    –Or–

- Click the tab in which the register appears and, from the tab's Acct section, click the down arrow and then click the account.

In all cases, the register opens. Figure 4-4 displays a register window for a checking account.

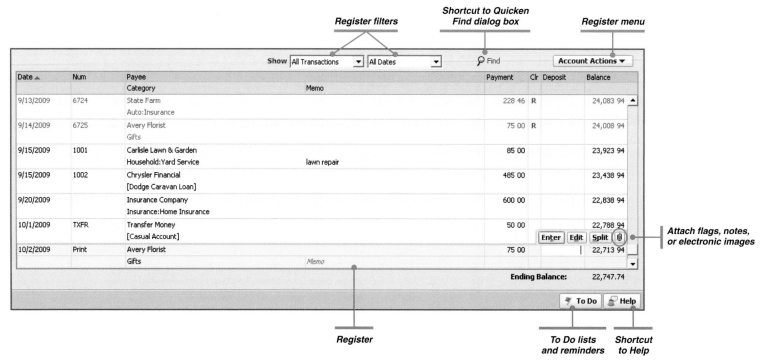

Figure 4-4: From the account register window, you can download transactions for that account, as well as view and record transactions.

Enter a Check

To enter a check into the register:

1. If it is not already selected, click at the top of the empty pair of lines at the bottom of the Date column. By default, this is highlighted in a light-orange color. This activates the transaction line.

2. Accept today's date, type a date using either the numeric keys at the top of the keyboard or the 10-key pad on the right of the keyboard (with **NUMLOCK** activated), or click the small calendar to the right of the field. (If the calendar does not appear in the field, double-click to open a calendar.) In the calendar, click the date you want using the arrows in the upper-left and upper-right corners to select a different month.

3. Press **TAB** to move to the Num field, or click in the **NUM** field. By default, a drop-down list of potential entries will display. Type the check number, if you haven't entered one before, or use the drop-down list by pressing the following keys on your keyboard:

   ● Press **N** to automatically enter the next sequential check number if you have been using the check register.

   ● Press **A** if you want "ATM" to appear in the Num field.

   ● Press **D** if you want "DEP" (for "Deposit") to appear in the Num field.

   ● Press **P** if you plan to print this check later and want "Print" to appear in the Num field.

   ● Press **T** if you want "TXFR" (for "Transfer") to appear in the Num field.

   ● Press **E** if you want "EFT" (for "Electronic Funds Transfer") to appear in the Num field.

4. Press **TAB** to move to the Payee field. Type the first letter of the payee's name to display a list of all the payees that start with that letter. Choose the name you want, or type a new payee name.

NOTE

When you enter a payee for the first time, you might notice that Quicken assigns it to a category. A special feature of Quicken, Automatic Categorization assigns a category based on a list of thousands of payees.

NOTE

Other transactions can be bank service charges, wire transfer fees, charges on your bank statement for checks or deposit slips, and ATM fees. Enter these transactions in the same way as you would checks that you write.

5. Press **TAB** to move to the Payment field. Type the amount of the check. You can use either the 10-key pad with **NUMLOCK** activated or the numbers at the top of the keyboard. If you have paid this payee before and have set your preferences to automatically enter it, the amount of the most recent transaction for this payee appears.

6. Press **TAB** to move to the Category field. Type the first letter of the category you want to use. By default, the category you used the last time you paid this payee appears in the Category field. If you want to change the category, click the name in the drop-down list. If the transaction is for more than one category, you can create a split transaction. See "Create a Split Transaction" later in this chapter.

7. Press **TAB** to move to the Memo field. Type any special information, such as an invoice number or what you purchased.

8. Press **ENTER** or click the **Enter** button to complete and save the transaction.

Print Checks with Quicken

Quicken will print checks for you if you have special Quicken paper checks for your printer. You can order these checks through your bank, through Quicken, or through third-party companies (do an Internet search on "Quicken checks"). Printing your checks makes them easier to read and potentially saves you time in that you can enter information directly into a check form or print checks already entered into the register. Before you start, you need to load the special paper checks into your printer.

PRINT CHECKS IN THE REGISTER

If you have transactions to print in your register with "Print" in the Num field, you can directly print them instead of entering them into the check form to be printed. When you use the form, however, the information is automatically entered into the register.

1. Click the **File** menu, and then click **Print Checks**. If you do not have transactions in your register with "Print" in the Num field, you will see a message stating that you do not have any checks to print. If you do have transactions with "Print" in the Num field, the Select Checks To Print dialog box will appear.

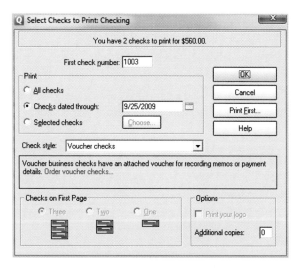

2. Enter the number of the first paper check in the printer.

3. Choose which checks to print.

- **All Checks** prints any checks that have not yet been printed. This includes any postdated checks you may have entered.

- **Checks Dated Through** allows you to print unprinted checks through a date you enter or select.

- **Selected Checks** allows you to choose which checks to print. Click Choose and clear the check marks for any checks you don't want to print at this time.

Print	Date	Payee	Category	Amount
✓	10/2/2009	**Avery Florist**	**Gifts**	**75.00**
✓	10/2/2009	**Chrysler Financial**	**[Dodge Caravan Loan]**	**485.00**

Select Checks to Print — Mark All   Clear All   Done   How Do I?

- Click **Mark All** to print all of the checks.

- Click **Clear All** to clear all of the listed checks, and then click in the **Print** column just the checks you want to print.

- Click **Done** to close the dialog box and print the checks.

4. Click the **Check Style** down arrow, and choose a style. Depending on the style you are using, click the number of checks on the first page with your style.

5. Click **Print First** to print the first check and see how it looks. Click **OK** if your check printed correctly. Otherwise, enter the check number of the check, and Quicken will reprint it. Make any necessary corrections to how checks are printed.

NOTE

Standard-style checks are normally thought of as business checks, and are 8½ × 3½ inches. Wallet-style checks are normally thought of as personal checks, and are 6 × 2¾ inches.

NOTE

Each check style shows a message "Order ....checks" in blue. This is a direct link to the Quicken check-ordering website.

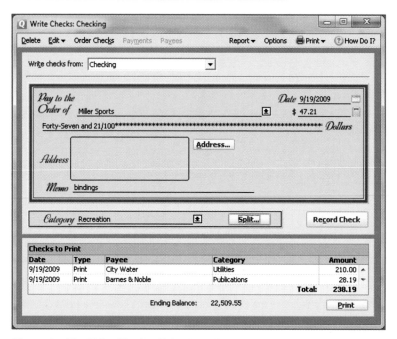

Figure 4-5: The Write Checks dialog box gives you a way to visualize the checks you are preparing.

6. Click **OK** to print all the checks you selected. When the printing is completed, click **OK** if all checks printed correctly. Otherwise, enter the check number of the check on which there was a problem so that Quicken can reprint it and any following checks.

PRINT CHECKS FROM THE CHECK FORM

If you would like to see a representation of the check you will be sending, Quicken provides a form into which you can enter the information you want on the final printed check, as shown in Figure 4-5. To use the check form:

1. From the Banking tab, select the account from which you want to write checks. Click **Account Actions** and click **Write Checks**. The Write Checks dialog box appears with a blank check displayed that you can fill in.

2. Click in the **Pay To The Order Of** line, or click the down arrow at the end of the line, to display a drop-down list of previous payees.

3. Type as much of the payee's name as needed to select the payee you want, or click the payee you want in the drop-down list.

4. Press **TAB** to move to the Amount field. If you have sent checks to this payee previously, the most recent amount you paid will be filled in. Press **TAB** again to accept the previous amount and move to the Address field. Otherwise, enter the new amount, and then press **TAB**.

5. Type the address, if one is not already attached to the payee. If you want to edit the address, click **Address** to open the Address Book. Make any changes or additions to the address, and click **OK**.

If you selected the Allow Entry Of Extra Message On Check check box in the Write Check Preferences dialog box, a Message field appears on the check. Because the Memo field can be visible when you use window envelopes, confidential information, such as your account number, can be entered into the Message field rather than the Memo field.

You may have noticed the effects of the "QuickFill" option in the Address Book, Write Checks window, Split Transaction window, or the register. QuickFill tries to complete each field after you type just a few letters. It also provides drop-down lists so that you can find items quickly. If you have activated QuickFill in the Preferences dialog box, Quicken memorizes each new transaction. For more information, refer to "Determine QuickFill Preferences" earlier in this chapter.

6. Press **TAB** to move to the Memo field. Type a memo entry, if you want, and press **TAB** again to move to the Category field.

7. Begin to type the category. If there is an existing category starting with the letters you've typed, it will be filled in. Alternatively, you can click the down arrow at the end of the **Category** line, and click the category you want to use.

8. If you want to have portions of the money you are paying go to different categories, click **Split** and follow the instructions in the section "Create a Split Transaction" later in this chapter.

9. If you don't want to use the default of today's date, click in the **Date** field, and enter a new date using any of Quicken's date-entering features described in "Enter a Check" earlier in this chapter.

10. When the check looks the way you want, click **Record Check**. The new check appears on a list of checks to be printed at the bottom of the window, and the check form is once more blank.

11. When you have entered all the checks you want to print, click **Print**. The Select Checks To Print dialog box appears. To continue, see "Print Checks in the Register," and complete the steps in that section (starting with step 2).

ENTERING A DEPOSIT

Entering a deposit is like entering a check, except that you enter the amount in the Deposit field rather than the Payment field. To enter a deposit:

1. If it is not already selected, click in the empty line at the bottom of the Date column.

2. If you want to change the date, use one of the techniques described in "Enter a Check."

3. Press **TAB** to move to the Num field, and press **D** to have "DEP" placed in the field.

4. Press **TAB** and enter the name of the payer, or select it from the drop-down list that is displayed.

5. Press **TAB** to move to the Deposit field, and enter an amount.

6. Press **TAB** to move to the Category field. Type a category or choose one from the drop-down list.

7. Click **Enter** to complete the transaction.

NOTE

The only register item you cannot change is the Balance column.

Create a New Transaction Category

When you enter a check or a deposit, you can easily create a new category if there isn't one in the Category List that you want to use.

1. Press **TAB** to move to the Category field and automatically open the list of existing categories, or click the **Category** down arrow to open the list.

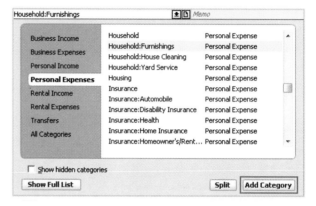

2. Click **Add Category**. The Set Up Category dialog box appears.

3. Type the name and description of the new category, and select the group you want it in. Press **TAB** to move from field to field.

4. Click **Income** or **Expense** or **Subcategory** and its name to tell Quicken what type of category this is.

5. Enter the tax-line item if this category has tax implications.

6. Click **OK** to close the dialog box.

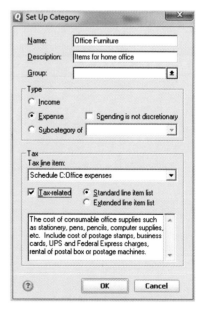

CHANGING, VOIDING, OR DELETING A TRANSACTION

From time to time, you may need to edit, or change, a transaction in your check register, as well as void or delete a transaction.

CHANGE A TRANSACTION

1. With the register containing the transaction you want to change displayed, click in any field of the transaction.

2. Type or select from drop-down lists the new or revised information.

3. Click **Enter** or press **ENTER** to save the changes.

VOID A TRANSACTION

You can void any transaction in an account register. Quicken keeps the check number, removes the dollar amount, and inserts ***VOID*** in front of the payee name. If you make a mistake, you can restore the transaction to the way it was originally.

| 1003 | **VOID**Avery Florist | |
| | Gifts | *Memo* |

1. With the register containing the transaction you want to void displayed, click the transaction.

2. Click the **Edit** menu on the Quicken Menu bar, and click **Transaction**, or right-click anywhere in the transaction, or click **Edit** in the transaction toolbar. From the context or regular menu that is displayed, click **Void Transaction(s)**. The transaction is voided.

3. If you have not yet pressed **ENTER** or clicked **Enter** and the transaction is still selected, you can restore it by clicking the **Edit** menu on the Quicken Menu bar and clicking **Transaction**. Or, you can click **Edit** on the transaction toolbar. After using either of these methods, click **Restore Transaction**.

| Enter |
| Restore transaction |
| Split |

Continued . . .

Perform Activities with Check Registers

Not all transactions in your register are as straightforward as a check or a deposit with one category. Some transactions require you to split categories or transfer funds from one account to another. Quicken makes all of these transactions easy to enter. Other activities you may want to perform are locating, sorting, or filtering transactions; attaching invoice copies or other images to your transactions; and printing your check register.

Create a Split Transaction

A *split* transaction is one that has more than one assigned category. For example, a check you write to the insurance company might be for both homeowners' and automobile insurance, or a deposit might be for both the principal amount of a loan and interest. You can assign up to 30 categories for any single transaction. To enter a split transaction:

1. Click the empty line at the bottom of your register.

2. Enter the date, check number, payee, and the total amount of the check, as described in "Enter a Check" earlier in this chapter.

3. Click **Split** in the transaction toolbar.

   –Or–

   Click the **Category** field drop-down arrow to open the Category List. Click **Split** at the bottom of the list.

   In either case, the Split Transaction dialog box appears, as shown in Figure 4-6.

4. The Category field on the first line may already be selected. If not, choose a category from the drop-down list, or type a category. Press **TAB**, type any additional information or notes in the **Memo** field, and again press **TAB**.

5. The total amount of the transaction appears under Amount on the first line. Over that amount, type the amount for the first category. Click **Next**.

QUICKSTEPS

CHANGING, VOIDING, OR DELETING A TRANSACTION (Continued)

4. Press **ENTER** or click **Enter** to complete the procedure.

DELETE A TRANSACTION

When you delete a transaction, Quicken recalculates all balances and permanently removes that transaction from the register.

1. With the register containing the transaction you want to delete displayed, click the transaction.

2. Press **CTRL+D** and click **Yes** to delete the transaction.

   –Or–

   Click the **Edit** menu, click **Transaction**, click **Delete**, and click **Yes** to delete the transaction.

   –Or–

   Right-click anywhere in the transaction, click **Delete** from the context menu, and click **Yes** to delete the transaction.

3. The transaction is completely deleted, and your balance is recomputed.

CAUTION

Quicken can restore a deleted transaction only in the Quicken session in which it was deleted (that is, before you exited Quicken). To restore a deleted transaction, click it, click the **Edit** menu on the Quicken Menu bar, and click **Transaction**; or click **Edit** on the transaction toolbar. After either step, click **Undo Delete**.

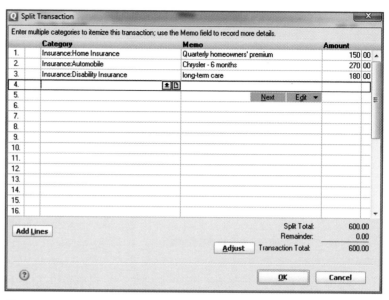

Figure 4-6: Splitting a transaction among multiple categories allows you to refine your accounting and better understand where your money goes.

6. Quicken computes the remainder and shows it in the Amount field of the second line. Enter or select the next category, press **TAB**, enter any information you want in the Memo field, press **TAB** again, and either accept the computed amount or type a new one. Click **Next**.

7. Repeat step 6 until you have all the categories you want. Then click **Next** once more. If you need to adjust any of the entries, click the amount that needs to be adjusted.

8. If the entries are correct and you have a difference, either positive or negative, from the original check amount, click **Adjust** to make the total for the transaction the sum of the split categories.

9. Click **OK** to close the Split Transaction dialog box. Instead of a single category appearing in the Category field, Quicken displays "--Split--" to remind you that there are multiple categories for this transaction.

10. Hover your mouse pointer over "--Split--" in the Category field to see the amounts in each split category.

11. Click the transaction and three buttons appear next to "--Split--".:

   a. Click ☑ to open the Split Transaction dialog box, where you can edit the split.

   b. Click ☒ to clear all of the split categories and amounts so that you can replace them with a single new category.

   c. Click 🔲 to open the Activity dialog box, where you can see the sum of the amounts in the categories used in this transaction.

Transfer Funds from One Account to Another

You can easily record the transfer of funds from one account to another in Quicken. The quickest way is to open the register of the account the money is from. Then:

1. Click **Account Actions** at the top of a register, and then click **Transfer Money**. The Record A Transfer Between Quicken Accounts dialog box appears.

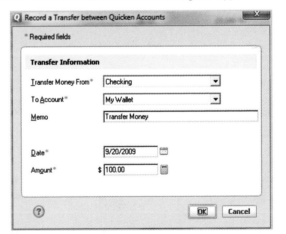

2. Click **Transfer Money From** to choose the account from which you are transferring the money.

3. Click the **To Account** down arrow, and select the account into which you are transferring the funds.

4. Press TAB if you want a different description other than the default: "Transfer Money." If so, type that description or edit the current text—for example, To vacation savings.

5. Press TAB and enter the date of the transfer if it is different from today's date.

6. Press TAB and type the amount.

7. Click **OK** to make the transfer and close the dialog box.

Locate Transactions

There are several ways to find a transaction within Quicken.

1. Click **Find** at the top of any register.

    –Or–

    Click **Edit** on the Quicken Menu bar, click **Find And Replace**, and then click **Find**.

    –Or–

    Press CTRL+F.

2. Click the **Search** down arrow to open a list of fields on which to search. Click the field you want to search on.

3. Click the **Match If** down arrow to open a list of expressions to use in the search. Click the expression you want to use.

4. Click in the **Find** text box, and type what you want to find.

5. Click **Find** to select the most recent transaction that matches your criteria. You may see a dialog box asking if you want to continue your search from the end of the register. If so, click **Yes**.

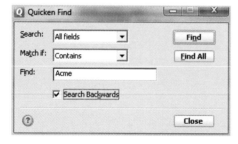

–Or–

Click **Find All** to open the Search Results dialog box showing all the transactions that match your criteria. Figure 4-7 shows all the transactions containing the word "Acme" in any field.

Select	Date ▼	Acct	Num	Payee	Cat	Memo	Clr	Amount
☐	9/8/2009	Brokerage (Cash)		Acme Tool	[Checking]		R	150.00
☐	9/8/2009	Checking	DEP	Acme Tool	--Split--		R	1,500.00
☐	9/4/2009	House		Acme Home Improveme...	[Money Market]	New Deck		3,250.00
☐	9/4/2009	Money Market	EFT	Acme Home Improveme...	[House]	New Deck		-3,250.00
☐	8/25/2009	Brokerage (Cash)		Acme Tool	[Checking]		R	150.00
☐	8/25/2009	Checking	DEP	Acme Tool	--Split--		R	1,500.00
☐	8/11/2009	Brokerage (Cash)		Acme Tool	[Checking]		R	150.00
☐	8/11/2009	Checking	DEP	Acme Tool	--Split--		R	1,500.00
☐	7/28/2009	Brokerage (Cash)		Acme Tool	[Checking]		R	150.00
☐	7/28/2009	Checking	DEP	Acme Tool	--Split--		R	1,500.00
☐	7/14/2009	Brokerage (Cash)		Acme Tool	[Checking]		R	150.00
☐	7/14/2009	Checking	DEP	Acme Tool	--Split--		R	1,500.00
☐	7/9/2009	Checking 6789	5040	Acme Home Improveme...	Household	New Deck	R	-123.94
☐	6/30/2009	Brokerage (Cash)		Acme Tool	[Checking]		R	150.00
☐	6/30/2009	Checking	DEP	Acme Tool	--Split--		R	1,500.00
☐	6/16/2009	Brokerage (Cash)		Acme Tool	[Checking]		R	150.00
☐	6/16/2009	Checking	DEP	Acme Tool	--Split--		R	1,500.00
☐	6/2/2009	Brokerage (Cash)		Acme Tool	[Checking]		R	150.00
☐	6/2/2009	Checking	DEP	Acme Tool	--Split--		R	1,500.00

☑ Sh*ow matches in split*

Item found in 40 transaction(s)

To select a range, click the first item you want then hold Shift while clicking the last item you want.

Edit Transaction(s)   **Close**

Figure 4-7: Quicken's ability to search transactions allows you to find, for example, all the transactions to a given payee or all transactions over a certain amount.

Filter Transactions for More Information

Quicken can filter the transactions displayed in a register so that only the ones you are interested in are shown. This can help you quickly locate specific information.

1. From the top of the register, click the **Show** filter to display the filter options.

2. Click the **Date** filter to narrow your choices to specific periods, like the current month or last quarter, or click **Custom** to enter or select a specific date range.

All Transactions
All Transactions
Uncategorized
Uncleared
Flagged
Payments
Deposits

SORTING TRANSACTIONS

You can sort your transactions by any of the columns in your register except the Balance column. Depending on your choices in Preferences, Quicken can keep the sorted column as you have set it or go back to its default of sorting by date.

- Click the column heading to sort by that column. A small triangle appears by the name to indicate that it is the sort column. Date ▲

- Click **Date** to sort first by date and then by check number. The oldest date is displayed at the top.

- Click **Num** to sort by check number. This places the words, such as "ATM" or "Deposit," first and then sorts the checks numerically, with the smallest check number at the top.

- Click **Payee/Category/Memo** to show payees displayed alphabetically, with "a" at the top.

- Click **Payment** to list payments, with the smallest payment amount at the bottom of the list.

- Click **Clr** to show all reconciled transactions first and then any unreconciled transactions.

- Click **Deposit** to show the deposits in descending order, with the largest deposits at the top.

- Click **Account Actions** and then click **Sorting Options** at the top of the register to see additional sort options.

Attach Digital Images to a Transaction

If you use Quicken 2010 Deluxe, Premier, or Premier Home & Business edition, Quicken works with your scanner, Windows Explorer, and the Clipboard in Windows so that you can attach digital images to each transaction in your register. You can attach any type of file that can be viewed in Microsoft Internet Explorer, such as .jpg, .gif, .txt, .html, .pdf, and .png. These attachments are then stored in the same file as your Quicken data. A digital attachment can be a picture of your new snowboard, a receipt for a donation, or any other item you may want to scan or download and keep with your transaction for tax or warranty purposes. You must first bring these items into Quicken and then attach them to a transaction.

ATTACH IMAGES TO TRANSACTIONS

1. Click the **Attach** icon (the small paper clip) on the transaction toolbar.

2. Click **Attach Electronic Image**.

3. Click the **Check**, **Receipt/Bill**, **Invoice**, **Warranty**, or **Other File** option, depending on the type of attachment you want to use.

4. Click in the **Attach New** field at the bottom of the window to choose the item you want to attach from the drop-down list.

5. Depending on how you intend to acquire the attachment, select one of the following:

   a. Click **File** to attach an image already in your computer.

      i. The Select Attachment File dialog box appears. Locate your file and click **Open**.

      ii. Your image appears on the screen with its default name, such as "Receipt/Bill" or "Warranty."

b. Click **Scanner** to see the Select Source dialog box. Select the scanner you wish to use to scan the item. Follow the directions for your scanner. The image will appear in the Transaction Attachments window.

c. Click **Clipboard** to attach an item you have copied to your Clipboard. The item appears in the Transaction Attachments window. For more information on using the Clipboard in Windows, see "Using the Windows Clipboard" QuickSteps later in this chapter.

6. When you have finished, the attachment appears in the window, as shown in Figure 4-8. Click **Done** when you have finished attaching documents.

7. A small attachment icon (a paper-clipped note) appears beneath the transaction's date.

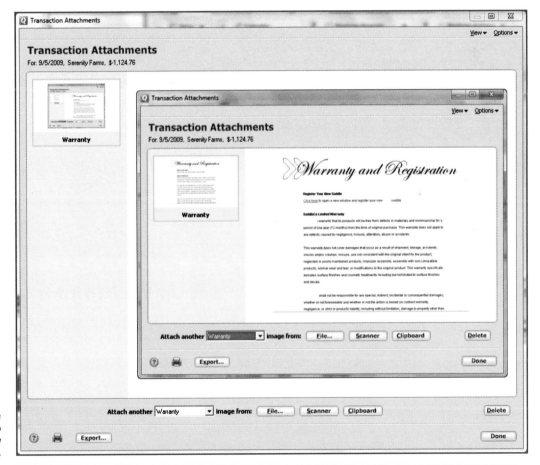

Figure 4-8: Attach electronic images to transactions in Quicken to keep transactions and their supporting documents together.

ADD A FOLLOW-UP FLAG OR NOTE TO A TRANSACTION

1. Click the **Attach** icon (the small paper clip) on the transaction toolbar.

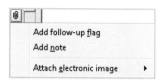

2. Click **Add Follow-Up Flag** or **Add Note**. Choosing either will cause the Transaction Notes And Flags dialog box to appear.

   a. Type any notes you want as part of this transaction.

   b. Click **Flag This Transaction** if you need to mark the transaction. Choose the color of the flag from the drop-down list.

   c. Click the **Alert For Follow-Up On** option, and enter a date to have this transaction appear on your Alert List in the Quicken Home tab.

3. Click **OK** to close the dialog box. A small flag appears beneath the date of the transaction.

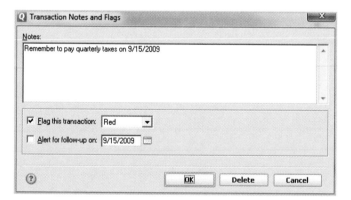

NOTE

Include alerts as part of the Main View subtab of your Home tab by customizing the Main View, as discussed in Chapter 1.

NOTE

To read any notes, click the small flag beneath the transaction date. Click the attachment icon to see the attachments.

Set Up Your Printer and Print a Register

As you continue to work with Quicken, you may want to print a register. Before you do, you may need to set up your printer to print reports or graphs.

SET UP YOUR PRINTER

1. Click the **File** menu, click **Printer Setup**, and click **For Reports/Graphs**. The Printer Setup For Reports And Graphs dialog box appears.

2. Click the **Printer** down arrow to show a list of your printers, and click the one you want to set up.

UICKSTEPS

USING THE WINDOWS CLIPBOARD

Microsoft Windows XP, Vista, and Windows 7, as well as other Windows operating systems, have some handy keyboard shortcuts to capture on-screen images and place them on the Windows Clipboard. An example of an on-screen image might be a scanned deposit slip from your bank's website. To capture this image directly from your screen:

1. Press the **PRINT SCREEN** button, usually located on the upper-right area of your keyboard, to capture the entire screen as shown on your monitor.

   –Or–

   Hold down the **ALT** button, usually located on either side of the **SPACEBAR**, and press the **PRINT SCREEN** button to capture a copy of the active window.

   Either action will put the image on the Windows Clipboard.

2. Use the **Clipboard** button in the Transaction Attachment view to attach your captured image to a transaction.

NOTE

Only you can decide whether you need a printed copy of your check register. If you back up your information on a regular basis, you may never need one. You might consider printing one at year-end and filing it with your tax information.

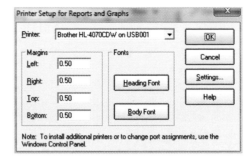

3. Click in each of the margin text boxes you want to change, and type the new margin.

4. Click **Heading Font** to change the font, font style, and size. Click the name of the font, the style, and the size from their respective lists, and then click **OK**.

5. Click **Body Font** and repeat step 4. The choices you make will be used with all of the reports or graphs you print on this printer.

6. Click **OK** to close the Printer Setup dialog box.

PRINT A REGISTER

1. With the register you want to print open, press **CTRL+P** to open the Print Register dialog box.

2. Type a title for the report. The name of the account appears on the report by default.

3. Select a time period for which you want to display the transactions.

4. Click the **Print Split Transactions** option if you want the multiple categories in your split transaction to be included on the report (this option is not selected by default).

5. Click **Print** to print the report. In the Print dialog box that appears, make any needed changes, and click **Print**.

Use Other Banking Tab Registers

When you first open the register for a credit card account, its appearance is much like a check register. However, there are a few differences that you should recognize, as described in Table 4-2.

CHECK REGISTERS	CREDIT CARD REGISTERS
Date: The date of the transaction.	**Date**: The date of the transaction.
Num: The check number or an alphabetic description of the transaction. There is a drop-down list to assist you in choosing.	**Ref**: The type of transaction, such as charge, payment, or finance charge. There is no drop-down list.
Payee/Category/Memo: The person or organization paid and its category. Drop-down lists are available for payees and categories.	**Payee/Category/Memo**: The person or organization paid and its category. Drop-down lists are available for payees and categories.
Payment: The amount of the check, charge, or deposit. There is a calculator available if you need it.	**Charge**: The amount of the charge, payment, or fee. There is a calculator available if you need it.
Clr: Whether a transaction has appeared on a statement from your financial institution and has been cleared.	**Clr**: Whether a transaction has appeared on a statement from your financial institution and has been cleared.
Deposit: The amount that has been deposited into this account. A calculator is available if you need it.	**Payment**: The amount you have paid on this credit card. A calculator is available if you need it.
Balance: The amount of money you have in this account after entering all of your deposits and checks.	**Balance**: The amount of money you owe on this credit card after entering all of your charges and payments.

Table 4-2: Differences Between Checking and Credit Card Registers

ENTER A CREDIT CARD CHARGE, FINANCE CHARGE, OR CREDIT

If you are familiar with entering checks into your checking account register, the process is similar in your credit card register.

1. Click the credit card account in the Account Bar to open that card's register. The empty transaction line at the bottom of the register should be selected, as shown in Figure 4-9.

2. If it isn't already selected and you want to change the date, click in the **Date** column, and used the date-picking techniques described in step 2 of "Enter a Check" earlier in this chapter.

3. Press TAB to move to the Ref column, and type a description of the transaction.

NOTE

Many people use "Chg" for a charge and "Cdt" for a credit. A credit could be something you purchased on your credit card and later returned to the store.

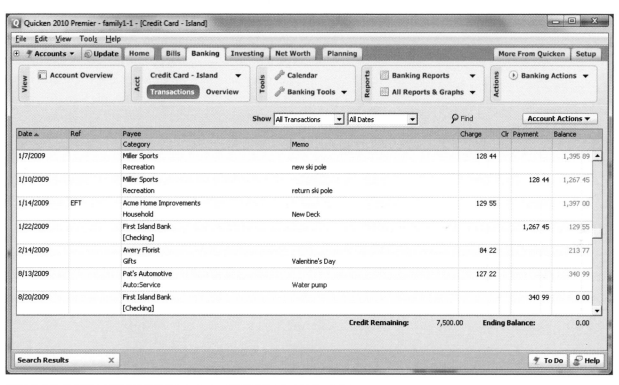

Figure 4-9: Credit card registers have many similarities to check registers.

4. Press **TAB** or click **Payee**, and enter the name of the business.

5. Press **TAB** or click **Charge**, and enter the amount of the charge.

6. Press **TAB** or click **Category**, and select from the drop-down list or type the category.

7. Press **TAB** or click **Memo**, and enter any identifying information, such as <u>Dinner with Megg and Cooper</u> or <u>School clothes for Sally</u>.

8. Click **Enter** or press **ENTER** to complete the transaction.

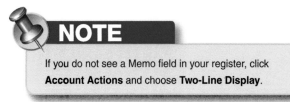

NOTE

If you do not see a Memo field in your register, click **Account Actions** and choose **Two-Line Display**.

WORK WITH A CASH ACCOUNT REGISTER

Creating an account to track your cash spending can be useful. It is a great learning tool for young people to track where they spend their money. You can enter data each time money is spent or add information in bulk at the end of each week or month. Many people who use this type of account enter only whole-dollar amounts. Use the same procedures described in "Enter a Check" earlier in this chapter.

1. Create a cash account, as described in Chapter 2. Open that account's register, and, if it isn't already selected, click in the empty transaction line.

2. If needed, change the date, press **TAB**, type a description in the Ref column, and select or type a payee to identify the transaction.

3. Enter the amount spent in the Spend column or the amount received in the Receive column.

4. Click **Enter** or press **ENTER** to complete the transaction.

Date ▲	Ref	Payee / Category	Memo	Spend	Clr	Receive	Balance
1/15/2009		[Checking]				250 00	295 00
1/27/2009		Dewey Tax Prep / TaxPreparation		125 00			170 00
3/23/2009		Community Church / Charitable Donations		50 00	✓		120 00
5/18/2009		Lion's Club / Charitable Donations		25 00	✓		95 00
8/27/2009		Island County Fair Assn / Charitable Donations		50 00	✓		45 00
9/20/2009		Transfer Money / [Checking]				100 00	145 00

Ending Balance: 145.00

Search Results ✕   ☀ To Do   🔖 Help

How to...

- Create a Memorized Payee
- Change Memorized Payees
- Use Renaming Rules for Downloaded Transactions
- Create and Memorize a Split Transaction Using Percentages
- Locking a Memorized Payee
- Understand Scheduled Transactions
- Schedule a Transaction
- Understanding Scheduled Transaction Methods
- Create a Scheduled Transaction from a Register
- Work with Scheduled Transactions
- Use the Calendar
- Showing Transactions on Your Calendar
- Scheduling Repeating Online Payments
- Set Report Preferences
- Create a Standard Report
- Creating a Mini-Report
- Create a Standard Graph

Chapter 5

Taking Control with Quicken

After using Quicken to enter your day-to-day transactions, you may want to step up to the next level and start using more of the features Quicken provides to help you save time as you manage your finances. In this chapter you will learn how to automate Quicken, memorize payees, schedule transactions, make more use of the Calendar, automate transactions or schedule your bills online, create reports, and produce useful graphs.

Memorize Your Entries

When you set your preferences (see Chapter 4), you told Quicken how to use QuickFill to make data entry faster and whether to automatically update new payees. You might recall that one choice was to automatically memorize new payees and then recall them when you next entered them. Whether or not you chose to have Quicken do this, you can also memorize transactions and payees manually.

Create a Memorized Payee

Memorizing saves you valuable data-entry time. Use the Memorized Payee List, shown in Figure 5-1, to create a memorization.

1. Click **Tools** and click **Memorized Payee List** to display the list.

   –Or–

   Press **CTRL+T**.

2. Click **New** on the Menu bar or at the bottom of the Memorized Payee List. The Create Memorized Payee dialog box appears.

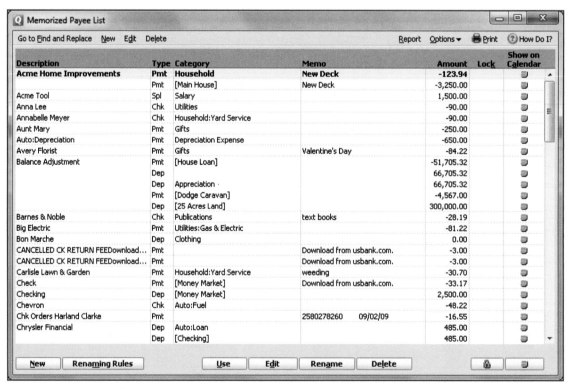

Figure 5-1: The Memorized Payee List lets you create, edit, use, rename, and delete your memorized payees.

3. Click the **Type Of Transaction** down arrow to choose the transaction type.

4. Press **TAB** and type the name of the payee in the Payee field.

5. Press **TAB** to go to the Address button if you have selected Print Check as the transaction type. Otherwise, click the **Category** down arrow, and choose a category from the list or type one in the Category text box.

6. Press **TAB** to move to the Split button. Click the button to open the Split dialog box if this is a transaction with several categories. If you choose to split the transaction into two or more categories, -*Split*- will appear in the Category field. Press **TAB**.

7. Enter any memo item you want to appear on the payment. Press **TAB** to move to the next field, and type an amount if you pay the same amount each time. If you entered a split transaction, the total amount of the splits will automatically appear in the Amount field.

8. To save the memorized payee and dismiss the dialog box, click **OK**.

Change Memorized Payees

You can work with the Memorized Payee List in several ways. As you look at the list shown in Figure 5-1, you see a Menu bar at the top of the list, as well as buttons on the bottom of the list. Some of the things you can do with the Memorized Payee List include:

- If your Memorized Payee List isn't already displayed, press **CTRL+T**.

- Click **Go To Find And Replace** on the Menu bar to find an existing transaction and replace any of its information.

- You can click **New**, either on the Menu bar or using the buttons at the bottom, to create a new memorized transaction.

- Select any payee on the list, and click **Edit**, either on the Menu bar or at the bottom of the screen, to make changes to existing information.

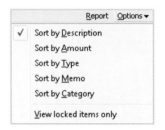

Q Quicken 2010

Ok to Delete 1 items?

OK   Cancel

- Select any payee and click **Delete**, either from the Menu bar or using the button at the bottom of the screen, to delete that payee. A dialog box appears prompting you to confirm this action. Click **OK**.

- Select any payee and click **Report** to create a report showing all transactions for that payee. However, if you have used a memorized payee only in hidden accounts, those transactions will not appear on a report.

- Click **Options** to tell Quicken how to sort the Memorized Payee List. Click **View Locked Items Only** to display only those items on the list that you have locked.

Report   Options ▾

✓ Sort by Description

Sort by Amount

Sort by Type

Sort by Memo

Sort by Category

View locked items only

- Click **Print** to open the Windows Print dialog box to print your Memorized Payee List.

- Click **How Do I?** to open the Quicken Help dialog box.

- Click the **Use** button at the bottom of the page to use the memorized payee as the next transaction in your current register.

- Click **Rename** to merge this payee with another one. See "Merge and Rename Payees" later in this chapter.

- Select a payee and click the **lock** icon to lock a payee's transaction. Select a payee and click the **note** icon to remove the transaction from the Quicken Calendar.

CAUTION

Use Memorized Payee will overwrite any transaction you happened to have selected. Be sure you have selected a blank line in the register before clicking Use.

NOTE

You can delete any transaction from a register by selecting it and pressing **CTRL+D**.

TIP

You can use your keyboard to access any menu item. Use the **ALT** key plus the underlined letter in the item to open the menu item.

Use Renaming Rules for Downloaded Transactions

When banks assign a payee name to a transaction, they may not use the name you want in your check register. Quicken allows you to establish renaming rules so that these transactions can be matched. You can add renaming rules from the Memorized Payee List or from the Quicken Preferences dialog box.

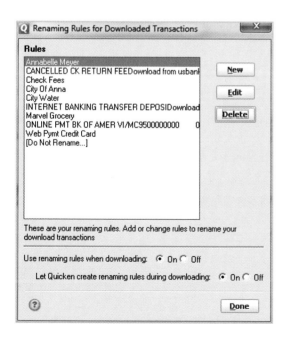

ADD RENAMING RULES FROM THE MEMORIZED PAYEE LIST

1. Click **Tools** and click **Memorized Payee List**.

   –Or–

   Press **CTRL+T**.

   In either case, the Memorized Payee List appears.

2. Click the name of one or more payees that you want to rename. To choose multiple names and rename them with the same name, hold down the **CTRL** key while clicking them.

3. Click **Rename** at the bottom of the window. The Merge And Rename Payees dialog box appears. Type the name you want to use in the New Name field. If you do *not* want all future downloaded transactions to use this name, clear that check box and click **OK**. The Edit Renaming Rule dialog box appears.

4. Make any changes to the rule, and, if needed, click **Add New Item** to add any names that should be renamed using this renaming rule. Click **OK** to close the Edit Renaming Rule dialog box.

WORK WITH RENAMING RULES FROM QUICKEN PREFERENCES

Quicken Preferences allow you to add a renaming rule when you don't have a current memorized name to work with. To add a renaming rule from Quicken Preferences:

1. Click **Edit** and click **Preferences.** Click **Quicken Preferences.**

2. Click **Downloaded Transactions** and then click **Renaming Rules**. The Renaming Rules For Downloaded Transactions dialog box appears.

3. Click **New**. The Create Renaming Rule dialog box appears. Enter the new payee name and the name or names that should be renamed to the new name. Then click **OK** to return to the Renaming Rules For Downloaded Transactions dialog box.

4. If you do *not* want Quicken to use renaming rules, click **Off** next to the Use Renaming Rules When Downloading radio button. The default is On.

5. If you do not want Quicken to create renaming rules when downloading, click **Off** next to that option as well.

6. Click **Done** to close the Renaming Rules For Downloaded Transactions dialog box, and then click **OK** to close Quicken Preferences.

Figure 5-2: *You can easily merge several spellings of the same payee in the Edit Renaming Rules dialog box.*

MERGE AND RENAME PAYEES

If you have more than one name for a specific payee, such as Cooper Store, Cooper's, and Coopers, you can merge these payees and still save all the detailed transaction information. To merge payees:

1. Press **CTRL+T** to open the Memorized Payee List.

2. To choose multiple names, hold down the **CTRL** key while clicking them.

3. Click **Rename** to open the Merge And Rename Payees dialog box.

4. In the **New Name** text box, type the name you want to use.

5. Click **OK**. The Edit Renaming Rules dialog box appears. Quicken shows each of the names you have selected to ensure you really want to include that name, as seen in Figure 5-2.

6. Click **Remove** to remove any of the names from this new name.

7. Click **Add New Item** to include additional items that may not have appeared on your Memorized Payee List.

8. Click **OK** when you have entered all the names you want to merge.

9. You are returned to the Memorized Payee List, and only the newly created name appears on it.

10. Click **Close** to close the Memorized Payee List.

Create and Memorize a Split Transaction Using Percentages

When you create a split transaction, there may be times when you want to use a percentage and have Quicken calculate an amount rather than entering the specific dollar amount for each category. To create such a transaction:

1. Open the account register that will contain the transaction, and enter the date, number or reference, payee, and total amount as you normally would.

2. Click **Split** on the Transaction toolbar.

   –Or–

   Click in the **Category** field, and click **Split**.

   –Or–

   Press **ALT+S**.

   In all cases, the Split Transaction dialog box appears, as shown in Figure 5-3.

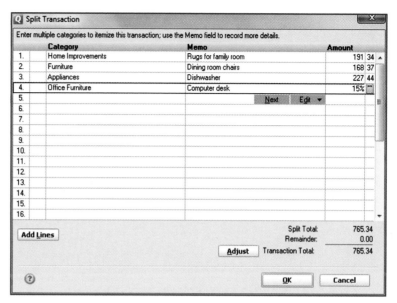

QUICKSTEPS

LOCKING A MEMORIZED PAYEE

If you choose to automatically memorize new payees in Quicken Preferences, each time you use a memorized payee, the transaction amount associated with that payee is updated. You can lock a memorized payee transaction so that the transaction amount won't change if you enter a transaction with a different amount for that payee. For example, let's say you send your son in college, Cooper Collegiate, an allowance of $150 per month for spending money and have locked that transaction. If you send him a birthday check for $250, the locked transaction will not change. If you do not lock it, the new memorized payee amount will be $250. To lock a transaction that is already in the Memorized Payee List:

1. Click **Tools** and click **Memorized Payee List**.

2. Click in the **Lock** column of the relevant transaction to lock the amount. The small lock icon is displayed.

   –Or–

   Select the transaction you want to lock, and click the **Lock** button at the bottom of the Memorized Payee List.

3. Click **Close** to close the list.

You can unlock a transaction in the same way. When a transaction is unlocked and your preferences are set to automatically memorize new payees, the next time you enter a transaction for this payee, the new amount is memorized.

Figure 5-3: The Split Transaction dialog box allows you to assign multiple categories to one transaction by either dollar amount or percentages.

3. Click the **Category** down arrow, and select a category. Press **TAB**, enter a memo or description if you choose, and press **TAB** again.

4. In the Amount field, which contains the total amount, replace the existing amount by typing a percentage as a number followed by the percent (%) sign. Quicken automatically calculates the dollar amount for the category by multiplying the total amount of the transaction by the percentage and then displays the balance on the next line. For example, if the check is for $200.00 and you type 75% on the first line, the amount displayed on the first line will be $150.00 and $50.00 will be displayed on the second line.

5. Press **TAB** to move to the next line, and repeat steps 3 and 4.

6. Click **OK** to apply the split and close the window.

7. Click **Edit** and then click **Memorize Payee** (or press **CTRL+M**) to memorize the transaction. A dialog box asks if you want to memorize the split payees as a percentage. If so, click **Yes**. Then click **OK** to complete the memorization.

Create Bill Reminders and Scheduled Transactions

Most of us have bills we pay every month. Your list may seem endless, with utility bills, rent or mortgage payments, property tax payments, and so on. Quicken's Bills And Reminders feature helps you automate the process. You can select and schedule all recurring transactions so that you don't accidentally overlook a regular payment. Quicken can even enter them automatically. You can set up reminders or record transactions several days earlier than they are actually due to remind yourself to put money in the bank to cover them. You can set up your paycheck using Quicken Paycheck Setup to keep track of your gross wages and deductions to help with tax planning. (See Chapters 9 and 10 for information on taxes and budgeting.) You can even enter the scheduled transactions 30, 60, or 90 days in advance to do cash-flow forecasting in your account register (that is my personal preference).

Understand Scheduled Transactions

Quicken has two types of scheduled transactions: recurring transactions, such as insurance or mortgage payments, and one-time transactions, such as the balance due on the new deck you're having built. You can also create a scheduled transaction to be paid later online. Other scheduled transactions can include:

- Income
  - Paychecks
  - Alimony or child support payments
  - Social Security or retirement checks
- Payments
  - Mortgage or rent payments
  - Car payments
  - Health and other insurance payments
  - Taxes
  - Membership dues

Schedule a Transaction

You can schedule payments and deposits at any time.

1. Click the **Bills** tab, and from the Actions Action Bar, click **Manage Reminders** to open the Bill And Income Reminders dialog box.

   –Or–

   Press **CTRL+J**.

   –Or–

   Click **Tools** and click **Manage Bill & Income Reminders**.

   In all cases, the Bill And Income Reminders dialog box appears.

2. If you have set up online bill payments, you will see the Schedule tab. Click the **Schedule** tab to see any transactions that are currently scheduled.

3. Click **Create New** and click **Scheduled Bill Or Deposit** to open the Add Transaction Reminder dialog box, as seen in Figure 5-4.

Tools	Help	
	Go to Setup	
	Account List	Ctrl+A
	Add Account	
	Calendar	Ctrl+K
	Alert Center (View and Setup)	
	Manage Bill & Income Reminders	Ctrl+J
	Loan Details	Ctrl+H

Bill and Income Reminders

Enter   Skip   Create New ▾   Edit   Delete   Options ▾   Print   How Do I?

Monthly Bills & Deposits | All Bills & Deposits | **Scheduled** | Repeating Online

☐ Show graph   ☐ Show calendar

Status	Due ▲	Pay To / Receive From	Amount	Show in List	#Left	Method	How Often	Web	Action
	10/25/2009	Acme Tool	1,500.00	22 days before		Deposit	Monthly		Enter Edit▾ Skip
	10/25/2009	First Community Bank	-516.39	3 days before	171	Payment	Monthly		
	11/3/2009	Acme Tool	1,500.00	1 days before		Paycheck D...	Every 2 weeks		
	11/5/2009	Big Company	1,800.00	3 days before		Paycheck D...	Twice a month		
	11/6/2009	Serenity Farms	-183.66	3 days before	35	Payment	Monthly		
Due Soon	11/6/2009	Western National Mortgage	-825.00	75 days before		Payment	Monthly		
	11/6/2009	Melody Flowers	518.80	3 days before		Paycheck D...	Every 2 weeks		
	11/14/2009	Credit Card Seattle	(no amount)	3 days before		Payment	Monthly		
	11/15/2009	Main Street Bank	-759.75	3 days before	59	Payment	Monthly		
	11/15/2009	First Community Bank	-1,249.50	3 days before	240	Payment	Monthly		
	11/15/2009	The Pool Guys Inc	-501.52	3 days before	11	Payment	Monthly		
	11/20/2009	Insurance Company	-600.00	3 days before		Payment	Monthly		
	11/24/2009	Chysler Financial, Inc.	-485.00	3 days before	33	Payment	Monthly		
	12/1/2009	Middletown Savings & Loan	-400.00	3 days before	82	Payment	Monthly		
	12/6/2009	Anna Lee	-90.00	3 days before		Payment	Monthly		
	12/6/2009	Avery Florist	-75.00	3 days before		Payment	Monthly		

Figure 5-4: The Add Transaction Reminder dialog box makes it easy to enter information about a payment, deposit, or transfer.

NOTE

All items marked with a red asterisk in the Add Transaction Reminder dialog box are required items.

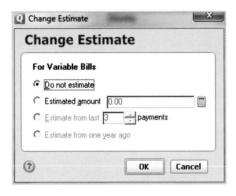

4. Choose the type of transaction.

- Click **Bill Or Payment** if the transaction you want to schedule pays a bill.
- Click **Income Or Deposit** to schedule funds coming into your accounts.
- Click **Transfer** to schedule a transfer from one account to another.

SCHEDULE A BILL OR PAYMENT

If you want to schedule funds going out of your accounts:

1. From the Add Transaction Reminder dialog box, choose **Bill Or Payment**.

2. In the Who section, type the name of the payee in the Pay To text box. A drop-down list will appear after you have typed one or two letters. Choose from the list, or type the entire name.

3. If the amount of the payment you are scheduling is the same each time, click the **Fixed Amount** radio button and enter the amount.

4. If the amount varies from payment to payment, click **Variable Amount**. The default is to give no estimate of the payment amount. If you want to change the default, click **Change**.

5. The Change Estimate dialog box appears.

- Choose **Do Not Estimate** if you want to leave the scheduled amount at zero.
- Click **Estimated Amount** and enter an amount if you want to "guesstimate" what you will be paying.
- Click **Estimate From Last *n* Payments**, and enter the number of payments that Quicken should use to estimate the scheduled payment. If you have not paid the scheduled bill the number of times that you enter, the amount may not be accurate.
- Click **Estimate From One Year Ago** to have Quicken look at the bills you paid to this payee last year to create the estimate. This choice might be useful for scheduled income or property tax payments.

6. In the How section, click the **Pay From Account** down arrow to open a list of accounts from which this bill is scheduled to be paid. Click the account name, and press **TAB** to continue.

7. Click the **Payment Method** down arrow to choose the way you will make this payment.

8. If you choose:

  - **Manual Payment** You can use the Address button to enter an address. Click **Address** to open the Address Book, and then enter the information. Click **OK** to close the dialog box, and press **TAB** to continue. This is the only payment method that allows you to enter information in the Address Book. If you choose one of the other two options, the Address button is grayed out.

  - **Online Bill Pay** Your payment will be sent from Quicken using the Online Bill Pay account you have set up.

  - **Print Check With Quicken** You may print the payment using checks specifically designed to be used with Quicken.

9. Continue to the **Delivery Method** drop-down box. If the payment method you chose was:

  - **Manual Payment** You may choose from six options, including Bank Web Site, Mail, and Payee Web Site.

  - **Online Bill Pay** You have only one choice: Send Via Bill Pay.

  - **Print Check With Quicken** You may select from three options: In Person, Mail, and Other.

  After you have chosen the delivery method for your scheduled payment, you have the option of entering the payee's website. If you enter the website address (often called the URL), click Go to use your Internet connection to open that website.

10. In the Track Spending section, type the category name in the Category field, or click the down arrow to choose one from the drop-down list.

11. Click **Split** if this transaction is divided into several categories, such as your house payment with principal, interest, and insurance. Enter the appropriate data, and then click **OK**.

12. Enter any memo information you want to appear on each check, such as an account or contract number.

13. In the When section, click the **Next Due Date** text box to enter the date the scheduled payment is due. You can also use the small calendar icon on the right side of the Date field to choose the date.

14. At the Remind Me *n* Days In Advance message, click **Change** to open the Change Reminder Options dialog box.

  - Click **Remind Me *n* Days In Advance** to enter the number of days in advance of the payment you want to be reminded.

- Click **Automatically Enter The Transaction In Register** *n* **Days Before The Due Date** to have Quicken enter the amount in the appropriate register.

- Click **Use Only Business Days For Reminder Days** if you want Quicken to ignore weekends and holidays when determining which day to remind you about a scheduled transaction.

15. Select the **How Often** drop-down box to show how often this transaction occurs. The default is **Monthly**, but you have other choices, as shown in Table 5-1.

FREQUENCY FOR SCHEDULED TRANSACTIONS	EXPLANATION
Only Once	This is for transactions that will only happen once, such as an upcoming balloon or final payment.
Weekly	Use this if the transaction occurs every week. Quicken uses the starting date of the transaction to determine which day of the week it will occur. With all frequencies other than Only Once, you have the option to set the date on which this transaction will end, the number of times it will occur, or no ending date.
Every Two Weeks Every Four Weeks	You have the same options as with the Weekly occurrence. The transaction repeats every two or four weeks from the start date.
Twice A Month	You tell Quicken on which two days each month to schedule this transaction.
Monthly	This is the default setting, since most recurring transactions happen monthly. You can designate a specific date or a specific day, such as the third Tuesday of each month.
Every Two Months	This option repeats the transaction bimonthly from the originally scheduled date. This frequency is often used for utility payments.
Quarterly	Use this if you have something that occurs every three months, such as estimated income tax payments.
Twice A Year	This option allows you to choose two days per year on which to schedule the transaction. Auto insurance and property tax payments are often paid twice each year.
Yearly	This option is for annual payments. You can set a specific date, such as August 10 or the second Wednesday of August.
Estimated Taxes	You can schedule four equal payments on your selected dates when you choose this option.
Variable Weeks	This option lets you schedule the transaction every set number of weeks. For example, if you choose to save $100 every seven weeks on Tuesday, you would select this option.
Variable Months	This option repeats the transaction every specified number of months. You have the same day and date choices as you do for the Monthly option.

Table 5-1: Choices for the Frequency of Scheduled Transactions

16. Choose how the date of the next payment is to be calculated. Your choices are:
    - The day of the month of the payment date
    - The day and the week of the payment date
    - The last day of every *n* months
    - Your last option is to set the schedule for this transaction.

17. Click **With No End Date** to have the transaction occur forever. Click **Change** to open the End Reminders dialog box.
    - Click **No End Date** to keep the scheduled transaction in your Reminders List forever.
    - Click **End On** to enter the date of the last payment.
    - Click **End After *n* Reminders** to enter the number of payments remaining to this payee.
    - Click **OK** to close the End Reminders dialog box.

18. Click **OK** to close the dialog box and return to the Bill And Income Reminders dialog box.

SCHEDULE A DEPOSIT

To schedule a receipt of funds into your accounts:

1. From the Add Transaction Reminder dialog box, choose **Income Or Deposit**.

2. In the Who section, click **Receive From** to enter the name of the entity that will be paying you. This could be a company, a person, or even the government.

3. If the amount to be deposited into your account is the same each time, click **Fixed Amount** and enter the amount. Use the small calculator to the right of the text field to enter the numbers, if you choose.

4. Click **Variable Amount** if the deposit varies from time to time. Follow the instructions in steps 4 and 5 in "Schedule a Bill or Payment" earlier in this chapter.

5. In the How section, click **Add To Account** to enter the account into which the funds will be deposited. Type the name of the account, or use the drop-down list to choose from all of the accounts you've entered into Quicken.

6. Click **Payment Method** and choose what type of payment you will be receiving from the drop-down list. See the QuickFacts "Understanding Scheduled Transaction Methods" later in this chapter for more information about the types of payments you may receive.

7. Click **Delivery Method** to enter how you will receive the funds.

8. Click **Web Site** to enter the URL of the entity paying you the money.

9. In the Track Spending section of the dialog box, click **Memo** to enter any additional information about this deposit, such as an account number or contract number.

10. In the When section, click **Next Due Date** to enter the next date you expect the payment.

11. Continue through the dialog box, as described in steps 14 through 17 in "Schedule a Bill or Payment" earlier in this chapter.

12. Click **OK** to return to the Bill And Income Reminders dialog box.

SCHEDULE A TRANSFER

To schedule a transfer between your accounts:

1. From the Add Transaction Reminder dialog box, choose **Transfer**, as seen in Figure 5-5.

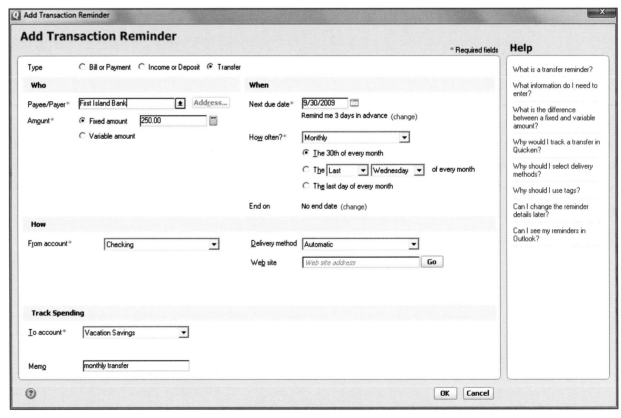

Figure 5-5: Scheduling transfers between accounts can help you save for a special event.

2. In the Who section, click **Payee/Payer** to enter the name of the bank or account that will be receiving or paying the transferred amount.

3. Click **Fixed Amount** to enter the amount of the transfer if it is the same each month.

4. Click **Variable Amount** if the amount varies.

5. Click **From Account** to enter the name of the account from which the funds will be transferred. Alternatively, click the down arrow to open the drop-down list from which you can choose. All of your accounts that are not hidden in Quicken are available on this list.

6. Click **Delivery Method** to enter how the transfer is to be done.

7. Click **Web Site** to enter the URL of any pertinent website.

8. In the Track Spending area, click **To Account** to enter the name of the account into which the transfer will be made.

9. Click **Memo** to enter any additional information.

10. Click **Next Due Date** to enter the date of the next transfer. Enter reminders as appropriate.

11. Click **How Often** to tell Quicken when to record the transfer. Click **End On** to set an ending date if necessary.

12. Click **OK** to return to the Bill And Income Reminders dialog box.

Create a Scheduled Transaction from a Register

You can create a scheduled transaction directly from a transaction in a register.

1. With a register open, right-click the transaction you want to schedule to display a context menu.

2. Click **Schedule Bill Or Deposit**. The Add Transaction Reminder dialog box appears, as described in "Schedule a Transaction" earlier in this chapter.

UNDERSTANDING SCHEDULED TRANSACTION METHODS

Quicken provides nine different methods for completing a scheduled transaction. These methods are based on the type of account the transaction affects and what version of Quicken you use, so not all choices are available for every transaction.

WORK WITH OUTGOING TRANSACTIONS

Scheduled disbursements can be used in all types of accounts. The methods for completing outgoing transactions vary, depending on the type of account, whether it is enabled for download, and so forth. These methods are:

- **Manual Payment** is used by Quicken for all transactions that pay money out of an account without using printed checks, including handwritten checks and direct charges, such as the deduction for your annual safe-deposit box fee.

- **Print Check With Quicken** is a check that is printed with Quicken.

- **Online Bill Pay** is the option you select when you use an online bill-paying service through your financial institution or Quicken Bill Pay. You can repeat this online payment automatically.

Continued . . .

UNDERSTANDING SCHEDULED TRANSACTION METHODS *(Continued)*

WORK WITH INCOMING TRANSACTIONS

The methods for completing incoming transactions are as follows:

- **Deposit** is used by Quicken to indicate any transaction that puts money into an account.

- **Transfer** is the method used when you move funds from one account to another, for example, from your checking account to your savings account each month.

- **Interest** is the method used when recording a repeating payment of interest, such as from a security.

- **Dividend** is used when you are scheduling a transaction in an investment account.

SCHEDULE A PAYCHECK

If you have not scheduled a paycheck in the Setup tab or elsewhere in Quicken, you can use the Bill And Income Reminders dialog box to do so.

1. Click the **Bills** tab, and from the Actions Action Bar, click **Manage Reminders** to open the Bill And Income Reminders dialog box.

2. Click **Create New** and click **Paycheck**.

3. The Manage Paychecks dialog box appears.

    a. Click **New** to open the Paycheck Setup wizard. Ensure you have your most recent paystub, and click **Next**.

    b. Click **This Is My Paycheck** or **This Is My Spouse's Paycheck**.

    c. Enter the company name and any optional information in the Memo field. Click **Next**.

    d. Click **I Want To Track All Earnings, Taxes, And Deductions** to simplify your tax preparation and have Quicken track your withholding amounts.

    e. Click **I Want To Track Net Deposits Only** if you only want to schedule the net amount of your paycheck each pay day. Click **Next** to continue.

    f. Enter all of the appropriate information in the Track All Earnings, Taxes And Deductions dialog box, as shown in Figure 5-6.

    g. Click **Done** to close the Paycheck Setup wizard.

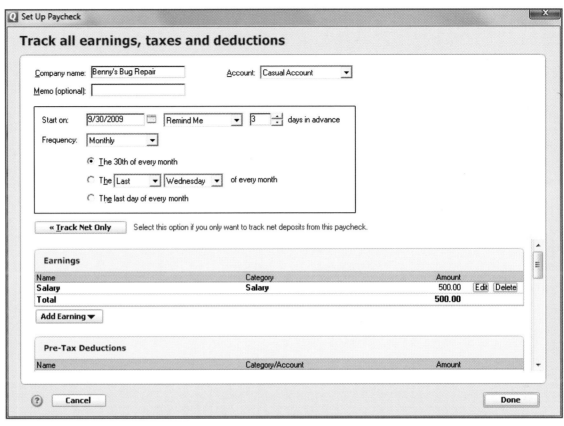

Figure 5-6: Tracking your earnings and deductions through Quicken can make tax time much easier.

h. The Enter Year-To-Date Information dialog box appears. Click **I Want To Enter Year-To-Date Information** if you choose to do so.

    i. Click **OK** to open the Paycheck Year-To-Date Amounts dialog box.

    ii. Using your most recent paystub, enter all of the appropriate information, and click **Enter** when you have completed the task. You are returned to the Manage Paychecks dialog box.

i. Click **I Do Not Want To Enter My Year-To-Date Information**, and click **OK** to return to the Manage Paychecks dialog box.

4. Click **Done** to return to the Bill And Income Reminders dialog box.

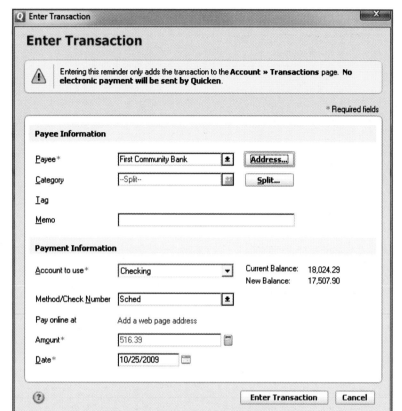

Figure 5-7: *The Enter Transaction dialog box reminds you to both enter a transaction into your register and physically complete the transaction.*

Work with Scheduled Transactions

In the Bill And Income Reminders dialog box, the Scheduled tab has several ways you can work with each scheduled transaction.

1. Click **Tools** and click **Manage Bill & Income Reminders** to open the Bill And Income Reminders dialog box.

2. Select a transaction to work with it.

3. Click **Enter** on either the Menu bar or the Transaction Tool Bar to open the Enter Transaction dialog box, as seen in Figure 5-7.

4. Verify the information that appears. If you want to enter this transaction into the referenced account, click **Enter Transaction**. Remember that just because you enter a transaction into a Quicken register, no payments or deposits have physically been made until you make them!

5. Otherwise, click **Cancel** to return to the Bill And Income Reminders dialog box.

6. Select a transaction and click **Skip** on either the Menu bar or the Transaction Tool Bar to open a message box asking if you want to skip the transaction for one time. Click **Yes** or **No**, depending on your decision.

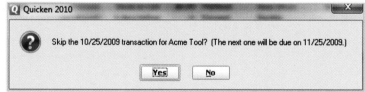

7. Select a transaction and click **Edit** on either the Menu bar or the Transaction Tool Bar to open the Edit Reminder dialog box. Make the appropriate changes, and click **OK** to close the dialog box. Depending on the type of reminder, the dialog may be titled Edit Bill Reminder, Edit Income Reminder, etc.

8. Select a transaction and click **Delete** on the Menu bar to delete a scheduled transaction. A warning message appears telling you that you are about to delete a scheduled bill or deposit. Click **OK** if that is your desire, or click **Cancel** to stop the deletion.

SORT BILL AND INCOME REMINDERS

When working in the Bill And Income Reminders dialog box, you can sort in three ways.

1. From the Menu bar, click **Options**.
2. Click **Sort By Payee** to sort alphabetically by the name of the payee.
3. Click **Sort By Amount** to sort by the amount of the payment or deposit, lowest to highest.
4. Click **Sort By Next Date** to return to the default setting. This option sorts in chronological order.

PRINT SCHEDULED TRANSACTIONS

Once you have scheduled all of your transactions in Quicken, to create a printed list:

1. Click **Print** from the Bill And Income Reminders Scheduled tab's Menu bar.
2. A Windows print dialog box appears. Enter the number of copies, the location of the printer, and so on.
3. Click **Print** to print the list.

Use the Calendar

Sometimes, it's helpful to see events on a calendar to reinforce them in your mind. The Calendar in Quicken lets you see at a glance your financial events for each month, as shown in Figure 5-8.

1. Press **CTRL+K**.

   –Or–

   Click the **Tools** menu, and then click **Calendar**.

   In both instances, the Calendar window opens.
2. Click the arrows to the left and right of the month on the Menu bar to move between months. The current month is displayed by default.

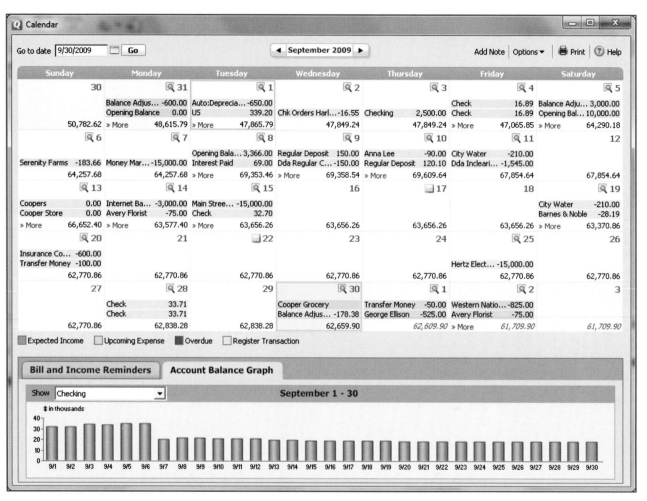

Figure 5-8: Quicken's Calendar helps you organize your financial transactions.

3. In the Go To Date text box, type a date or click the calendar icon on the Menu bar to open a small calendar from which you can select any specific date you want to view. Use the right and left arrows to go to other months. Click **Go** to display that date in the large calendar.

WORK WITH SPECIFIC DATES

To work with a specific date:

1. Right-click the date on the Calendar to display a context menu. Click **Transactions** to display the Transactions On: *this date* dialog box.

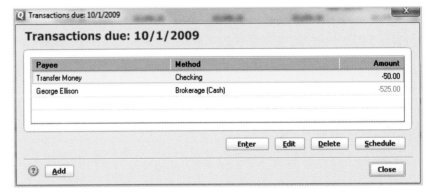

a. Click **Add** to display the Add Transaction dialog box. This dialog box is similar to the Schedule Transactions dialog box, except it asks if you would like to set up a reminder for this transaction or enter it now. If this is a one-time transaction, click **Enter Now**. If you want to schedule this transaction, click **Remind Me**, fill in the applicable transaction fields, and click **OK** when you are finished. If the radio button is set to Remind Me, the dialog is titled Add Transaction Reminder.

b. Click **Enter** to enter a transaction into the register for that day. The Enter Transaction dialog box appears. Fill in the applicable fields, and click **Enter Transaction** when you are finished.

c. Click **Edit** to edit a transaction. A dialog box appears. What dialog box you see depends on the type of transaction you have clicked. This dialog box requires the same information as the Create A Scheduled Transaction dialog box (see "Create a Scheduled Transaction from a Register" earlier in this chapter). Click an existing transaction, and click **Edit** to change it for the future. Make the needed changes, and click **OK** to close the dialog box.

NOTE

To delete a note from a specific date, right-click the date on the Calendar, click **Note**, and then click **Delete Note**.

NOTE

You can also add a note to a specific date by selecting **Add Note** on the Calendar Menu bar. This option adds a note to the current (today's) date, which is the default date on the Calendar.

CAUTION

Each date can hold only one note; however, you can combine several reminders into one note.

NOTE

You can also choose which accounts to display on the Calendar from the Calendar Menu bar. Click **Options** and click **Select Calendar Accounts**.

d. Click **Schedule** to open the Add Transaction Reminder dialog box. Follow the instructions in "Schedule a Transaction" earlier in this chapter.

e. If you have not scheduled the transaction for Online Bill Pay and sent the information to your bank, you may have the option to delete it by clicking **Delete**. The deletion warning message will appear. Click **OK** to delete the transaction, or click **Cancel** to close the warning box without deleting the transaction.

f. Click **Close** to close the Transactions On: *this date* dialog box.

2. Click **Note** on the context menu to add a reminder note to the date. The Add Note dialog appears.

   a. Type the note you want on that date.

   b. Select the color of the note from the drop-down box if you want a color other than the default one of yellow.

   c. Click **OK** to close the dialog box.

3. Click **Previous Month** or **Next Month** on the date's context menu to see this account's Calendar for the previous or next month.

4. Click **Calendar Accounts** on the context menu to select the accounts to include on this Calendar.

   a. Click **Mark All** to have scheduled transactions for all accounts display on the Calendar.

   b. Click **Clear All** to clear all selected accounts.

   c. Click **OK** to close the Calendar Accounts dialog box.

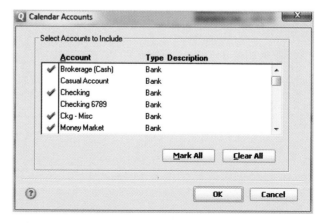

SHOWING TRANSACTIONS ON YOUR CALENDAR

When you are using your Calendar, you can easily add memorized transactions to any date on it. From your Calendar:

1. Click **Options** and click **Show Memorized Payee List** to display the list of memorized items displayed on the right side of your Calendar.

2. Drag any item on the list to the date on which you want the transaction to take place. The Add Transaction Reminder dialog box appears. You may click **Enter Now** to open the Add Transaction dialog box.

3. Complete any changes and click **OK**.

4. The transaction now appears on your Calendar on the date you chose.

USE THE CALENDAR OPTIONS

The Options menu on the Calendar Tool Bar allows you to tailor the Calendar to meet your needs.

1. Click **Show Recorded Transactions In Calendar** to display all of the transactions for each date.

2. Click **Show Bill And Income Reminders In Calendar** to display upcoming expenses or income that you have scheduled.

3. Click **Show Daily Balances In Calendar** to display the total balance each day for all of the accounts you have selected.

4. Click **Show Snapshots Below Calendar** to display the Scheduled Bills & Deposits and Account Balance Graph below the Calendar.

5. Click **Show Memorized Payee List** to display a list of your memorized transactions, which you can drag onto specific dates on your Calendar. See the "Showing Transactions on Your Calendar" QuickSteps for further information.

6. Click **Edit Memorized Payee List** to display the Memorized Payee List so that you can make necessary changes.

7. Click **Select Calendar Accounts** to open the Calendar Accounts dialog box to choose which accounts to be included in your Calendar.

IDENTIFY THE COLOR CODES USED ON YOUR CALENDAR

Quicken color-codes information on your calendar to make it easier to quickly spot specific types of transactions.

- Deposits or payments that have been recorded in your account register are displayed in black text on a clear background.

- Pending transactions you have scheduled appear in black text on a grey background.

- Any scheduled transaction that is overdue displays with a red background.

- Income items scheduled in the future display on a green background.

- Payment items scheduled in the future display on an orange background.

Use Reports and Graphs

After you have been working with Quicken for a while, it may be easier to see information in a report or graph format rather then viewing the various registers and lists. You can create reports directly from registers or transactions, use one of the many standard reports included with Quicken, customize an existing report in a number of ways, and memorize the reports you use regularly. You can print reports and graphs, and you can copy or transfer the data on a report to other programs, such as Microsoft Excel or TurboTax. By setting your preferences, you can change how reports use color and display information, and you can set the default date range for your reports. In this chapter we discuss some of the standard reports and graphs available. In later chapters we discuss ways you can customize and change reports, and you'll learn about reports you can create regarding your investments, taxes, and net worth.

Set Report Preferences

You can determine how each report displays your data from two different locations in Quicken: the Preferences menu and from within the Reports Action Bar in the various tabs. To set how your reports display:

1. Click **Edit**, click **Preferences**, click **Quicken Preferences**, and click **Reports And Graphs**. The Quicken Preferences Reports And Graphs Preferences dialog appears, as seen in Figure 5-9.

   - Click the **Default Date Range** down arrow to choose the range you will most often use when running reports. Year To Date is selected by default.

SCHEDULING REPEATING ONLINE PAYMENTS (Continued)

10. Enter the phone number of the payee, and click **OK**. The Confirm Online Payee Information summary appears. Click **Accept** if the information is correct. Click **Cancel** to return to the Set Up Online Payee dialog box to correct the information.

11. The instruction is listed in the Repeating Online tab as a repeating online payment.

12. To send the instruction, from the Bill And Income Reminders dialog box, click the **Repeating Online** tab, select the payment to be made, and click **Pay**. The One Step Update Settings dialog appears.

13. Click **Update** to open the One Step Update Settings dialog. Click the check box of the account from which the repeating payment will be paid, and click **Update Now** to complete the setup.

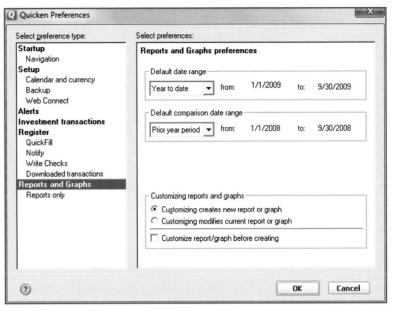

Figure 5-9: *Use Quicken Preferences to set the default report and graph displays.*

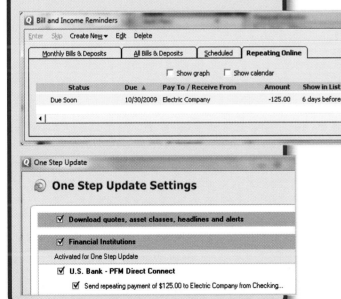

- Click the **Default Comparison Date Range** down arrow to choose the range that you will compare the current data to when creating a report. Prior Year Period is selected by default.

- In the Customizing Reports And Graphs area, click **Customizing Creates New Report Or Graph** or **Customizing Modifies Current Report Or Graph**. Customizing Creates New Report Or Graph is selected by default. You can also click **Customize Report/Graph Before Creating** to customize reports or graphs before creating them.

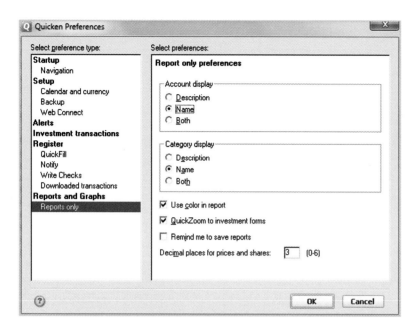

2. Click **Reports Only** to view the options for how reports will display information. For the display of both accounts and categories:

   - Click **Description** to include each account's or category's description in your reports.

   - Click **Name** (selected by default) to include the name of an account or category.

   - Click **Both** to include the name and description in each report.

3. For other display options:

   - Clear the **Use Color In Report** check box if you want to print your report in black and white.

   - Click **QuickZoom To Investment Forms** to see what information makes up each line of data on an investment report.

   - Clear the **Remind Me To Save Reports** check box if you don't want Quicken to remind you to save any reports you have created.

   - Type a number in the **Decimal Places For Prices And Shares** field if it is different from the default choice of 3.

4. Click **OK** to close the Quicken Preferences dialog box.

Create a Standard Report

To create a standard report in Quicken:

1. In any tab that contains a Reports Action Bar, click **All Reports & Graphs**.

2. Click **Reports And Graphs Center** to display the Reports & Graphs window (see Figure 5-10).

3. Click the small triangle icon in the area from which you want the report created. The standard reports available in this area are displayed in the window.

4. Click the report you want to create.

5. Choose the date range if it is different from the default range you set under Preferences.

Repeating online payments do not appear in your account register or the transaction lists until they are processed by your financial institution.

QuickZoom is a Quicken feature that allows you to see more detail about items in a report or graph. In some reports and graphs, this feature opens the original transaction.

Quicken's standard reports are designed to give you broad information about your accounts and activities. However, sometimes you might only want to find out how much you have paid to one payee to date or how much money you have spent eating out during the last three months. You can create a mini-report from any register regarding a payee or a category.

1. Open a register that has either the category or the payee on which you want your mini-report.

2. Click in either the **Payee** or the **Category** field.

3. Click the mini-report icon (it looks like an orange square with one corner folded down). You will see a small report on your screen displaying the last few transactions for this category or payee. The time period for the mini-report will vary based on the amount of matching transactions. If there are many recent transactions, the time period will be the last 30 days. If there are only a few transactions, the time period could be the last three years.

Continued . . .

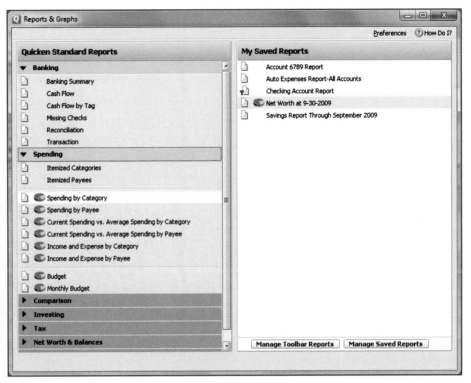

Figure 5-10: Quicken's Standard Reports help you create detailed information about your finances.

6. Click **Customize** to open the Customize dialog box for this report (see Chapter 6 for more information.)

7. Click **Show Report** to see the report.

8. Click **Print** on the Menu bar to print the report.

9. Click **Save Report** on the Menu bar to save the report. Close the Reports & Graphs window.

Create a Standard Graph

Quicken supplies you with several standard graphs for each report area, some of which can be customized. On the Standard Reports List, if there is a standard

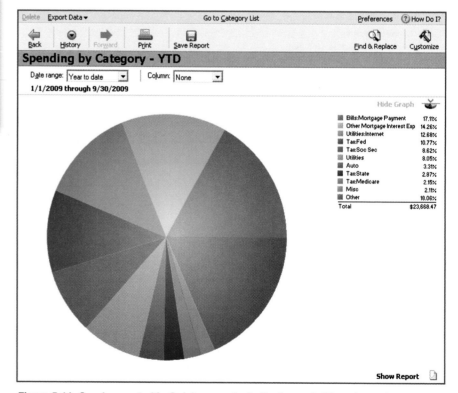

QUICKSTEPS

CREATING A MINI-REPORT (Continued)

4. Click **Show Report** to see a full report. However, Show Report defaults to the last 12 months, no matter what the time period for the mini-report was, so you may end up with no transactions in the full report. This can be confusing if you have transactions in the mini-report but get no transactions in the full report.

5. In the Transaction Report window, a standard report appears about this payee or category. From this window, you can:

- Change the date range from the default settings.

- Determine how the report calculates subtotals.

- Edit individual transactions within the mini-report and edit one or more transactions in the full report.

- Click **Close** to close the Transaction Report window.

graph associated with a report, you will see both a report and a graph icon by the report name. To create a graph:

1. In any tab that contains a Reports Action Bar, click **All Reports & Graphs**.

2. Click **Reports And Graphs Center** to display the Reports & Graphs window.

3. Choose a report that has a small graph icon to its left, as seen in Figure 5-10.

4. Click the graph you want, and click **Show Graph**. The standard graph will appear, as shown in Figure 5-11.

5. If you want to customize the graph, click **Customize**. (Customizing graphs is discussed further in Chapter 6.)

6. Click **Print** on the Menu bar if you want to print the graph.

7. Click **Close** to close the graph.

Figure 5-11: Graphs created in Quicken can be in the form of either pies or bars.

How to...

- *Link an Asset to a Liability Account*
- *Linking Multiple Liability Accounts to One Asset Account*
- *Adjust the Value of an Asset*
- *Understanding Depreciation*
- *Adjust the Interest Rate on a Loan*
- *Handle Other Loan Functions*
- *Making Additional Principal Payments*
- *Deleting an Alert*
- *Set Up Alerts*
- *Customize an Existing Report*
- *Save a Customized Report*
- *Manage Custom Folders for Saved Reports*
- *Recalling a Saved Report*
- *Add a Report to the Quicken Toolbar*
- *Create a Net Worth Report*
- *Use the Refinance and Loan Calculators*

Chapter 6
Tracking Your Assets and Liabilities

In the last chapter you learned how to memorize and schedule transactions and were introduced to reports and graphs. In this chapter you use those skills as you work with Property & Debt transactions in the Net Worth tab. This chapter will teach you how to link your assets with the related liabilities, enter information that affects the value of your assets, track your loans, and record other liabilities or payments. You'll find out how to customize reports, set alerts, and display your net worth. You will also learn to use the Quicken Refinance Calculator and the Quicken Loan Calculator.

Work with Asset and Liability Accounts

When you used the Quicken Setup tab (see Chapter 1), you may have set up your house and its accompanying mortgage accounts. It is a good idea to track the asset value in one account and the liability, or amount you owe, in another. While you may not have an asset account for every liability account, review your accounts now to ensure that you include all of the assets you want to watch. Quicken can track any loan type you may have, as described in Table 6-1.

For most of us, our biggest asset is our home, so much of the information in the following section is focused on that. However, you can make adjustments to any asset in the same way as described here.

LOAN TYPE	DESCRIPTION
Mortgage	A long-term loan, secured by real property, such as your house. A mortgage can have a *fixed* or an *adjustable* interest rate. Fixed rate means the amount of interest you pay is set at the beginning and stays at that rate for the life of the mortgage. Adjustable rate means that the rate of interest is adjusted at regular intervals throughout the life of the mortgage. Adjustable-rate mortgages are sometimes called variable-rate or floating-rate mortgages.
Home Equity	This type of loan is secured by the equity in your house. It is sometimes called a *second mortgage*. In some cases, the interest you pay on this type of loan may be tax-deductible. Consult with your tax professional for more information. Home equity loans can also have either a fixed or variable interest rate.
Reverse Mortgage	This type of loan allows homeowners with no mortgage to borrow against the equity in their home. The homeowner is paid regular monthly payments, and the loan is paid off when the home is sold. A reverse mortgage is often used by people on a fixed income to provide additional income, such as during retirement.
Vehicle Loan	This type of loan uses a vehicle—such as a boat, automobile, or recreational vehicle—as the *collateral* for the loan. Collateral is property used as security for a loan. The interest is normally not tax-deductible, but check with your tax professional to be sure.
Personal Loan	A loan that usually requires no collateral, and interest is often charged at a higher rate than with the other types of loans.

Table 6-1: Types of Loans You Can Track in Quicken

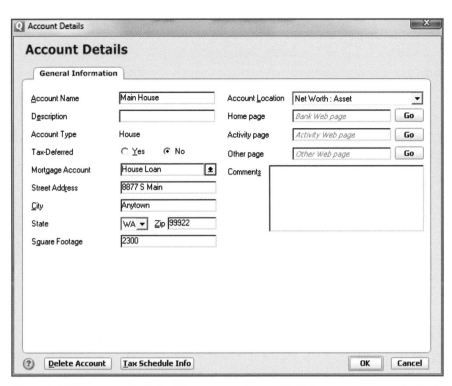

Figure 6-1: The Account Details dialog box can be used to link an asset account with a liability account, as well as to enter other information.

NOTE

The account-linking feature is available in Quicken Deluxe, Premier, and Home & Business versions.

Link an Asset to a Liability Account

If you have created your mortgage account but not the asset account, create the asset account now and then link them. If you have not yet created your house or mortgage account, do it now, following the directions in Chapter 3. If you have created both accounts but not yet linked them, you can do so quickly.

1. Click the **Tools** menu, and click **Account List**.

   –Or–

   Press **CTRL+A** to see the Account List.

2. Click the asset account with which you want to work. Click **Go To Register** to open the account register.

3. Click **Account Actions** and choose **Edit Account Details**. The Account Details dialog box appears, as shown in Figure 6-1.

4. Click the **Mortgage Account** down arrow to see a list of liability accounts. If the asset is not a house, the list will be called Linked Liability Account or, if the asset is a vehicle, Vehicle Loan Account.

5. Click the relevant liability account, and click **OK**.

LINKING MULTIPLE LIABILITY ACCOUNTS TO ONE ASSET ACCOUNT

If you have a second mortgage or line of credit secured by your home, you can track this information in Quicken.

1. Press **CTRL+A** to open the Account List.

2. Click the liability account you want to link with your asset account.

3. Click **Edit Details**.

4. Click the **Linked Asset Account** down arrow to open a list of assets.

5. Click the asset to which this liability is to be linked.

6. Click **OK** to close the Account Details dialog box.

7. Click the asset account you just linked.

8. Click **Edit Details** to open the Account Details dialog box. Note that the linked liability account now reads "Multiple," indicating that there are more than one liability accounts associated with this asset.

9. Click **OK** to close the dialog box.

10. To unlink a liability account, reverse this process.

Adjust the Value of an Asset

As time passes, you will probably add improvements to your home, thereby increasing its value. Furthermore, in many areas, real-estate market values fluctuate over time. You may want to record this information in your Asset Account register.

Account Details

Account Details

General Information

Account Name	Home Equity Loan
Description	
Account Type	Liability
Interest Rate	9.28 %
Linked Asset Account	Main House

Account Details

Account Details

General Information

Account Name	Main House
Description	
Account Type	House
Tax-Deferred	○ Yes ⦿ No
Mortgage Account	(multiple)

RECORD IMPROVEMENTS

An improvement such as remodeling a bathroom or adding a garage is called a *capital improvement* and adds to the value of your home. For example, if you purchased your home for $180,000 and added a garage for $25,000, the adjusted basis, or cost, of your home is $205,000. For additional information on how capital improvements may affect you, consult your tax professional. To record an improvement in your Asset Account register:

1. Open the account from which you want to pay for the improvement, for example, **Checking**.

2. Enter the transaction in the normal manner.

3. In the Category field, select **Transfers**, and select the name of the asset account.

4. The transaction appears in the Checking Account register, and the improvement is automatically added to the value of the house in the House Asset register.

| 9/25/2009 | 6731 | Hertz Electrical Contracting | | 15,000 00 | | 58,852 08 |
| | ✎ | [Main House] | rewire office and family room | | | |

| 9/25/2009 | | Hertz Electrical Contracting | | | 15,000 00 | 265,000 00 |
| | | [Savings] | rewire office and family room | | | |

USE THE UPDATE BALANCE DIALOG BOX

As your assets increase and decrease in value, you may want to adjust the account balances to ensure your financial net worth shows properly in Quicken. To access the Update Balance dialog box:

1. From the Account Bar, in the Property & Debt section, click the account you want to update.

   –Or–

   From the Net Worth tab's View Action Bar, click **Account Overview** and select the account by clicking the account name.

   In either case, the account register displays.

2. Click **Account Actions** and then click **Update Balance** to open the Update Balance Dialog Box.

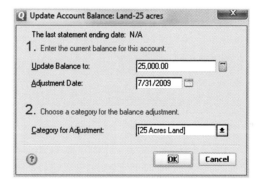

3. Enter the new total value of the asset in the Update Balance To field.

4. Enter the adjustment date if it is different from today's date.

5. Click the **Category For Adjustment** down arrow to open a list of categories for this adjustment. Quicken uses "Misc" as the default category. Consult your tax professional for a recommendation if needed. Personal net worth statements often show the market value of assets, as opposed to business balance sheets, which, by business accounting standards, show the historical cost of an asset.

7/31/2009	Balance Adjustment	R	15,000 00	25,000 00
	Appreciation			

6. Click **OK** to close the dialog box. You are returned to the account register, where your updated information appears on the next register line.

Work with Loans

Whether you used Quicken Setup to set up your loans or manually entered the information regarding your debts (other than credit cards), you may have to change interest rates or otherwise work with your loan information on occasion.

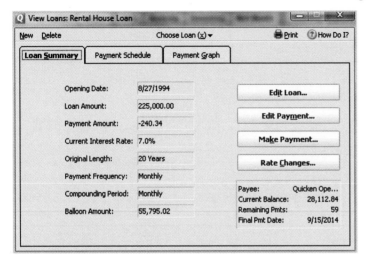

Adjust the Interest Rate on a Loan

From time to time, your lender may adjust interest rates on loans. The rate change may take effect at some future date, or it may be effective immediately with the next payment.

CHANGE THE INTEREST RATE IN THE FUTURE

To adjust your loan when the change takes effect with future payments:

1. From the Tools menu, click **Loan Details**.

    –Or–

    Press **CTRL+H** to open the View Loans dialog box.

2. Click **Choose Loan** on the Menu bar to display a list of all your loans. Click the loan whose rate you want to change.

3. Click **Rate Changes**. The Loan Rate Changes dialog box appears.

4. Click **New** to open the Insert An Interest Rate Change dialog box.

5. Type a date in the Effective Date field. Press **TAB** to move to the next field.

6. Type the new interest rate in the Interest Rate field. Press **TAB**, and Quicken calculates the new payment amount without changing the length of the loan.

CAUTION

If you have set up a liability account without setting up an amortized loan, this liability will not be visible in the View Loans dialog box.

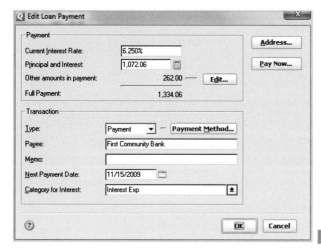

7. Click **OK** to close the Insert An Interest Rate Change dialog box, and click **Close** to
   close the Loan Rate Change dialog box. Finally, click **Close** to close the View Loans
   dialog box. The Current Interest Rate field will change after the date of the interest rate
   change.

CHANGE THE INTEREST RATE FOR THE NEXT PAYMENT

If your new interest rate is effective with the next payment:

1. Open the **View Loans** dialog box, and select your loan, as described in the first two
   steps of "Change the Interest Rate in the Future."

2. Click **Edit Payment** to open the Edit Loan Payment dialog box.

3. Type the new rate in the Current Interest Rate field.

   Quicken calculates the principal and interest payment for you using the next payment
   date as the effective date of the change without changing the length of the loan.
   However, if you change the payment amount (Principal And Interest field), Quicken
   changes the loan's length to accommodate the new payment.

4. Click **OK** to close the Edit Loan Payment dialog box, and click **Close** to close the View
   Loans dialog box.

Handle Other Loan Functions

In addition to changing the interest rate, you may need to handle other loan
functions, including changing the loan balance, making additional principal
payments (including tax and insurance payments), handling interest-only or
balloon payments, and printing a loan summary.

CHANGE LOAN BALANCES

Periodically, you may get statements from your lender showing the current
balance of a loan or the balance as of a specific date. If you want to change the
loan balance in Quicken to match the lender's record:

1. From the Net Worth tab's View Action Bar, click the **Account Overview** subtab and
   select the debt with which you want to work. Click **Account Actions** and then click
   Loan Details.

   –Or–

   Press **CTRL+H** to display the View Loans dialog box.

   –Or–

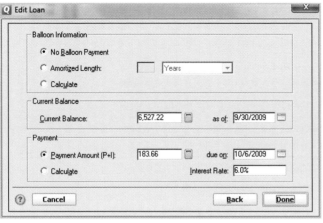

Click **Tools** and click **Loan Details**.

In all cases, the View Loans dialog appears.

2. Click **Choose Loan** and click the loan with which you want to work.

3. Click **Edit Loan** to open the Edit Loan dialog box.

4. Click **Next** in the lower-right corner.

5. Type the balance shown by the lender in the Current Balance field.

6. Click **Done** to close the dialog box, and click **Close** to close the View Loans dialog box.

INCLUDE TAX AND INSURANCE PAYMENTS

Many mortgages, and some home equity loans, include other amounts with each payment, such as property taxes, *PMI* (private mortgage insurance), or homeowners' insurance. The property taxes and insurance payments are then paid by the lender directly to the taxing authority and insurance company. If these amounts are changed, you should reflect that information in your loan payment.

1. Press **CTRL+H** to open the View Loans dialog box.

2. Click **Choose Loan** and click the loan with which you want to work.

3. Click **Edit Payment** to open the Edit Payment dialog box.

4. Click **Edit** to open the Split Transaction window.

5. Fill in the **Category** and **Amount** fields for each of the fees included in your payment.

   a. You may want to use the standard Quicken category of Insurance: Home Insurance for the insurance portion of your payment.

   b. Quicken's standard category for property taxes is Taxes:Property.

6. Click **OK** to close the Split Transaction window, click **OK** once more to close the Edit Payment dialog box, and click **Close** to close the View Loans dialog box.

QUICKSTEPS

MAKING ADDITIONAL PRINCIPAL PAYMENTS

Making additional principal payments can reduce the amount of interest you pay over the term of a loan. To record these additional payments:

1. Press **CTRL+H** to open the View Loans window.

2. Click **Choose Loan** and click the loan with which you want to work.

3. Click **Make Payment**. The Loan Payment dialog box appears. Click **Extra**.

4. Click the **Account To Use** down arrow, and select the account you want.

5. Click the **Type Of Transaction** down arrow, and choose how you want to make the payment.

Continued . . .

HANDLE INTEREST-ONLY LOANS AND BALLOON PAYMENTS

While not the safest type of loans, some mortgages are interest-only, with the full amount of the loan payable at the end of the loan's term. In this way, consumers have a lower monthly payment in the short-term and can make principal payments whenever they choose or refinance the loan at the end of the interest-only term. To enter a new loan of this type:

1. Press **CTRL+H** and click **New**. The Loan Setup wizard starts. Click **Next**.

2. Click **Borrow Money**, click **Next**, and enter an account name. Click **Next**, tell Quicken if payments have been made on this loan by clicking **Yes** or **No**, and click **Next** again.

3. Enter the date of the loan and the original balance, and click **Next**.

4. You are asked if this loan includes a balloon payment at the end. Click **Yes** and then click **Next**.

5. In the Original Length field, enter the length of time in which payments are to be made on the loan, *not* the length of time over which it is amortized, and click **Next**.

6. Enter the number of years over which the loan is to be amortized in the Amortized Length field. If you are not sure of the amortized length, click **Please Calculate The Amortized Length For Me**, and Quicken will compute the amortization period based on the amount of the payments and the interest rate. Click **Next** to continue.

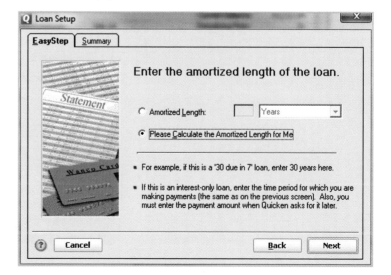

MAKING ADDITIONAL PRINCIPAL PAYMENTS *(Continued)*

6. Type a value in the Amount field, click the **Number** down arrow, and select how you will reference the payment.

7. If you want to include your account number or other information on the check, enter it into the **Memo** field.

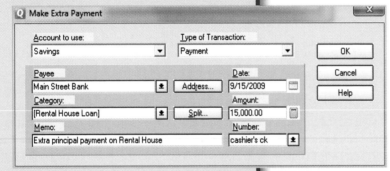

8. Click **OK** to close the dialog box, and click **Close** to close the View Loans dialog box.

The transaction is entered in the relevant checking account and is reflected as an additional principal payment in the Liability Account register.

7. Enter the payment period for this loan.

   a. Click **Standard Period** if you make regular payments—usually monthly. If you will be making payments other than monthly, use the drop-down list to choose the interval at which you will be making the payments.

   b. Click **Other Period** if you will not be making regular, periodic payments. Enter the number of payments per year you will be making.

8. Click **Next**. Enter the compounding period for this loan. This describes the way your lender calculates interest owed. Many institutions compound interest daily; however, "Monthly" is the default. Click **Next**.

9. If you answered "Yes" in step 2, that payments have been made on this loan, you are asked if you know the current balance. If you know it, click **Yes**; if you do not know the current balance, click **No**. In either case, click **Next** to continue.

10. If you answered "Yes," that you know the current balance, you are asked to:

    a. Enter the date of the current balance in the Current Balance Date field.

    b. Enter the amount of the current balance in the Current Balance Amount field.

    c. Click **Next** to continue.

11. If you answered "No," that you do not know the current balance, you are asked to enter the date of the next payment.

12. If you answered "No" in step 2, that no payments have been made on this loan, you are asked to enter the date of the first payment if it is different than a month from today. Click **Next**.

13. You are asked if you know the amount of either the first payment (if no payments have been made on this loan) or the next payment (if payments have been made on this loan). Click either **Yes** or **No**.

14. If you chose Yes, enter the amount in the Payment Amount field, and click **Next** to enter the interest rate for this loan.

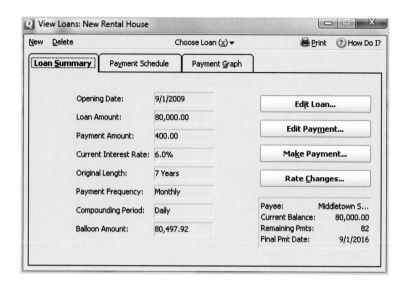

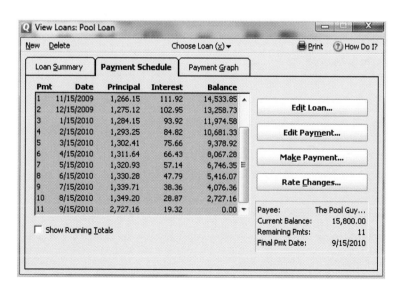

15. Independent of whether you answered "Yes" or "No" to knowing the payment amount, the Interest Rate dialog box will appear. Enter the interest rate as a percent (you don't need to include the percent sign), and click **Next**.

16. The first Summary dialog box will appear. Confirm the information it contains, and click **Next**. A second Summary dialog box will appear. Again, confirm the information it contains, and click **Next**.

17. The third Summary dialog box will appear. Confirm the information it contains, and click **Done**. Depending on how you entered the information, Quicken may display a message stating that it has calculated either the amortization period or the payment.

18. The final Summary dialog box displays the information you have entered or that Quicken has calculated. Click **Done** to display the Set Up Loan Payment dialog box.

19. Enter the payee information in the Set Up Loan Payment dialog box, and click **OK**. Click either **Yes** or **No** when asked if you want to create an asset account for this loan. If you click **No**, you will see a summary of your loan. Click **Close** to close the View Loans dialog box.

PRINT A LOAN SUMMARY

The View Loans dialog box allows you to print a summary of each loan, the payment schedule, and a graph that shows the progress of the loan repayment. To access this dialog box:

1. Press **CTRL+H** to open the View Loans dialog box. Click **Choose Loan** and select the loan you want to print.

2. Click **Print** on the Menu bar to open a Windows Print dialog box.

3. Click **Preview** to see how the report will look when it is printed. Figure 6-2 shows an example of this report.

4. Click **Print** to print the report, or click **Close** to close the Print Preview dialog box without printing the report.

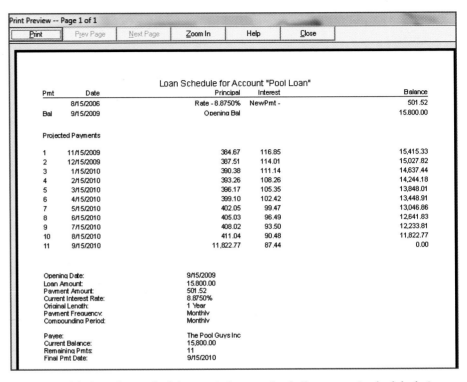

| | Print | Prev Page | Next Page | Zoom In | Help | Close | |

Loan Schedule for Account "Pool Loan"

Pmt	Date		Principal	Interest		Balance
	8/15/2006		Rate - 8.8750%	NewPmt -		501.52
Bal	9/15/2009		Opening Bal			15,800.00

Projected Payments

1	11/15/2009		384.67	116.85		15,415.33
2	12/15/2009		387.51	114.01		15,027.82
3	1/15/2010		390.38	111.14		14,637.44
4	2/15/2010		393.26	108.26		14,244.18
5	3/15/2010		396.17	105.35		13,848.01
6	4/15/2010		399.10	102.42		13,448.91
7	5/15/2010		402.05	99.47		13,046.86
8	6/15/2010		405.03	96.49		12,641.83
9	7/15/2010		408.02	93.50		12,233.81
10	8/15/2010		411.04	90.48		11,822.77
11	9/15/2010		11,822.77	87.44		0.00

Opening Date:	9/15/2009
Loan Amount:	15,800.00
Payment Amount:	501.52
Current Interest Rate:	8.8750%
Original Length:	1 Year
Payment Frequency:	Monthly
Compounding Period:	Monthly
Payee:	The Pool Guys Inc
Current Balance:	15,800.00
Remaining Pmts:	11
Final Pmt Date:	9/15/2010

Figure 6-2: **Printing a loan schedule report shows not only the payment schedule, but also a summary of the loan itself.**

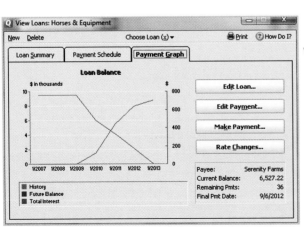

VIEW A PAYMENT GRAPH

The payment graph allows you to see the history of your loan, interest, and future balance displayed in a line graph. While you cannot print this directly, it is a useful tool. To see the payment graph:

1. Press **CTRL+H** to open the View Loans dialog box. Click **Choose Loan** and select the loan you want to view.

2. Click the **Payment Graph** tab to view it. The colored legend on the bottom of the graph shows what each line means.

3. Click **Close** to close the View Loans dialog box.

Understand Alerts

One of the most powerful features in Quicken Premier and Home & Business editions is the ability to set up *alerts,* or reminders. Not all alerts are available in Quicken Deluxe or Quicken Starter edition. Alerts remind you to download transactions, pay bills, know when your credit card balance is nearing its limit, know when an account is near its minimum balance, or know when your auto insurance is approaching its renewal date, among other things. With Quicken .com, you can create a Watch List for securities you want to track. Chapter 7 discusses investments and securities in further detail. There are four major categories of alerts.

- **Banking alerts** let you monitor minimum and maximum balances, credit card limits, monthly expenses, and savings goals, as shown in Figure 6-3. You can even check your financial institutions for new services they offer.

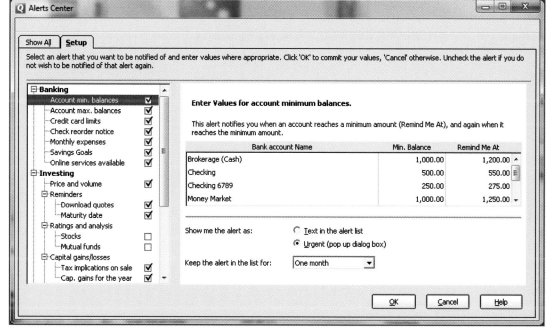

- **Investing alerts** remind you to download quotes and prices, notify you when earnings fail to meet or exceed projections, give you useful information about mutual fund distributions, and identify the holding periods for your securities.

- **Tax alerts** notify you when you have either over- or under-withheld income tax from your paycheck, remind you about upcoming tax dates, and provide useful tax information about personal deductions.

- **General alerts** remind you to download transactions and notify you that scheduled transactions are soon due, that insurance policies are approaching renewal dates, and that a mortgage interest rate may be changing.

*Figure 6-3: **Alerts help you manage your finances.***

Enter Values for credit card limits.

This alert notifies you when you've charged close to the limit on a credit card (Remind Me At), and again when you charged over the limit

Credit Card Name	Credit Limit	Remind Me At
Credit Card - Island	7,500.00	0.00
Credit Card - Seattle	10,000.00	0.00

QUICKSTEPS

DELETING AN ALERT

To delete an alert:

1. Click the **Tools** menu, and click **Alert Center (View And Setup)** The Alerts Center window opens with the Show All tab displayed.

2. Click the check box next to the alert you want to delete, and click the **Delete** button at the bottom of the window. A dialog box will appear warning that you are about to delete an alert.

3. Click **OK** to verify the deletion.

4. Click **Close** to close the window.

Set Up Alerts

To set up an alert:

1. Click the **Tools** menu, and then click **Alert Center (View And Setup)**.

2. If the Setup tab is not already displayed, click it. You should see a window similar to the one shown in Figure 6-3.

3. Select the type of alert you want to set, and click the plus sign (+) to the left of it.

4. Click the check box corresponding to the alert you want. The values that can be entered appear on the right side of the window.

5. If you can enter values in the alert with which you are working, click in the limit box to type in your values. Click the individual categories for which you want to receive alerts, and enter the required information.

6. Click either **Text In The Alert List** or **Urgent (Pop-Up Dialog Box)** to tell Quicken how you want the alert displayed.

7. Click the **Keep The Alert In The List For** down arrow, and choose how long you want the alert to remain in the list.

8. Click **OK** to save the alert and close the window.

Create Custom Reports

In Chapter 5 you learned how to create standard Quicken reports and graphs. The following sections will discuss how to customize reports so that they provide exactly the information you want. You can review your spending, learn your net worth, and get ready for taxes. You can save reports, or you can tell Quicken to save new reports automatically. You can export your reports to the Clipboard in Windows or to Microsoft Excel. You can also export them to a PDF file format that can be read with Adobe Acrobat Reader on any computer, even if Quicken is not installed.

Customize an Existing Report

The easiest way to make a report your own is to start with an existing report and customize it to meet your needs. We'll start with one report (the Banking

Transactions report) and create a report based on what we want to know. Each standard report may have slightly different options.

1. From the Banking tab's Reports Action Bar, click **Banking Reports** and click **Transaction**. A Transaction report appears, with the date range set as the default year-to-date.

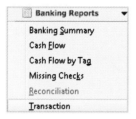

2. Click **Customize** to open the Customize Transaction dialog box.

   a. Click the **Date Range** down arrow, and choose from a list of preset periods.

   b. Click **Custom Dates** from the Date Range list to set your own date range.

3. Click the **Display** tab to tell Quicken how to lay out your report.

   a. Click in the **Title** field, and type a new title.

   b. Click the **Subtotal By** down arrow, and choose to subtotal by one of several time periods or by category, class, payee, account, or tax schedule.

   c. Click the **Sort By** down arrow, and choose how you want your data sorted.

   d. Click the **Organization** down arrow, and choose whether the report is organized with income at the top and expenses at the bottom or with income items interspersed with expense items to show the cash flow at any period.

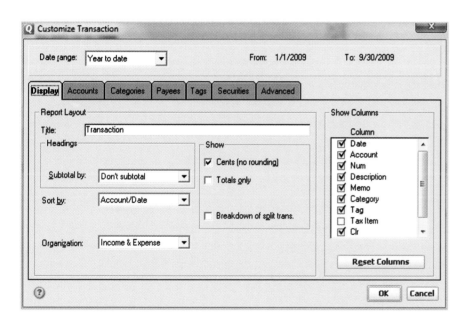

1 2 3 4 5 **6** 7 8 9 10

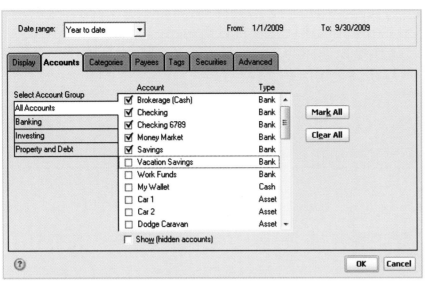

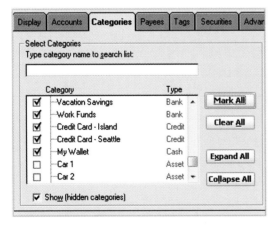

e. Click **Cents (No Rounding)** if you want to see transactions to the nearest penny, or clear this check box to round items to the nearest dollar.

f. Click **Totals Only** if you want only the summary categories displayed. Clear this check box if you want all transactions displayed.

g. Click **Breakdown Of Split Trans.** if you want to show how split transactions were categorized.

h. Click the columns you do not want displayed in the Show Columns area; by default, all columns are displayed. To reselect all the columns, click **Reset Columns**.

4. Click the **Accounts** tab to choose the accounts included in the report. You can choose to use all accounts or specific Banking, Investing, or Property & Debt accounts.

a. Click **Mark All** to choose all accounts.

b. Click **Clear All** to clear all accounts and select the ones you want to use. This is the quickest way to select only one or two accounts.

c. Click **Show (Hidden Accounts)** to include accounts that normally aren't displayed in Quicken.

5. Click the **Categories** tab to select the categories included in your report.

a. Click **Mark All** to choose all accounts.

b. Click **Clear All** to clear all accounts and select the ones you want to use.

c. Click **Expand All** if you want details about subcategories included, or click **Collapse All** if you want only the main category information to be displayed.

d. Enter information into the Category, Payee, or Memo Contains fields if you want to include only those transactions that contain specific information in the Category and/or Memo fields.

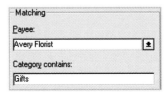

NOTE

It may be confusing why you can enter a payee in the Customize Transaction Category tab or enter a category in the Payee tab. The answer is that the Category tab allows you to select all the categories in the report and to select a single payee in those categories. Step 7 allows you to select all the payees in the report and to select a single category for those payees. In most instances, the payee is left blank in the Category tab and the category is left blank in the Payee tab so that you can create a report with both multiple categories and multiple payees.

TIP

Expand the date range if your payee name does not appear and you are sure you have paid this payee.

TIP

If the payee name does not appear, review the list again. You may have misspelled the name the first time you entered it.

6. Click the **Payees** tab to select the payees to include in the report. Type a payee name, or choose one from the list. Click **Clear All** to clear the payee check boxes and select the ones you want.

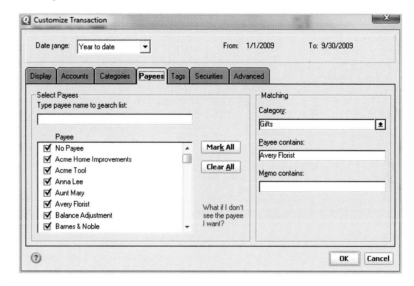

7. Click the **Tags** tab to select tags, if you use them.

8. Click the **Securities** tab to choose the securities included in the report.

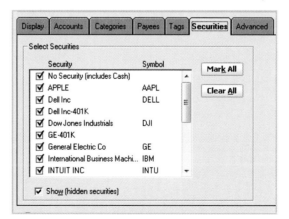

9. Click **Show (Hidden Securities)** to include securities you have chosen not to display in your report, or clear the check box if you do not want them included.

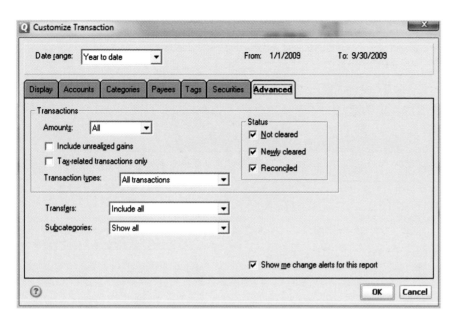

10. Click the **Advanced** tab to further refine your report.

   a. Click the **Amounts** down arrow, and click a criterion for selecting the amounts you want to include.

   b. If you choose a criterion other than All, enter an amount to use with the criterion.

   c. Click **Include Unrealized Gains** if you have set up investment accounts and want to include paper gains and losses in your report (see Chapter 8 for more information).

   d. Click **Tax-Related Transactions Only** to include only those transactions that relate to income tax.

   e. Click the **Transaction Types** down arrow, and choose **All Transactions** (selected by default), **Payments**, **Deposits**, or **Unprinted Checks**.

   f. Clear the check boxes in the Status area to limit your report to transactions that have cleared but are not reconciled.

11. Click **OK** to display the report after you have finished customizing it.

12. Click the **Print Report** icon on the toolbar to print the report.

Save a Customized Report

After you have created your custom report, you can save it to your My Saved Reports folder, recall it, revise it, and resave it with either a new name or as a replacement for the original saved report.

To save a customized report when you first create it:

1. Click the **Save Report** icon on the toolbar to open the Save Report dialog box.

2. Type a name in the Report Name field to identify this report, press **TAB**, and type a description if you want. The description will appear in your list of saved reports under the title of the report.

TIP

A "paper" gain or loss is an unrealized gain or loss that you might have realized if you had sold the security at today's price. The word "paper" comes from getting today's price from the newspaper.

CAUTION

The Description field in the Save Report dialog box holds only 21 characters, including spaces. If you choose to create a description for a saved report, make it short.

3. Click the **Save In** down arrow, and click the folder in which you want your report stored. If you do not create a separate folder, the report will be displayed on the right side of the Report & Graph window under My Saved Reports.

4. Click **Save Report History** if you want to save all versions of this report. By default, Quicken does not save this history.

5. Click **OK** to save the report, and click **Close** to close the report window.

Manage Custom Folders for Saved Reports

You might want to organize your saved reports into different folders so that you can easily retrieve them. To create a folder:

1. In any tab except the Bills tab, in the Reports Action Bar, click **All Reports & Graphs** and click **Reports & Graphs Center**. The Reports & Graphs window opens.

2. On the right side of the Reports & Graphs dialog box, click the **Manage Saved Reports** button. The Manage Saved Reports dialog box appears.

3. Click **Create Folder**. The Create New Report Folder dialog box appears.

4. Type a new folder name, and click **OK**.

RENAME A FOLDER OR REPORT

1. In the Manage Saved Reports dialog box, click a folder, click **Rename Folder**, type a new name, and click **OK**.

2. To change the name of a report, select the report, and click **Edit** to change its name or description.

DELETE AND MOVE FOLDERS AND REPORTS

1. Click a report or a folder, and click **Delete** to delete it.

2. Click a report and click **Move To Folder** to move a report to another folder.

3. Type or select the name of the folder, and click **OK**.

Click **Done** when you have finished organizing your saved reports. Click **Close** to close the Reports & Graphs window.

You cannot delete a folder from your Saved Reports screen without moving or deleting all of the reports in that folder.

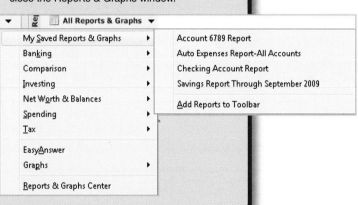

QUICKSTEPS

RECALLING A SAVED REPORT

Once you have customized and saved a report, you can easily retrieve it.

1. From any tab except the Bills tab, from the Reports Action Bar, click **All Reports & Graphs** and click **My Saved Reports & Graphs**. A list of your saved reports will appear.

2. Click the name of the report you want to view.

3. Click **Show Report** to open the report.

4. Click **Close** to close the report, and click **Close** to close the Reports & Graphs window.

Add a Report to the Quicken Toolbar

If you choose to display the Quicken toolbar, you can save your reports or your report folders to the toolbar. To save a report to the Quicken toolbar:

1. Click **View** and click **Show Tool Bar** to display the Quicken toolbar.

2. From any tab except the Bills tab, from the Reports Action Bar, click **All Reports & Graphs** and click **My Saved Reports & Graphs**.

3. Click **Add Reports To Toolbar** at the bottom of the submenu. The Manage Toolbar Reports dialog box appears.

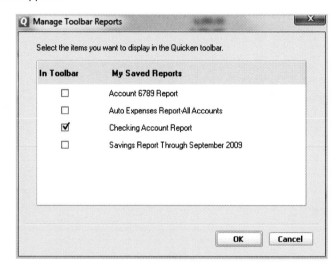

4. Click the small arrow to the left of each folder's check box to display the reports in that folder.

5. Click the check box of the reports (or folders) you want to appear on the Quicken toolbar.

6. After you have made your selections, click **OK** to close the dialog box.

7. Your selections appear on the Quicken toolbar.

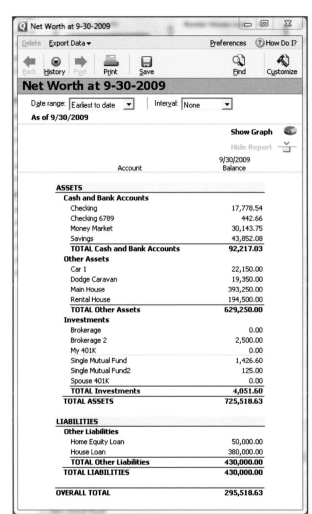

Net Worth at 9-30-2009

Delete   Export Data ▼   Preferences   ⑦ How Do I?

Back   History   Fwd   Print   Save   Find   Customize

Net Worth at 9-30-2009

Date range: Earliest to date ▼ | Interval: None ▼
As of 9/30/2009

Show Graph
Hide Report

| | 9/30/2009 |
| Account | Balance |

ASSETS | |
Cash and Bank Accounts | |
Checking | 17,778.54 |
Checking 6789 | 442.66 |
Money Market | 30,143.75 |
Savings | 43,852.08 |
TOTAL Cash and Bank Accounts | 92,217.03 |
Other Assets | |
Car 1 | 22,150.00 |
Dodge Caravan | 19,350.00 |
Main House | 393,250.00 |
Rental House | 194,500.00 |
TOTAL Other Assets | 629,250.00 |
Investments | |
Brokerage | 0.00 |
Brokerage 2 | 2,500.00 |
My 401K | 0.00 |
Single Mutual Fund | 1,426.60 |
Single Mutual Fund2 | 125.00 |
Spouse 401K | 0.00 |
TOTAL Investments | 4,051.60 |
TOTAL ASSETS | 725,518.63 |

LIABILITIES | |
Other Liabilities | |
Home Equity Loan | 50,000.00 |
House Loan | 380,000.00 |
TOTAL Other Liabilities | 430,000.00 |
TOTAL LIABILITIES | 430,000.00 |

OVERALL TOTAL | 295,518.63 |

Figure 6-4: A Net Worth report shows all of your assets minus all of your liabilities for a "net" financial "worth."

Create a Net Worth Report

Your *net worth* is the difference between the value of what you own (your assets) and what you owe (your liabilities). From time to time, you may want to print a report of your net worth, and Quicken makes this easy to do. An example of a Net Worth report is shown in Figure 6-4.

1. To create a Net Worth report, in the Net Worth tab's Reports Action Bar, click **All Reports & Graphs** to open a menu.

2. Click **Net Worth & Balances** to display the related reports.

3. Click **Net Worth**. In the **Report Balance As Of** text box, enter the as-of date for which you want the report, and click **Show Report**. If you have any accounts set to Don't Include in Totals or Don't Show In Bar, you may receive a prompt explaining how to exclude these accounts from your Net Worth report.

4. Click the **Date Range** down arrow, and choose from a list of preset periods. The default is from the earliest date to today's date.

5. Click **Interval** to choose the period of time that this report will cover. There may be times that creditors or others will ask for a "net worth statement" covering just a specific period. When that is the case, use this option.

6. Click **Print** on the Report toolbar to print your report.

7. Click **Customize** to change the date or other items within the report, as described in "Customize an Existing Report" earlier in this chapter.

8. Click **Save Report** to open the Save Report dialog box, as described in "Save a Customized Report."

9. Click **Close** to return to Quicken.

Use the Refinance and Loan Calculators

As you continue to work with your assets and debts, you may want some answers to financial questions about your mortgage or other debt. The Refinance and Loan Calculators can help you make good decisions.

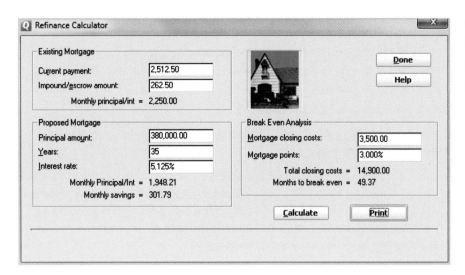

USE THE REFINANCE CALCULATOR

With the Refinance Calculator, you can easily see how much you would save or gain by refinancing your current mortgage. To use the Refinance Calculator:

1. From the Net Worth tab's Tools Action Bar, click **Property & Loan Tools**, and click **Refinance Calculator**. The Refinance Calculator dialog box appears.

2. Click **Current Payment** to enter your current payment, including any escrow amounts.

3. Click **Impound/Escrow Amount** to enter the escrow portion of the payment you entered in step 1.

4. Click **Proposed Amount** to enter the amount of the proposed mortgage, the years of payments, and the new interest rate. The new monthly principal and interest amount will be calculated, as well as the monthly savings over your current monthly payment.

5. Enter any closing costs and points in the appropriate fields, and Quicken will calculate the total closing costs, as well as how many months it will take you to break even if you decide to refinance.

6. Click **Print** to open a Windows Print dialog box to print this proposal.

7. Click **Done** to close the Refinance Calculator.

WORK WITH THE LOAN CALCULATOR

Whether you are considering borrowing money or loaning it to someone else, the Quicken Loan Calculator is a handy tool. To work with the Loan Calculator:

1. From the Net Worth tab's Tools Action Bar, click **Property & Loan Tools**, and click **Loan Calculator**. The Loan Calculator dialog box appears.

2. You can use the Loan Calculator to determine either the amount of each loan payment or the total principal. To calculate the loan payment amount:

   - In the Calculate For section, click **Payment Per Period**.

   - Click **Loan Amount** and enter the total dollar amount of the proposed loan.

   - Enter the annual interest rate in the relevant field. In the Number Of Years field, enter the number of years for the loan, and click **Periods Per Year** to enter the number of payments to be paid each year.

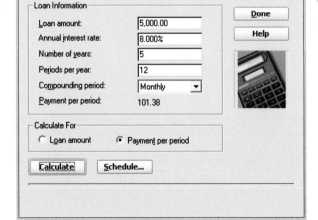

- Click **Compounding Period** to indicate how the interest will be calculated. If the compounding period is something other than monthly, choose it from the drop-down list.

- Click **Calculate**, and Quicken will display the amount of each payment.

3. To calculate the total loan amount by entering the payment amount:

   - In the Calculate For section, click **Loan Amount**.

   - Enter the annual interest rate, number of years, periods per year, and compounding period, as described previously.

   - Enter the payment per period, and click **Calculate**. Quicken will display the total loan amount.

   - Click **Schedule** to open the Approximate Future Payment Schedule dialog box.

   - Click **Print** to open a Windows Print dialog box to print the schedule.

4. Click **Done** to close the Loan Calculator.

How to...

- *Reconcile Quicken with Your Bank's Paper Statement*

- *Make Corrections in the Statement Summary Window*

- *Reconciling for the First Time*

- *Deal with Unrecorded Items*

- *Reconcile Credit Card Statements*

- *Using a Quicken Adjustment*

- *Activating Automatic Reconciliation*

- *Finding and Resolving Credit Card Errors*

- *Reconcile an Investment Account to a Paper Statement*

- *Reconcile a Single Mutual Fund Account*

- *Updating Prices Manually from a Paper Statement*

- *Update 401(k) Accounts*

- *Understanding How Quicken Works with 401(k)/403(b) Accounts*

- *Update an Asset or Liability Account*

- *Use the Find And Replace Dialog Box*

- *Watch for Escrow Discrepancies*

Chapter 7

Keeping Your Records Up to Date

What does it mean to reconcile an account? Why should you do it? *Reconciling* is the process of verifying that what is in your Quicken register is the same as what the bank or other financial institution shows in their records. Reconciling, or *balancing*, your checking and other accounts ensures that you have entered any fees and charges, that all deposits have been credited to your account (banks do make errors), and that your records accurately reflect what has happened during the period since you last balanced your account. This chapter will discuss how to reconcile and update checking and savings accounts, credit card statements, and investment accounts from paper statements as well as from online ones.

Reconcile Checking and Savings Accounts

You are probably familiar with the checking and savings account statements sent by your bank. They show the balance at the beginning of the month, all of the transactions for the account that occurred since the last statement, any fees charged to your account, and the bank's balance for the account at the end of the month. This section will show you how to reconcile your Quicken checking and savings accounts with your bank's paper statements and online information. It will also discuss how to deal with items that appear on the bank statement that aren't recorded in Quicken, what to do if the account doesn't balance the first time, and how to find discrepancies.

Reconcile Quicken with Your Bank's Paper Statement

One of the great features of Quicken is its ability to quickly reconcile or balance your bank's statement to your Quicken account. You may reconcile bank accounts to a paper statement, whether they have been enabled for online services or you enter your transactions manually.

RECONCILE AN ONLINE-ENABLED ACCOUNT TO A PAPER STATEMENT

To reconcile an account that has online services with the bank's paper statement:

1. Click the name of the account you want to reconcile in the Account Bar to open its register.

2. Click **Account Actions** and, from the menu, click **Reconcile**. You are prompted to download the latest transactions.

3. If you want to stop the reconciliation process, click **Yes**. The One Step Update dialog box appears. Enter your password and click **Update Now**. After the update, restart the reconciliation at step 2. If the account uses Web Connect rather than Direct Connect, you will be prompted with a screen to log in to your bank's website.

4. To continue reconciling with the paper statement, click **No**.

5. The Reconcile Online Account dialog box appears. Type the date of the paper statement in the Ending Statement Date text box.

6. Confirm the amount in the Opening Balance field. If the statement opening balance is not what Quicken shows, type the statement amount. Press **TAB** to continue.

7. Type the amount from your bank statement in the Ending Balance field, and click **OK** to close the dialog box and open the Statement Summary window. All of the transactions you have entered into this Quicken account that you have not yet reconciled to the statement appear in this window, an example of which is shown in Figure 7-1.

8. Check **Clr** (for "cleared") by each deposit and check that appears on the bank statement. After you have selected all the cleared checks and deposits, the difference shown in the bottom-right corner of the window should be zero. If it does, you're done reconciling. If you don't have a zero difference, see "Make Corrections in the Statement Summary Window" next in this chapter.

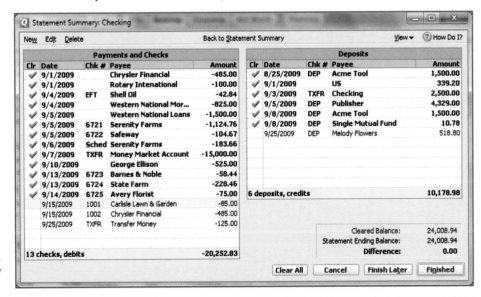

Figure 7-1: The Statement Summary dialog box makes quick work of reconciling your accounts.

9. Click **Finished** to open the Reconciliation Complete dialog box.

10. Click **Yes** to create a Reconciliation Report, or click **No** if you don't want to create one.

11. If you do not want to be asked this question again, click **Don't Show Me This Screen Again**.

12. Click **Yes** to display the Reconciliation Report Setup dialog box.

13. Type a title in the Report Title field if you choose. If you leave this field blank, Quicken uses the default title "Reconciliation Report."

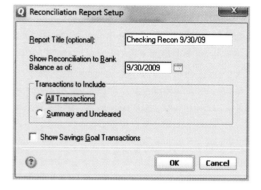

14. Change the date in the Show Reconciliation To Bank Balance As Of field if you want it to be the statement date instead of today's date.

15. Click **All Transactions** to create a report that includes all transactions through today.

16. Click **Summary And Uncleared** to include only a summary of the cleared transactions and details about uncleared items. This choice creates a shorter, more concise report.

17. If you have established savings goals and want to include them in the report, click the **Show Savings Goal Transactions** check box. Chapter 9 discusses savings goals and other financial-planning matters in more detail.

18. Click **OK** to open a print dialog box. Click **Preview** to see how the report will appear when printed.

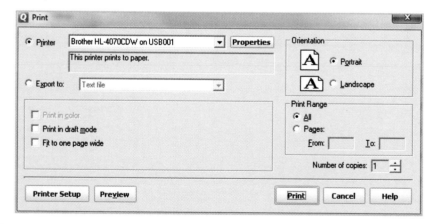

19. From the Preview window, click **Print**.

20. If you have not chosen to see a preview of your report, from the Print dialog box, click **Print** to print the report.

You may choose to reconcile your accounts to the balance shown by your bank. Before you reconcile online, ensure that all of your transactions have been downloaded and that you have reviewed and accepted them. When you update your Quicken register, the transactions can be automatically reconciled (see the QuickSteps "Activating Automatic Reconciliation"). There are two methods for reconciling online:

- You can update several times during a month and then reconcile to the paper statement at the end of the month.
- You can reconcile each time you download transactions.

Whichever method you use, stick to that method.

To perform the online reconciliation after you have downloaded and accepted all of the transactions:

1. Click the name of the account you want to reconcile in the Account Bar to open its register.
2. Click **Account Actions** and, from the menu, click **Reconcile**. You are prompted to download the latest transactions.
3. If you have not yet downloaded the latest transactions, and you want to stop the reconciliation process to download these transactions, click **Yes**. The One Step Update dialog box appears. Enter your password and click **Update Now**. After the update, restart the reconciliation.
4. To continue reconciling with the online bank balance, click **No**.
5. Click **Online Balance**. If you choose to automatically reconcile the account after you compare the transactions to the ones in your register, click the **Auto Reconcile** check box.
6. Click **OK** to close the dialog box and open the Statement Summary window. All of the transactions you have entered into this Quicken account that you have not yet marked as having been cleared by the bank appear in this window, an example of which is shown in Figure 7-2.
7. The difference should be zero. Click **Finished** to open the Reconciliation Complete dialog box, and proceed as described in steps 8 through 14 in "Reconcile an Online-Enabled Account to a Paper Statement" earlier in this chapter.

CAUTION

Working back and forth between reconciling online and with a paper statement can be confusing. Transactions that appear on your paper bank statement may not appear in the Statement Summary window, since Quicken has already reconciled them.

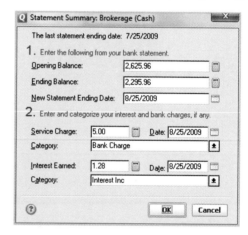

RECONCILE A MANUAL ACCOUNT TO A PAPER STATEMENT

If you have chosen to enter your transactions manually, or if your financial institution does not provide any online services, reconcile the account as follows:

1. Click the name of the account you want to reconcile in the Account Bar to open its register.

2. Click **Account Actions** and, from the menu, click **Reconcile**. The Statement Summary dialog box appears.

Figure 7-2: When reconciling to your online balance, all of the items that have cleared the bank are marked as such.

3. Confirm the amount in the Opening Balance field. If the statement opening balance is not what Quicken shows, type the statement amount. Press **TAB** to continue.

4. Type the amount from your bank statement in the Ending Balance field, and press **TAB**.

5. Enter the ending date shown on your paper bank statement. Press **TAB** to continue.

6. Enter any service charge shown on the bank statement in the Service Charge field, and enter the date on which it was charged. Press **TAB**.

7. Click the **Category** field to enter or select the category for the service charge. By default, Quicken uses Bank Charge. Press **TAB**.

8. Enter the amount of interest shown on the statement in the **Interest Earned** field and the date the bank credited the account, and press **TAB**.

9. Enter or select the category for the interest in the Interest Earned field. By default, Quicken uses Interest Inc as the category.

NOTE

"Interest Inc" in Quicken is an abbreviation for "Interest Income."

10. Click **OK** to close the dialog box and open the Statement Summary window. All of the transactions you have entered into this Quicken account that have not yet been marked as having been cleared by the bank appear in this window, as seen in Figure 7-1.

11. Check **Clr** (for "cleared") by each deposit and check that appears on the bank statement. After you have selected all the cleared checks and deposits, the difference shown in the bottom-right corner of the window should be zero. If it does, you're done reconciling. If you don't have a zero difference, see "Make Corrections in the Statement Summary Window" next in this chapter.

12. Click **Finished** to open the Reconciliation Complete dialog box.

13. Click **Yes** to display the Reconciliation Report Setup dialog box.

14. Type a title in the Report Title field if you choose. If you leave this field blank, Quicken uses the default title "Reconciliation Report."

15. Change the date in the Show Reconciliation To Bank Balance As Of field if you want it to be the statement date instead of today's date.

- Click **All Transactions** to create a report that includes all transactions through today.

- Click **Summary and Uncleared** to include only a summary of the cleared transactions and detail about uncleared items. This choice creates a shorter, more concise report.

16. If you have established savings goals and want to include them in the report, click the **Show Savings Goal Transactions** check box. Chapter 9 discusses savings goals and other financial-planning matters in more detail.

17. Click the printer icon to open a print dialog box. Click **Preview** to see how the report will appear when printed.

- From the Preview window, click **Print**.

- If you have not chosen to see a preview of your report, from the Print dialog box, click **Print** to print the report.

Make Corrections in the Statement Summary Window

If your transactions do not immediately balance, you can make corrections in the Statement Summary window to eventually reconcile the account.

- Click **New** to enter a transaction into the register that appears on the bank statement but that has not been entered into the register. This could be a charge for new checks or money withdrawn using a cash machine or a debit card. See "Deal with Unrecorded Items" next in this chapter.

- Select a transaction and click **Edit** to make changes to that transaction in the register. This is great for fixing transpositions or penny errors.

- Select a transaction and click **Delete** to permanently remove a transaction from the register.

- Click **Back To Statement Summary** to go back to the Statement Summary dialog box to make changes to the opening or ending balance.

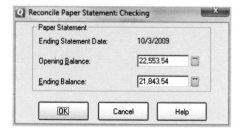

- Click **View** to change how Quicken sorts the transactions in this window.

- Click **How Do I?** to display a Help screen.

- Click **Mark All** to mark all of the transactions displayed in the window. If Mark All has already been clicked, Clear All is displayed to perform the reverse operation.

- Click **Cancel** to stop the reconciliation. This opens a dialog box that asks if you want to save your work or close the window without saving it. Click **Yes** to close the window without saving your work.

- Click **Finish Later** to save what you have done so far. When you return to the register, you will notice that any transactions you have selected now display a "c" in the Clr column. When you have finished the reconciliation, the "c" turns into an "R," and, if you have set the preferences to their default setting, the transaction text will be grey or dimmed.

- Click **Finished** to complete the reconciliation and open the Reconciliation Complete dialog box.

Deal with Unrecorded Items

Items may appear on your bank statement that do not appear in Quicken. Some examples can be automatic withdrawals, such as payments for your safety deposit box, or withdrawals from the cash machine you forgot to record. To enter an item from the Statement Summary window:

1. Click **New** on the menu bar to open the account register.

2. Enter the date on which the transaction occurred. The default is today's date, but you probably want to use the actual transaction date.

3. Enter the type of transaction in the Num field, and then fill in the **Payee**, **Category**, and **Amount** fields.

4. Click **Enter** and then click **Return To Reconcile** to return to the Statement Summary window.

> | Return to Reconcile |

FIND STATEMENT DISCREPANCIES

Several things need to be considered when trying to find a discrepancy between a bank statement and your Quicken account register.

- Ensure you are working with the right account. It's easy to click the wrong name if you have several accounts.

- Verify that the "Deposits, Credits" total amount and the "Checks, Debits" total amount displayed at the bottom of the Statement Summary window match the total amounts shown on the bank statement.

- Check the Difference amount in the lower-right corner of the window. If the difference is evenly divisible by nine, you may have transposed an entry. For example, if the difference is $0.63, you may have entered a check into Quicken as $29.18 and written the actual check for $29.81.

- If the difference is not a transposition, you may have neglected to enter a transaction, or you entered a deposit as a check or vice versa. If the difference does not equal a check amount on either your bank statement or your register, look in both for a transaction equaling half the amount of the difference. You may have entered a deposit as a payment or vice versa.

NOTE

You might want to use a split transaction for cash withdrawals so that you can keep track of how much money you are paying, if any, to use the cash machine.

Using Quicken's Scheduled Transactions feature can ensure that all of your transactions are entered into your check register.

When you pay your credit card or other bills, take the envelopes directly to the post office rather than leaving them in the mailbox. This ensures that anyone stealing mail from the boxes cannot get your information.

QUICKSTEPS

USING A QUICKEN ADJUSTMENT

If you do not want to locate a discrepancy between the bank and your Quicken register, Quicken will enter an adjusting entry for you.

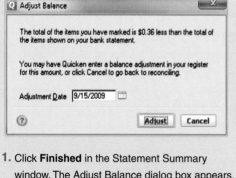

1. Click **Finished** in the Statement Summary window. The Adjust Balance dialog box appears.

2. Click in the **Adjustment Date** field, and enter the date of the adjustment. This can be the date of the paper statement or today's date, whichever makes more sense to you.

Continued . . .

- Determine if the difference is positive or negative. If the difference is negative, the bank shows more money than your register does. The bank may have a deposit you haven't entered, or you may have cleared checks the bank hasn't received. If the difference is positive, the bank shows less money than your register does. You may have neglected to enter a fee or an automatic withdrawal in your register.

- Watch for pennies. If your handwriting is not clearly legible, the automated machinery used by the bank for clearing checks may not read the amount correctly, for example, it might mistake an eight as a three.

- Take a time out. If you've been looking at your account for some time and can't locate the discrepancy, walk away for a few minutes. Often, when you come back after a break, the difference seems to appear as if by magic.

Reconcile Credit Card Statements

Reconciling your credit card statement is similar to reconciling your checking or savings account statement, especially if you enter your credit card purchases as you make them. If you wait until the credit card statement arrives to enter the charges and categorize them, however, the process takes a bit longer.

RECONCILE A PAPER CREDIT CARD STATEMENT

To reconcile your credit card account to a paper statement:

1. From the Account Bar, click the account with which you want to work.

    –Or–

    Click the **Banking** tab, and in the View Action tab, click **Account Overview** to display all of the accounts. Click the name of the account in the Credit Card Accounts section to open the register.

2. Click **Account Actions** and click **Reconcile** to open the Credit Card Statement Summary dialog box.

3. Enter the total from the statement in the Charges, Cash Advances field.

4. Click in the **Payments, Credits** field, and enter the total from the statement.

5. Click in the **Ending Balance** field, and enter the balance due on the statement.

6. Click in the **New Statement Ending Date** field, and enter the ending date of the statement.

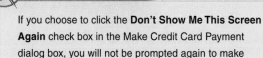

QUICKSTEPS

USING A QUICKEN ADJUSTMENT

(Continued)

3. Click **Adjust**.
4. A Reconciliation Complete dialog box appears. Click **Yes** if you want to create a reconciliation report; click **No** if you do not. If you click No, the dialog box closes and you are returned to the register.

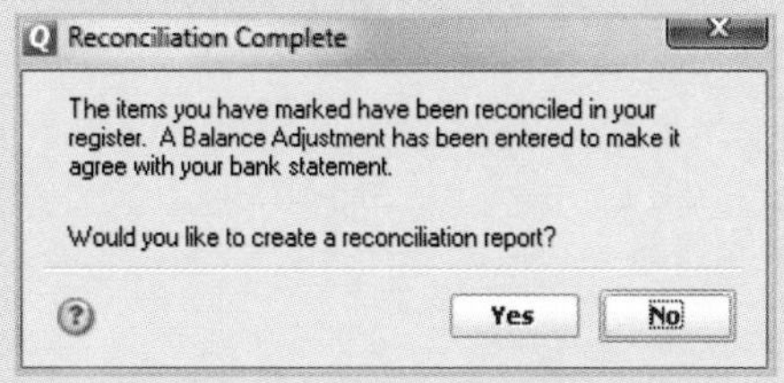

5. In your register, locate the balance adjustment that Quicken just created, and, if you want, change the category by clicking in the **Category** field and entering a new one. Click **Enter** to save the change.

NOTE

If you choose to click the **Don't Show Me This Screen Again** check box in the Make Credit Card Payment dialog box, you will not be prompted again to make a credit card payment.

7. Click in the **Finance Charges** field, and enter the amount of finance charges, if any. Click in the **Date** field, and change the date of the charges from the default of today's date if needed.
8. Click in the **Category** field, and either choose a category from the drop-down list or type the category for the finance charges.
9. Click **OK**. The Credit Card Statement Summary window opens.

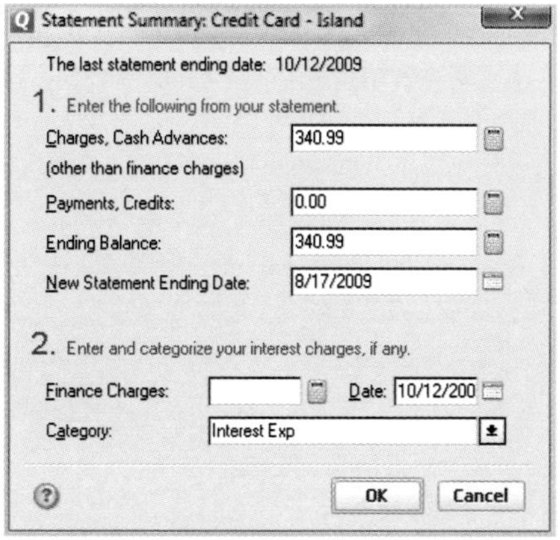

10. Proceed as described in "Reconcile Quicken with Your Bank's Paper Statement" earlier in the chapter.
11. If zero appears in the Difference field, click **Finished** to open the Make Credit Card Payment dialog box. You are asked if you want to make a payment on the balance now. If so:

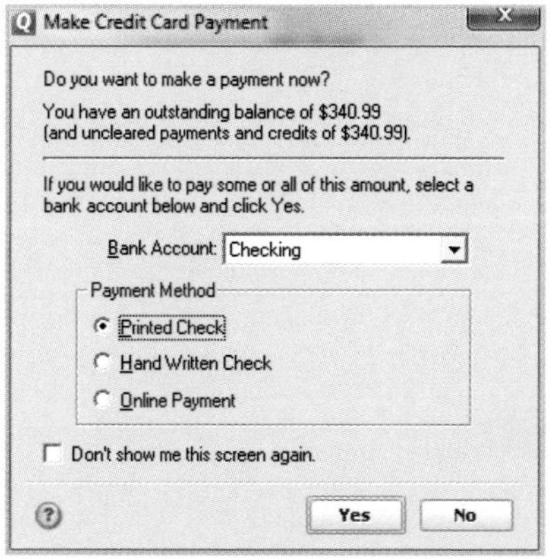

a. Click **Bank Account** to choose the account from which to write the check.

b. Choose the method of preparing the check, and click **Yes**.

- If you click **Printed Check**, a check facsimile opens for you to fill in. The default category is the credit card account.
- If you click **Hand Written Check**, the check is entered into the register and pauses for you to enter the check number.
- If you click **No**, the window closes and you are returned to the register.

QUICKSTEPS

ACTIVATING AUTOMATIC RECONCILIATION

When you have activated the downloading of transactions from your bank accounts, you can use a Quicken feature that makes reconciling automatic each time you download.

1. Open the register of the account you want to use.

2. Click **Account Actions** and click **Reconcile**.

3. Click **Online Balance**.

4. Click **Auto Reconcile After Compare To Register**.

The setting takes effect after the next time you go online. Quicken will automatically reconcile the downloaded transactions after you have accepted them. If the balances do not match, Quicken displays a Statement History dialog box to help you find the problem.

TIP

If you want to keep track of your credit card spending by category, you will need to enter each transaction separately, both charges and credits, so that you can categorize them.

RECONCILE A CREDIT CARD ACCOUNT ONLINE

As with reconciling bank accounts, if your credit card company offers it, downloading and reconciling transactions directly into your credit card register is the most efficient way to reconcile your account. However, if you want to keep track of your spending by category, you must remember to enter the category for each downloaded transaction, although if your transactions are to the same establishment for the same purpose, the category will carry over from transaction to transaction. The process for performing an online reconciliation of your credit card account is the same as those described in "Reconcile an Online-Enabled Account to a Paper Statement" and "Reconcile an Online-Enabled Account to the Online Balance" earlier in the chapter. If you choose to reconcile your paper credit card statement manually, follow the directions described in "Reconcile a Manual Account to a Paper Statement," also in this chapter.

MAKE CREDIT CARD STATEMENT ADJUSTMENTS

Sometimes, you just don't want to take the time to find all the discrepancies in a credit card register. Perhaps you've just started entering transactions and some of the beginning balances aren't right. Quicken can help you fix these problems.

1. When you have completed the reconciliation as far as you want, click **Finished** in the Statement Summary window. The Adjusting Register To Agree With Statement dialog box appears.

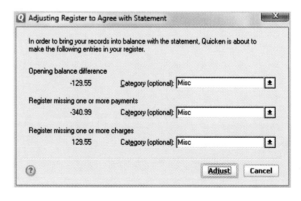

QUICKSTEPS

FINDING AND RESOLVING CREDIT CARD ERRORS

Using Quicken to reconcile your credit card statements may help you find errors in your account. To ensure there are no errors on your statement and that your account is protected:

- Check each item on the statement as soon as you get it.

- Ensure that each charge is the amount you expected.

- Know the date on which your statement usually arrives. Set an alert in Quicken to remember that date. If your statement has not arrived, call the credit card company to advise them the statement has not been delivered.

- If the credit card company provides online access to your account, go online on a regular basis to ensure that each charge to your account is valid.

RESOLVE CREDIT CARD ERRORS

If you do find an error, or if you have a dispute with a seller, take the following steps:

- Call the seller that charged you to see if the issue can be resolved between the two of you. Document the call; the name of the seller's agent; and the date, time, and nature of the problem.

Continued . . .

2. In the Opening Balance Difference text box, if there is one in your dialog box, click in the **Category** field, and change the category from the default "Misc" if you choose.

3. In the Register Missing One Or More Payments area, if there is one in your dialog box, click in the **Category** field, and change the category from the default "Misc" if you choose.

4. In the Register Missing One Or More Charges area, if there is one in your dialog box, click in the **Category** field, and change the category.

5. Click **Adjust** to have the entries recorded in the credit card account register.

6. If you want to apportion each entry between several categories, make no changes to the categories in the Adjusting Register To Agree With Statement dialog box. When you return to the register, locate each adjustment and select the first one with which you want to work.

   - Click **Split** to open the Split Transaction window, and assign the categories you choose.

   - Select the other adjustments you want to change, and assign categories to them.

Reconcile Investment Accounts

You use the same process to reconcile an investment account as you do with a checking account, except you have to balance to both a cash balance and a share balance. If your financial institution offers it, the easiest way to reconcile each account is to sign up for their download services. That way, you can download each transaction directly from your broker and use Quicken's Compare To Portfolio feature to monitor the account.

Reconcile an Investment Account to a Paper Statement

The process of reconciling an investment account is the same as described in "Reconcile a Manual Account to a Paper Statement" earlier in the chapter. To reconcile an investment account to a paper statement:

1. Click the Investing tab's View Action Bar, and click **Account Overview** to display all of your investing accounts.

QUICKSTEPS

FINDING AND RESOLVING CREDIT CARD ERRORS *(Continued)*

- Call the credit card company to tell them of the problem. Document the call as to date, time, and the name of the person with whom you spoke.

- Write a letter to the credit card company explaining the same information. The Fair Credit Billing Act requires that you notify your credit card company in writing. Make sure it is addressed to the correct address for billing inquiries. This address is usually listed on the back of your credit card. Include any supporting information. For further protection, send this letter via certified mail and ask for a return receipt as proof. This verifies both that you sent the letter within 60 days of the statement date and that your credit card company received the letter.

- Your credit card company must respond to your dispute letter, in writing, within 30 days. The credit card company then has two billing cycles or 90 days—whichever is less—to determine if the charge was in error. They are required to notify you in writing of their determination. If the charge was correct but there is still a dispute, write the credit card company again. They are not allowed to charge interest or require payment until the issue has been resolved.

2. Select the account you want to reconcile. The Overview subtab in the Acct Action bar will be highlighted and you see a window, as shown in Figure 7-3. From the Overview subtab, click **Options** in the Account Status section, and click **Reconcile This Account**.

–Or–

Click **Actions**, click **Investing Activities**, and click **Reconcile An Account**.

3. In either case, the Statement Summary dialog box appears.

4. Click in the **Starting Cash Balance** field, and enter the beginning balance amount from your paper statement.

5. Click in the **Ending Cash Balance** field, and enter the ending cash balance from your paper statement.

6. Click in the **Statement Ending Date** field to type the date of the statement.

7. Click **OK**. The Statement Summary window opens. This is similar to the Statement Summary window for your checking account; however, instead of showing checks and deposits, it shows increases and decreases to the account.

8. Click each transaction to note that it has cleared.

9. Click **Finished** to complete the reconciliation. The Reconciliation Complete dialog box appears.

10. Click **Yes** to create a reconciliation report. Click **No** to close the dialog box and return to the Investing tab.

Reconcile a Single Mutual Fund Account

Since single mutual fund accounts have no cash balances, you reconcile only the share balances. There are two ways of updating this type of account: with and without transaction detail.

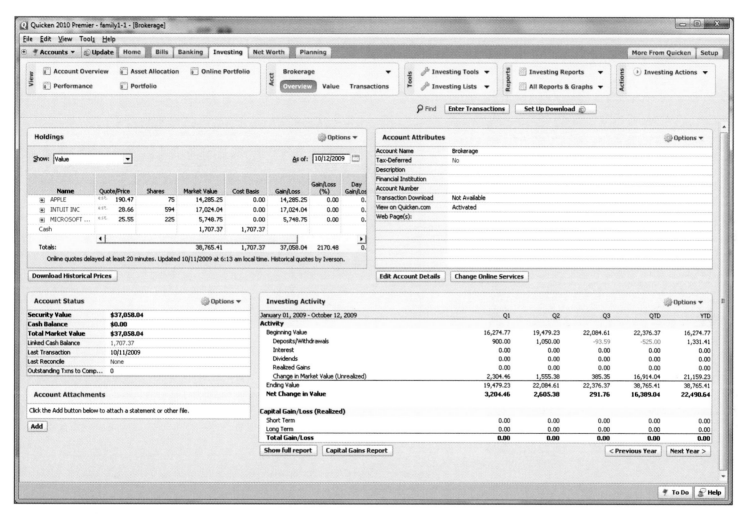

Figure 7-3: The Overview subtab of the Investing tab showing the holdings, account attributes, account status, and investing activity of this investment account

USE A STATEMENT THAT SHOWS TRANSACTION DETAIL

If your mutual fund statement includes the transaction detail:

1. Click the Investing tab's View Action Bar, click the **Account Overview** subtab, and click the account with which you want to work.

–Or–

From the Account Bar, select the account.

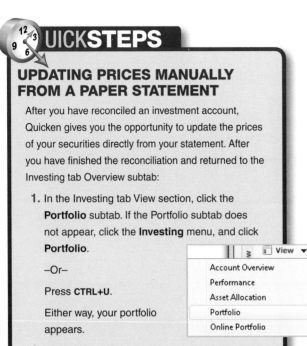

QUICKSTEPS

UPDATING PRICES MANUALLY FROM A PAPER STATEMENT

After you have reconciled an investment account, Quicken gives you the opportunity to update the prices of your securities directly from your statement. After you have finished the reconciliation and returned to the Investing tab Overview subtab:

1. In the Investing tab View section, click the **Portfolio** subtab. If the Portfolio subtab does not appear, click the **Investing** menu, and click **Portfolio**.

   –Or–

   Press **CTRL+U**.

   Either way, your portfolio appears.

2. Change the **As Of** date to the date of the paper statement.

3. Click in the **Quote/Price** column for each security, and enter the price shown on the statement.

2. From the Acct Action Bar, click the **Transactions** subtab. Click the **Enter Transactions** button to open the Buy - Shares Bought dialog box, which is displayed in Figure 7-4.

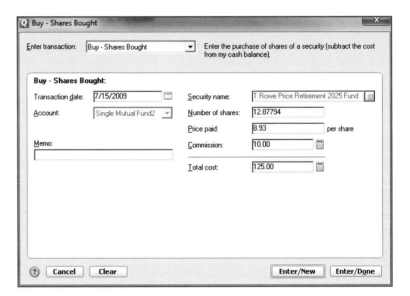

Figure 7-4: Use the Buy - Shares Bought dialog box to enter transactions into your single mutual fund account.

3. Enter each transaction listed on your statement. Click **Enter/New** to move to a new transaction. Click **Enter/Done** when you have entered all of the transactions shown on the statement.

4. You are returned to the Transaction List for the account. Click **Overview** in the Acct Action Bar, and from the Account Status section, click **Options** and click **Reconcile This Account**.

5. You are returned to the Transaction List for the account. Click **Overview** and from the Account Status section, click **Options** and click **Reconcile This Account**.

6. Follow the procedure in "Reconcile an Investment Account to a Paper Statement" earlier in this chapter.

Some brokerage and mutual fund statements only show transactions in terms of shares and not the dollars relating to those shares. To reconcile that type of statement:

1. In the Investing tab, click the account with which you want to work.

2. Click **Options** in the Account Status section, and click **Reconcile This Account**. The Reconcile Mutual Fund Account dialog box appears.

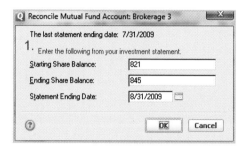

3. Enter the starting share balance and ending share balance from the statement in the relevant fields.

4. Enter the statement ending date.

5. Click **OK**. The Reconcile Mutual Fund Account window opens.

6. Click each transaction that appears in the window. Note that the balance is displayed in number of shares rather than in dollars. The ending balance in the Reconcile Mutual Fund Account window should be the same as the ending balance on the statement.

7. Click **Finished** when you have reconciled the account. The Reconciliation Complete dialog box appears. Click **OK** to close the dialog box.

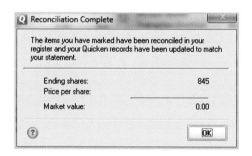

Update 401(k) Accounts

401(k) accounts are tracked a bit differently from other investment accounts. If you have Quicken Deluxe, Premier, or Quicken Home and Business edition, you can track actual shares or dollar amounts. If your financial institution offers it, you can even download your transaction details. You can also manually enter the information from a paper statement or use the 401(k)/403(b) Update dialog box. The easiest method to use is the download option; however, the 401(k)/403(b) Update lets you track the performance of funds in your 401(k) or 403(b).

USE THE 401(K)/403(B) UPDATE

1. From the Investing tab's View section, click the **Account Overview** subtab, and from the Retirement section, click the account with which you want to work.

2. Click the **Update 401(k) Holdings** button. The 401(k)/403(b) Update dialog box appears.

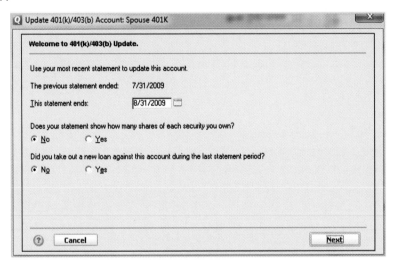

3. Enter the date of the statement in the This Statement Ends field.

4. Click either **Yes** or **No** in response to the question Does Your Statement Show How Many Shares Of Each Security You Own?, depending on which is correct.

5. Click either **No** or **Yes** in response to the question Did You Take Out A New Loan Against This Account During The Last Statement Period?, and then click **Next**.

6. Enter the amount in the Employee Contributions field, as shown on the statement.

7. Enter the amount in the Employer Matching Contributions field, as shown on the statement.

8. If needed, click in the **Other Contributions And Payments** field, and enter those amounts from the statement. Quicken adds all of these transactions, which should match your paper statement.

9. Click **Next**. The Total Withdrawals This Period dialog box appears.

10. Enter the amount in each of the fields from the statement that are applicable to you. Quicken shows the total, which should match the statement. Click **Next**.

11. If you took out a loan during this period, you are asked to enter the purpose of the loan and the loan amount. You may also choose to set up an account to track the loan balance. Enter the relevant information, and click **Next**.

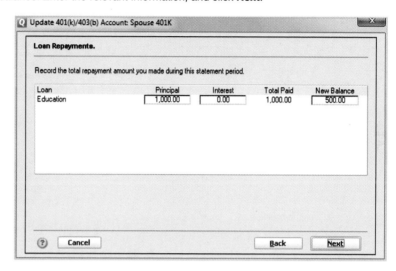

UNDERSTANDING HOW QUICKEN WORKS WITH 401(K)/403(B) ACCOUNTS

When you add a 401(k)/403(b) account in Quicken Deluxe, Premier, and Home and Business editions, Quicken adds a special tax-impact account. This account is not visible on the Account List, but you can see it on tax reports. (Learn more about taxes in Chapter 10.) This tax account tracks any transaction in this retirement account that may have an effect on your income taxes, such as early withdrawal of funds. Quicken uses the information in this hidden account in both reports and its tax planning tools. To ensure your tax planning tools and reports are as accurate as possible, do not change or remove any of the transactions in this account, or in the account itself.

12. The Loan Repayments dialog box appears. Enter the amount of principal and interest paid, as shown on the statement, and then click **Next**.

13. The name of each security held in the account is displayed in the next dialog box. Click **Add New Security** if there is a security on the statement that does not appear on this list. Otherwise, click **Next**.

14. Click either **No** or **Yes** in response to the question Did You Move Any Money From One Security To Another?

15. If you clicked Yes, enter the number of transfers on the statement in the How Many Transfers Appear On Your Statement? field. Click **Next**.

16. If you selected Yes in step 5, enter the number of ending shares shown on your statement. If you selected No in step 5, you do not have that option. Enter the value in the Market Value field from the statement for each security in the account. Click **Next**.

17. Verify that the amount in the Total Market Value field shown on the statement matches the 401(k)/403(b) Update Summary.

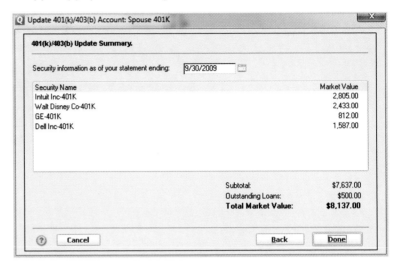

18. Click **Done**.

Reconcile Property & Debt Accounts

You may note that asset and liability accounts are called Property & Debt accounts in the Account Bar. Each of these accounts can be reconciled or updated in much the same way as other accounts. If you choose to update an asset account based on current market value, you can use documentation such as a property tax statement or valuation summary from a commercial appraisal. You may get monthly statements from a financial institution showing loan balances and loan payments due so that these accounts can be updated. While you can update these accounts without documentation, it is usually best to wait until you have written proof of your change before you make it. You can include the written proof as an attachment in Quicken, as described in Chapter 4.

NOTE

Some companies allow loans of up to 50 percent of your 401(k) account. However, the interest on these loans is not deductible on your income tax.

NOTE

If your home has increased in value or if your boat's value has decreased and you want to enter the increase or decrease, check with your tax professional for a category.

Update an Asset or Liability Account

You use the same process to update either an asset or a liability account.

1. From the Property & Debt section on the Account Bar, click the account you want to update.

   –Or–

   Click the **Net Worth** tab, and in the View area, click the **Account Overview** subtab. From the list of accounts, click the account you want to update.

   In either case, the account's transactions register appears.

2. Click **Account Actions** and click **Update Balance**.

   –Or–

   From the Account Status section, click **Options** and click **Update My Account Balance**.

   In both cases, the Update Account Balance dialog box appears.

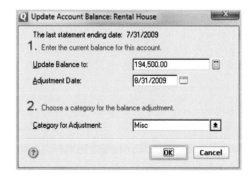

3. In the Update Account Balance dialog box, click in the **Update Balance To** field, and enter the balance from the statement or other documentation. For an asset, this is the current value of the asset. For a loan, this is the balance due on the loan.

4. Click in the **Adjustment Date** field, and enter the date of the documentation.

5. Click the **Category For Adjustment** down arrow, and choose the category in which the adjustment will be entered. You might choose **Interest Exp** to reflect additional interest being added to a loan.

6. Click **OK** to return to the Net Worth tab, Acct:Overview view. The adjustment has been added to the account.

Use the Find And Replace Dialog Box

When you need to locate a number of transactions for one payee, one category, or one amount, Quicken has a useful Find utility.

1. Click the **Edit** menu, click **Find & Replace**, and click **Find/Replace**. The Find And Replace dialog box appears (see Figure 7-5).

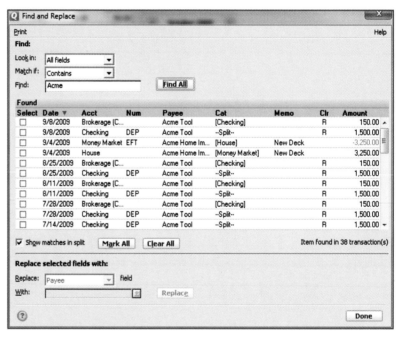

Figure 7-5: Use the Find And Replace utility to locate transactions for one payee, category, or amount.

2. Click the **Look In** down arrow, and click the field where Quicken is to look for the data (you can also click **All Fields**).

3. Click the **Match If** down arrow, and click the type of match.

4. Click in the **Find** text box, and enter the information for which you want to search, which will depend on the field you are searching.

5. Click **Find All**. A list of all matching transactions is displayed in the Found List.

6. Click **Show Matches In Split** if you want Quicken to include information shown in the Split Transactions window.

7. Click **Mark All** to select all the items on the list, or choose only the transactions you want to change.

8. Click the **Replace** down arrow, and choose a field whose contents you want to replace.

9. Click in the **With** text box and type the replacement text, or choose it from the drop-down list. Then click **Replace** to change the transactions.

10. Click **Done** to close the dialog box.

Watch for Escrow Discrepancies

If your financial institution pays real estate taxes or insurance premiums from the payments you send them each month, you may get an escrow statement from them each year. If you have set up your mortgage loan account using the Split Transactions window and have been tracking the portion of each payment that goes to insurance and the portion that goes to real estate taxes, as well as the portion that goes to principal and interest, it is an easy task to reconcile the escrow statement you receive.

1. In the Banking tab's Reports Action Bar, click the **Banking Reports** subtab to open a menu. Click **Transaction**, and click **Customize** on the far right of the toolbar. The Customize Transaction dialog box appears.

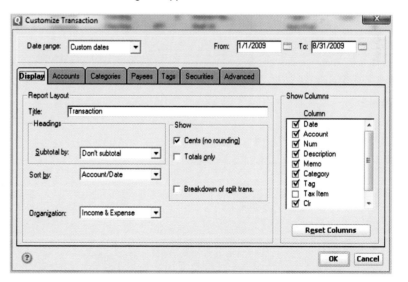

2. Click the **Date Range** down arrow, and click the date range of the escrow statement. Click the **Display** tab if it is not already selected.

3. Click the **Subtotal By** down arrow, and click **Category** from the list.

4. Click the **Accounts** tab, click **Clear All**, and click the account from which you pay this loan.

5. Click the **Categories** tab, click **Clear All**, and click the categories that are on the escrow statement. Click the **Payee** down arrow to select the payee.

6. Click **OK** to display your report. If you want to save this report, click **Save** in the Save Report dialog box that appears on the toolbar. Otherwise, click **Don't Save**. If you click Save, you will be prompted to name the report and designate the folder into which it should be saved.

7. Match the totals on the report to your paper escrow statement, and make any changes to the loan account.

8. Click **OK** to close the Customize Transaction dialog box, and click **Close** in the Transaction window.

How to...

- **Download Current Quotes**
- **Set Up Quicken.com**
- **Customizing the Quicken Toolbar**
- **Use Quicken.com**
- **Understanding Quicken.com Tools**
- **Use the Growth Of $10,000 Utility**
- **Customizing the Date Range**
- **Filter the Average Annual Return Anaylsis**
- **Allocate Your Assets**
- **Scheduling One Step Updates**
- **Understand Portfolio Terms**
- **Customize Your Portfolio View**
- **Setting Options in Your Portfolio View**
- **Work with Investing Tools**
- **Use the Buy/Sell Preview Tool**
- **Estimate Capital Gains**
- **Use the Portfolio Analyzer**
- **Open Online Research Tools**
- **Manage Your Security List**
- **Working with Your Watch List**

Chapter 8
Managing Your Investments

Your investments help shape your financial future. Whether you are saving for a new home, your children's education, or your own retirement, Quicken can help you with your investments in many ways. You can obtain a quick online quote for a specific security or learn the historical value of your portfolio. You can use Quicken to monitor prices on securities you already own or are thinking about purchasing. You can download information from your broker, analyze your asset allocation, estimate your capital gains, or use other sophisticated analysis tools included with Quicken. Whatever your financial position today, Quicken can help you strengthen it for tomorrow. The Investing tab not only gives you access to all of your investment accounts, it also provides links for downloading transactions, online quotes, and other investment services. You can set alerts and establish a Watch List, track the performance of both individual securities and your mutual funds, and get an analysis of your entire portfolio.

Understand the Investing Tab

When you first click the **Investing** tab, it opens to the View Action Bar's Account Overview subtab. This view lists all of your investment accounts as well as the securities you have told Quicken to watch for you in the Quicken Watch List. To open the Account Overview subtab:

1. Click the **Investing** tab on the Account Bar. The Account Overview subtab in the View Action Bar is highlighted, as seen in Figure 8-1. Listed first are the Investment and Retirement accounts you have entered, showing the cost basis of the investment, the historical gain or loss in both dollars and percentages, and the daily gain or loss in dollars and percentages.

2. To work with any of the accounts, click that account name.

*Figure 8-1: **Use Account Overview to look at your current investments as well as securities you are watching.***

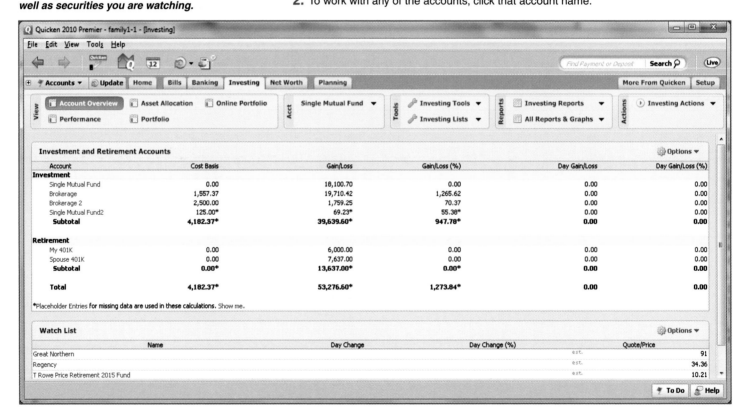

Download Current Quotes

Quicken provides the means to ensure you have up-to-date information about your investments. With your Internet connection, Quicken will download the most current *quotes,* or prices, for all of the securities in your portfolio. (A quote is the highest price being offered by a buyer or the lowest price being asked by a seller for a security at a given point in time.) To download quotes from the Investing tab's Account Overview subtab:

Options ▼
Add an account
Show Report
Setup / Edit Investing Alerts
View Account List
Download Latest Quotes

1. In the Investment And Retirement Accounts section, click the **Options** button. From the menu, click **Download Latest Quotes**.

   –Or–

   Click the **Options** button in the Watch List area of the Account Overview subtab, and choose **Download Latest Quotes**.

2. Once you are connected to the Internet, the Quicken Update Status dialog box appears. The latest quotes for your selected securities are downloaded to your computer.

3. If you are having trouble connecting and downloading, click **Help** to display Quicken Help.

4. Click **Stop Update** to stop the download before it is complete.

5. When all of your quotes have been downloaded, the Quicken Update Status dialog box closes and you are returned to the Account Overview subtab.

Set Up Quicken.com

When you registered Quicken, you may have created a Quicken.com account. With this account, you can keep an eye on your investments from any computer with Internet access. To set up Quicken.com for your investment information:

1. Ensure you are connected to the Internet. Click the **Quicken.com** icon on the Quicken toolbar. If the Quicken toolbar is not displayed:

   a. Click **View**.

   b. Click **Show Tool Bar**.

2. The Quicken.com page opens. Click **Sign In** and click **Investment Portfolio** to work with your investment portfolio at Quicken.com.

CAUTION

If you have set your web browser to show a pop-up warning when a web page address changes from http to https (or vice versa), you may have to go to Quicken.com from your web browser rather than from Quicken.

3. The Quicken.com registration dialog box appears, as seen in Figure 8-2. Enter your member ID and password if you have already registered, and click **Sign In**.

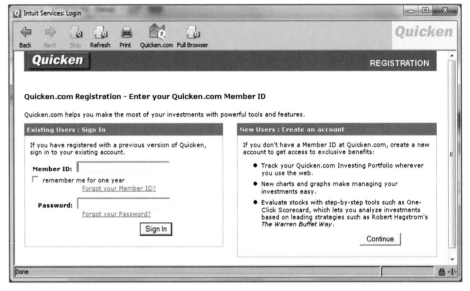

Figure 8-2: ***Register with Quicken.com to track your investments from anywhere with an Internet connection.***

4. If you have not yet created a Quicken.com account, click **Continue** to create one.

5. At the registration dialog box, enter your information and click **Submit**.

The Quicken Investing home page opens to My Portfolio.

Use Quicken.com

Once you have registered with Quicken.com, you can use the investing tools available online from any computer with an Internet connection. You can manually create a web portfolio rather than download your portfolio directly into Quicken .com should you choose to do so:

1. If this is the first time you have accessed Quicken .com, at the Quicken Investing Home tab, click **Add New Portfolio**. Otherwise, to add a new portfolio, click the **Portfolio Analysis** tab, and click **Manage Web Portfolios And Watchlists** to add your new portfolio.

QUICKSTEPS

CUSTOMIZING YOUR QUICKEN TOOLBAR

In Chapter 1, you learned to turn on the Quicken toolbar and use the default tools. However, you can customize it as well. To customize the Quicken toolbar:

1. Click **View** and click **Show Tool Bar**. The default tools appear, as discussed in Chapter 1.

2. Right-click anywhere in the toolbar, and click the **Customize Tool Bar** button. The Customize Toolbar dialog box appears.

Continued . . .

2. The Create New Portfolio dialog box appears. Type a name for this portfolio, and click **Save Changes**.

3. The Manage Web Portfolio dialog box appears, displaying your new portfolio, as shown in Figure 8-3. Click **Make This My Default Portfolio** if you choose.

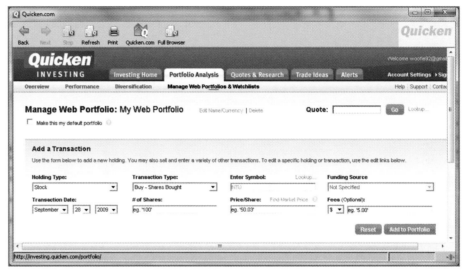

Figure 8-3: ***You can create one or more personal web portfolios at Quicken.com.***

4. Click **Edit Name/Currency** to open the Edit Name/Currency dialog box.

5. Click **Delete** to delete this web portfolio.

6. Click the **Holding Type** down arrow to begin entering your web portfolio holdings.

7. Click **Transaction Type** to choose a type of transaction from the drop-down list.

8. Click **Enter Symbol** to enter the ticker symbol for your new holding. If you do not know the correct symbol, click **Lookup** to open the Quicken Symbol Lookup dialog box.

9. Click **Transaction Date** to enter the date of the transaction you are entering.

10. Continue through the dialog box, entering the number of shares, what you paid per share, and any fees. Click **Add To Portfolio** to complete the process. Your holdings information appears in the Transactions For [your portfolio] section of the web page.

Transactions for My Web Portfolio						Collapse All	Expand All
▼ **Stocks**							
Symbol	Name	Shares	Price/Share	Transaction Amt	Current Price	Market Value	
⊕ INTU	Intuit Inc	50	--	--	$29.87	$1,494	✎ Edit
Data is delayed by at least 15 min.							

11. To add additional holdings, repeat steps 6 through 10.

To review downloading your portfolio information into Quicken.com, see the QuickSteps "Scheduling One Step Update" later in this chapter.

SIGN OUT OF QUICKEN.COM

After you have completed your work online at Quicken.com, be sure to sign out. This is especially important if you are working from a public computer, such as a library, or if you are working on your own laptop in a public place. To exit Quicken.com:

1. Click **Sign Out** at the upper-right corner of the window.
2. Ensure the Quicken registration dialog appears. Click **Close**.

Explore the Performance Subtab

Another useful tool in the Investing tab's View Action Bar is the Performance subtab. To use these utilities:

1. Click the **Investing** tab.
2. In the View Action Bar, click the **Performance** subtab. The Performance tools display, as seen in Figure 8-4.

Use the Growth Of $10,000 Utility

Quicken uses a utility called the Growth Of $10,000 that you can use to see how your portfolio compares to the main market indexes. This utility shows the value of $10,000 invested in your selected accounts compared to the same $10,000 invested in one or more of the market indexes over the same time period. To use and customize this utility:

1. At the top of the Performance subtab, click one of the Show Account options—**All**, **Investment**, or **Retirement**—or choose an individual account from the drop-down list to tell Quicken which accounts to include in the graph. Or, choose **Multiple Accounts** and select the desired accounts via the Customize dialog.

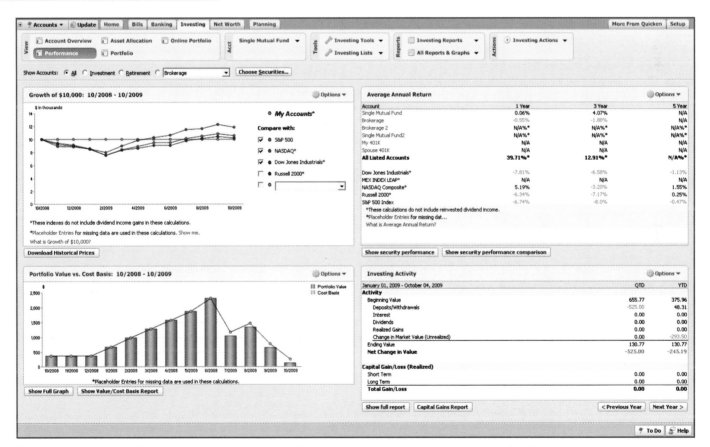

Figure 8-4: **The Growth Of $10,000 analysis tool, along with several others, shows your investments graphically.**

2. Click **Choose Securities**. The Customize dialog box appears. Select the securities you want to compare in the graph.

   a. Click **Mark All** to choose all the securities on your Security List, or click **Clear All** to clear all selections and choose just a few.

   b. Click **OK** to close the dialog box and return to the graph.

3. Click **Download Historical Prices** below the chart. The Get Historical Prices dialog box appears.

   a. Click the **Get Prices For The Last** down arrow, and click **Month**, **Year**, **Two Years**, or **Five Years**, depending on the time period for which you want to download prices.

   b. Select the securities for which you want to download prices, or click **Mark All** to include all of your securities. Click **Clear All** to start again.

   c. Click **Update Now** to download the information. When the information has been downloaded, the One Step Update Summary dialog box appears.

   d. Click **Close** to return to the graph.

Filter the Average Annual Return Analysis

The second analysis tool in the Performance subtab is the Average Annual Return tool. This shows the return on your investments as an annualized figure. To filter and customize this:

1. At the top of the Performance subtab, click one of the Show Account options—**All**, **Investment**, or **Retirement**—or choose an individual account from the drop-down list to tell Quicken which accounts to include. (See "Use the Growth Of $10,000 Utility" earlier in the chapter.) Or choose **Multiple Accounts** and select the desired accounts from the Customize dialog box.

2. In the Average Annual Return title bar, click **Options** and click **Show Security Performance**. The Security Performance dialog box appears.

TIP

After you have downloaded all of the historical information, you can click the names of market indexes to select and deselect them for comparison.

QUICKSTEPS

CUSTOMIZING THE DATE RANGE

The default view for the Growth Of $10,000 snapshot is the last 12 months; however, you can customize the date range.

1. In the Investing tab's View Action Bar, click the **Performance** subtab.

2. Click **Options** and then click **Customize This Graph**. The Customize dialog box appears.

3. Click the **Date Range** down arrow to see the list of possibilities, or click **Custom Dates** to determine your own dates.

4. Click **OK** to close the dialog box.

Include all dates
Include all dates
Monthly
Quarterly
Yearly
Month to date
Quarter to date
Year to date
Earliest to date
Custom to date
Last month
Last quarter
Last year
Last 30 days
Last 12 months
Custom dates

Security Performance

Name	Industry/ Category	Avg. Annual Return (%) 1-Year	Avg. Annual Return (%) 3-Year	Avg. Annual Return (%) 5-Year
Single Mutual Fund		0.06	4.07	N/A
⊞ INTUIT INC		0.36	4.20	N/A
⊞ MICROSOFT CORP		N/A	N/A	N/A
Cash				
Brokerage		-0.55	-1.88	N/A
⊞ INTUIT INC		0.36	-1.67	N/A
⊞ MICROSOFT CORP		-5.16	-2.99	N/A
Cash				
Brokerage 2		N/A*	N/A*	N/A*
Totals:		39.71*	12.91*	N/A*

Customize View... 10/4/2009

*Placeholder Entries for missing data are used in these calculations.

Online quotes delayed at least 20 minutes. Updated 10/4/2009 at 1:07 am local time. Historical quotes by Iverson.

3. Click **Customize View** to open the Customize Current View dialog box. Name this view and follow the instructions in "Customize Your Portfolio View" later in the chapter, and then click **OK**.

4. Click in the **Date** field to enter the date for which you want to see the data. The default is today's date.

5. Click **Close** when you are finished.

6. Click **Options** and click **Show Security Performance Comparisons** to work with the Security Performance dialog box. You can customize this view as well. Click **Close** when you are finished.

7. Click **Historical Prices** to open the Get Historical Prices dialog box. Click **Update Now** to download these prices. When the One Step Update Summary dialog box appears, click **Close**.

USE THE PORTFOLIO VALUE VS. COST BASIS GRAPH

You can see how the value of your portfolio compares to your cost basis in the Portfolio Value Vs. Cost Basis graph at the bottom-left area of the Performance subtab. To work with this graph:

1. At the top of the Performance subtab, click one of the Show Account options—**All**, **Investment**, or **Retirement**—or choose an individual account from the drop-down list to tell Quicken which accounts to include. (See "Use the Growth Of $10,000 Utility" earlier in the chapter.) Or choose **Multiple Accounts** and select the desired accounts via the Customize dialog.

2. Click **Options** and then click **Customize This Graph**. The Customize dialog box appears.

3. Click the **Date Range** down arrow to see the list of possibilities, or click **Custom Dates** to determine your own dates. Click **OK** to close the dialog box.

4. Click **Show Full Graph** to show the graph on a full screen.

5. Click **Show Value/Cost Basis Report** to show the information in report (text) form.

REVIEW THE INVESTING ACTIVITY SECTION

The final Performance subtab section displays all of the activity for your investment accounts for a specified period. To review this activity:

1. At the top of the Performance subtab, click one of the Show Account options—**All**, **Investment**, or **Retirement**—or choose an individual account from the drop-down list to tell Quicken which accounts to include. (See "Use the Growth Of $10,000 Utility" earlier in the chapter.) Or choose **Multiple Accounts** and select the desired accounts via the Customize dialog.

2. In the Investing Activity section, click the **Show Full Report** button to display the information in a Quicken report format.

3. If you have sold any securities, click the **Capital Gains Report** button to see any capital gains on the transactions. If you have no realized gains, there will be no information in the Capital Gains report. If you have the Customize Report Or Graph Before Creating preference selected in the Reports And Graphs preferences, you will see the Customize Capital Gains dialog.

4. Click **Previous Year** to display last year's information. Click **Next Year** to see information for next year.

Allocate Your Assets

Quicken provides an Asset Allocation Guide to help you structure your portfolio. From the Investing tab's View Action Bar, click the **Asset Allocation** subtab to see the tools Quicken provides to help you allocate your assets appropriately. To work with the allocation of your assets:

1. Click the **Investing** tab.

2. In the View Action Bar, click the **Asset Allocation** subtab. Your current allocations display in graphical format.

3. Click **Show Allocation Guide** at the bottom of the Asset Allocation area. The Asset Allocation Guide displays the How Can Quicken Help With Asset Allocation? dialog box. Click **Print** to print a page of the guide. Figure 8-5 shows the first page. If you have downloaded quotes or other information from your brokerage firm or Quicken .com, this page displays your current asset allocation. If you don't see your asset allocation, click the **Replace It With An Example** or **Set Up Quicken So You Can** link.

Figure 8-5: *The Asset Allocation Guide shows you how to determine if your securities meet your risk and return objectives.*

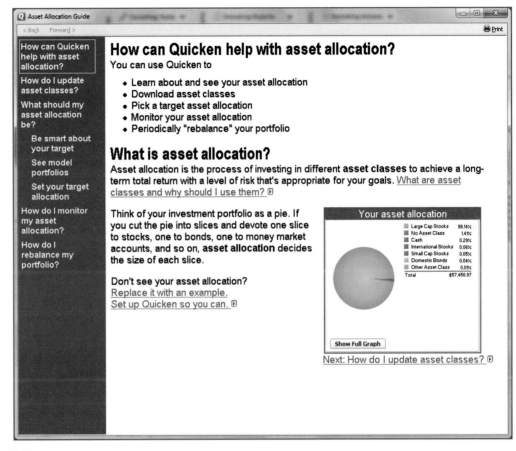

4. On the left side of the Asset Allocation Guide, click **How Do I Update Asset Classes** to display the next page.

5. Click **Go Online And Update Asset Classes** to open the Download Security Asset Classes dialog box.

   a. Click to the left of each security name for which you want the asset class downloaded, or click **Mark All** to choose each security in the list.

   b. Click **Update Now** to update your asset classes. After the transmission window has closed, the One Step Updates Summary dialog box may display what was downloaded. If you don't need to see this summary each time, click **Show This Dialog Only If There Is An Error**. Otherwise, click **Close** to return to the Asset Allocation Guide.

c. Click **Common Questions About Downloading Asset Classes** to display a list of frequently asked questions.

d. Click **Back: How Do I Update Asset Classes?** to return to that page.

e. Click **Next: What Should My Asset Allocation Be?** to continue. On this page of the guide, two sample asset allocation graphs are displayed: a current allocation and a target allocation, as shown in Figure 8-6.

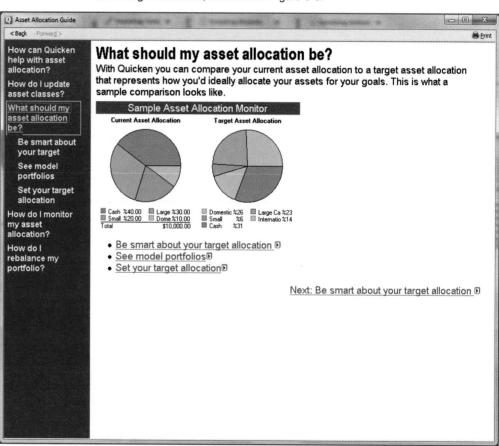

Figure 8-6: The What Should My Asset Allocation Be? page of the guide helps you set your allocation.

f. Click **Be Smart About Your Target Allocation** or **See Model Portfolios** to read advice about your allocation.

g. After you have read the material, click **Set Your Target Allocation**.

h. Click **Set**. The Set Target Asset Allocation dialog box appears.

CAUTION

Remember that investments in mutual funds are composed of several asset classes. While the allocation of classes within the fund changes from time to time, you really have no control over that mixture, and it may not meet your target allocation.

i. Click **Percentage** for each of the various asset classes to enter the percentage you want to achieve. Click **OK** when finished.

j. If this is the first time you've allocated your assets, click **How Do I Rebalance My Portfolio**. *Rebalancing* means moving money between investments so that your total investments are allocated in the best way for you to achieve your goals, as shown in Figure 8-7. Goal setting and planning is discussed in Chapter 9. Follow the instructions on the page to rebalance your assets.

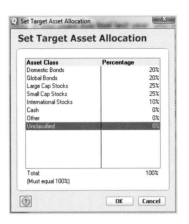

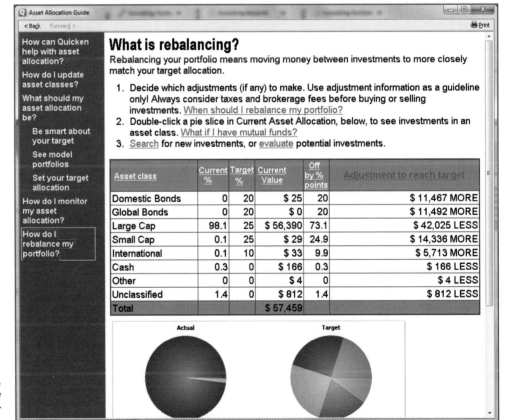

Figure 8-7: Periodically reviewing how your investments are balanced can help you better achieve your goals and objectives.

k. Click **How Do I Monitor My Asset Allocation** to understand more about your asset allocation.

l. Click **Close** to close the guide.

Work with the Portfolio Tab

The Portfolio subtab in the Investing tab's View Action Bar displays all of your investment information. By customizing the way you see this information, you can make educated decisions about the performance of each investment. To view your portfolio, press CTRL+U.

Understand Portfolio Terms

You can include several different columns of information in a custom view of your portfolio. To find what the column headings mean:

1. Click **Glossary** on the Menu bar. The Help screen is displayed.   `Options ▾` `Glossary`

2. If necessary, in the text box in the upper-left area of the Help screen, type <u>investment terms</u>, and press **ENTER**.

3. Click **Quicken Help Glossary** on the right side of the Help dialog box.

4. Click the first letter of the word you want to look up, and then scroll to the term you want to find, and click it to read the definition.

5. Close the Help window when you are finished.

Customize Your Portfolio View

Quicken has nine standard views for the portfolio, and you can customize up to nine others. All of the views can use any of up to 32 column headings. Before you create a customized view, make sure you download both the latest quotes and historical prices. To customize a view in your portfolio:

1. In Portfolio subtab, click the **Show** down arrow to select the view you want to customize.

SCHEDULING ONE STEP UPDATES

(Continued)

7. Enter the time in the At field.

Schedule

On: ☐ Mon ☐ Tues ☐ Wed ☐ Thurs

☐ Fri ☐ Sat ☑ Sun

At: 4:00 AM ▼ Note: Updates will run within 15 minutes of time specified.

8. If you are asking Quicken to update from your financial institutions, you must have stored your password for each institution in the Quicken Vault. To ensure proper security, select the time when Quicken will ask for your Vault password.

a. Click **Before Each Scheduled Update** to be prompted as the scheduled update begins.

b. Click **At Windows Startup** to have the password available the entire time you are working in Quicken.

9. Click **OK** to close the Schedule Updates dialog box.

2. Click **Customize View** to open the Customize Current View dialog box (see Figure 8-8). The name of the current selected view is displayed in the Name field. Type a new name for this view if you want.

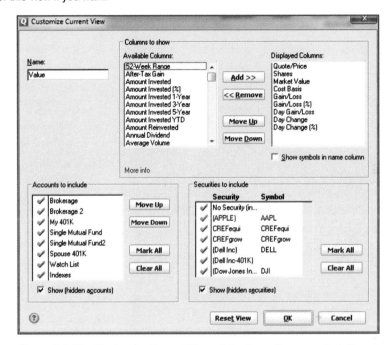

Figure 8-8: The Customize Current View dialog box allows you to tailor how you view your portfolio.

3. In the Accounts To Include list, click to the left of the accounts to select the ones you want to use. Click **Show (Hidden Accounts)** to include hidden accounts.

4. By default, your accounts are displayed alphabetically. If you want to change this, click an account, and then click **Move Up** or **Move Down** to change that account's position in the list.

5. To choose all of the accounts in the list, click **Mark All**.

SETTING OPTIONS IN YOUR PORTFOLIO VIEW

The Portfolio subtab in the Investing tab's View Action Bar allows you to set the display options for each view you display. From your Portfolio subtab:

1. Click **Options** on the Menu bar, and then click **Preferences**. The Portfolio View Options dialog box appears.

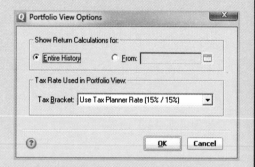

2. Click **Entire History** to include all transactions for your securities. This is the default setting. The alternative is to click **From** to enter a beginning date from which to display the information. The ending date is always today's date.

3. Click the **Tax Bracket** down arrow to choose a tax rate. The tax rate for short-term gains is shown first, and the rate for long-term gains is shown second. For example, (15%/5%) indicates that short-term gains are calculated at a 15-percent tax rate and long-term gains are calculated at a 5-percent tax rate.

4. Click **OK** to close the dialog box.

6. In the **Securities To Include** list, click to the left of the securities that you want to show. Click **Show (Hidden Securities)** to include hidden securities. You cannot change the order in which securities are displayed; they are always displayed in alphabetical order.

7. The columns that appear by default for this view are shown in the Displayed Columns list. To remove a column, click its name and then click **Remove**. The column heading moves from the Displayed Columns list to the Available Columns list.

8. Click a column in the Available Columns list, and click **Add** to include it in the Displayed Columns list.

9. Click a column heading in the Displayed Columns list, and click **Move Up** or **Move Down** to change its position in the list.

10. Click **Show Symbols In Name Column** to display the ticker symbol rather than the name of your security.

11. Click **Reset View** if you want to return to the original default settings.

12. Click **OK** when you are finished.

USE THE ONLINE PORTFOLIO

The final subtab in the Investing tab's View Action Bar is the Online Portfolio subtab. This is a direct link to the Quicken.com Investing center. To go to your Quicken.com page:

1. At the Investing tab's View Action Bar, click the **Online Portfolio** subtab.

2. Click **Start Here** if you have not set up Quicken.com as shown in "Set Up Quicken.com" earlier in this chapter.

3. Click **Log In** to log into your Quicken.com Investing center.

Work with Investing Tools

In the Investing tab's Tools Action Bar, Quicken provides a number of useful tools for your investing analysis. Each tool gives you a slightly different perspective on your investments or potential investments.

Use the Buy/Sell Preview Tool

1. In the Investing tab's Tools Action Bar, click **Investing Tools**.

2. Click **Buy/Sell Preview** to open the Buy/Sell Preview dialog box.

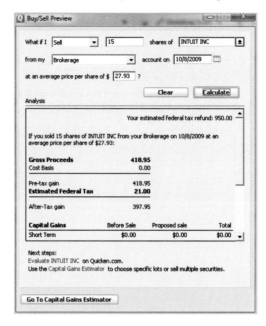

3. In the What If I text box, choose **Buy** or **Sell** from the drop-down box.

4. Complete the rest of the information as appropriate.

5. Click **Calculate** to have Quicken calculate the tax and capital gains effects.

6. Click **Clear** to add new information or **Close** to return to the Investing tab.

Estimate Capital Gains

The Capital Gains Estimator helps you determine how much tax you might have to pay if you sell a security.

1. From the Tools Action Bar in the Investing tab, click **Investing Tools** and click **Capital Gains Estimator**. The Capital Gains Estimator wizard appears, as seen in Figure 8-9. If you have previously used the Capital Gains Estimator, the screen may open to the What If scenarios.

CAUTION

Before using the Capital Gains Estimator, make sure you have set up your Tax Planner. See Chapter 10 for more information on setting up the Tax Planner.

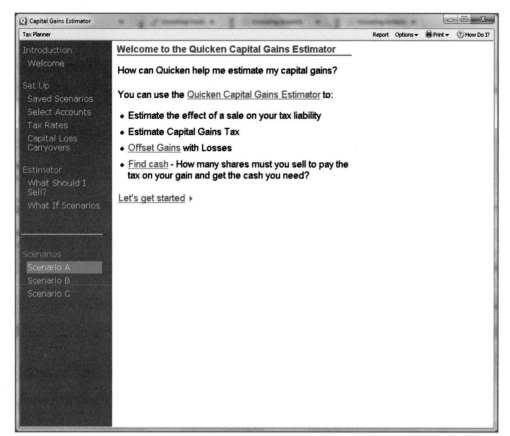

Figure 8-9: Use the Capital Gains Estimator to determine the tax consequences of your investment transactions.

2. Click **Let's Get Started** at the bottom of the Welcome message to start the wizard.

3. You can create up to three scenarios for comparison. Click one of the scenarios, and then click **Next** to continue.

4. Click to the left of the account name you want to include in the scenario. Click **Next**.

5. Continue through the Estimator by clicking **Next** and entering all relevant information.

6. Click the goal you want to achieve, such as **Maximize After-Tax Return** or **Balance My Year-To-Date Capital Gains**. The default is **Maximize After-Tax Returns And Minimize Fees**.

7. Click **Search** to have Quicken find the best way to meet your goal. When the Search dialog box has reached 100%, click **View Results**. The What Should I Sell? dialog box may appear and notify you that Quicken could not complete the scenario as you requested. Click **OK** and click **Settings**. Then:

   a. Click in the **% Of Your Target Goal** text box, and enter a percent of your target goal. Ten is the default percentage.

   b. Click in the **Seconds** text box, and enter the maximum number of seconds you want Quicken to try to meet your goal.

   c. Click in the **Optimal Solutions** text box, and enter the maximum number of possible solutions.

   d. Click **Stop As Soon As The First Acceptable Answer Is Found** to have Quicken end the search when any answer is found matching your criteria.

   e. Click **Quick Search** to choose one best method, or click **Exhaustive Search** to have Quicken merge a number of searches to give you a result.

   f. Click **OK** to return to the Search dialog box, and click **Start**.

CAUTION

Investment accounts that have missing cost-basis information or that are hidden in Quicken will not appear in the Capital Gains Estimator. Also, the Estimator does not include IRA or 401(k) accounts.

8. After the search is complete, you may see a dialog box stating that Quicken was not able to complete the task. Otherwise, click **View Results** to display the Capital Gains Estimator.

9. In the Current Holdings area, click to the left of the name of the security you want to sell. A check mark appears. If you have several lots of this holding, select the lot or lots from which you want to sell your shares.

10. In the Step 2 area, click in the **Shares To Sell** column opposite the stock you want to sell, and enter the number of shares you will be selling.

11. In the Step 3 area, view the potential taxable gains from your proposed sales. Read the bottom of the page to see detailed information about the proposed sale.

12. Click **Close** to return to the Investing Tools subtab.

Use the Portfolio Analyzer

The Portfolio Analyzer helps you review the risks and performance of your holdings. You can customize which accounts are being analyzed.

1. From the Tools Action Bar of the Investing tab, click **Investing Tools** and click **Portfolio Analyzer**.

2. Click **Customize** on the Menu bar to open the Customize Portfolio Analyzer dialog box. If not all of your investments appear in the list, click **Show Hidden Investment**.

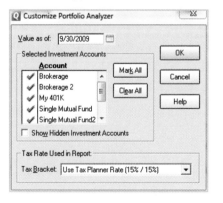

a. Click to the left of each account to select it for analysis, or click **Mark All** to choose all of the accounts on the list.

b. Click the **Tax Bracket** down arrow to select the tax rate used in the report. (See Chapter 10 for a complete discussion of tax planning.)

c. Click **OK** to close the dialog box.

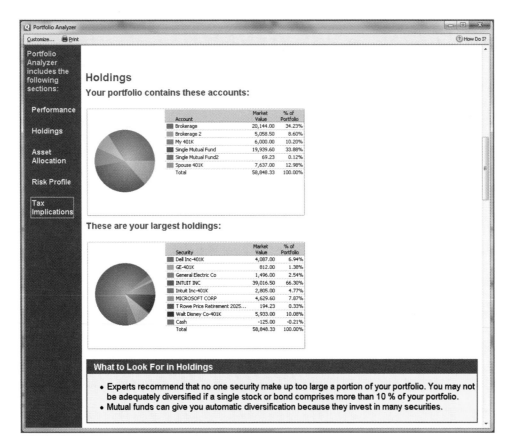

Holdings

Your portfolio contains these accounts:

Account	Market Value	% of Portfolio
Brokerage	20,144.00	34.23%
Brokerage 2	5,058.50	8.60%
My 401K	6,000.00	10.20%
Single Mutual Fund	19,939.60	33.88%
Single Mutual Fund2	69.23	0.12%
Spouse 401K	7,637.00	12.98%
Total	58,848.33	100.00%

These are your largest holdings:

Security	Market Value	% of Portfolio
Dell Inc-401K	4,087.00	6.94%
GE-401K	812.00	1.38%
General Electric Co	1,496.00	2.54%
INTUIT INC	39,016.50	66.30%
Intuit Inc-401K	2,805.00	4.77%
MICROSOFT CORP	4,629.60	7.87%
T Rowe Price Retirement 2025...	194.23	0.33%
Walt Disney Co-401K	5,933.00	10.08%
Cash	-125.00	-0.21%
Total	58,848.33	100.00%

What to Look For in Holdings

- Experts recommend that no one security make up too large a portion of your portfolio. You may not be adequately diversified if a single stock or bond comprises more than 10 % of your portfolio.
- Mutual funds can give you automatic diversification because they invest in many securities.

Figure 8-10: The Portfolio Analyzer has several sections, each one designed to help you with your financial investments.

3. A discussion of your holdings' performance displays. This can include a graphic presentation of your returns, your five best and five worst performers, tips on what to look for, and actions you can take to improve performance. Figure 8-10 shows a page of the Portfolio Analyzer.

4. Click **Holdings** to go directly to the graphic representation and accompanying tips on your holdings. Continue through the Portfolio Analyzer, clicking the items you want to view.

5. Click **Close** to close the Portfolio Analyzer.

Open Online Research Tools

To access additional Quicken investment tools, you must go online.

1. From the Tools Action Bar in the Investing tab, click **Investing Tools** and click **Online Research**.

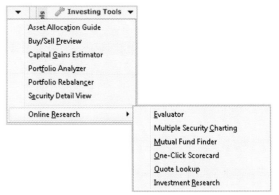

2. Click **Evaluator** to open the Quicken Investing Quotes And Research tab discussed earlier in this chapter.

3. Click **Multiple Security Charting** to find information on more than one security. With your Internet connection, the Multiple Security Charting dialog box appears, as shown in Figure 8-11.

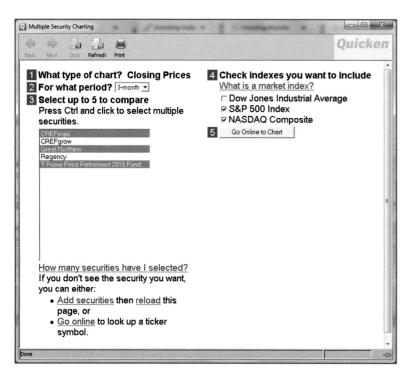

Figure 8-11: **You can compare up to five securities at the same time with the Multiple Security Charting utility in Quicken.**

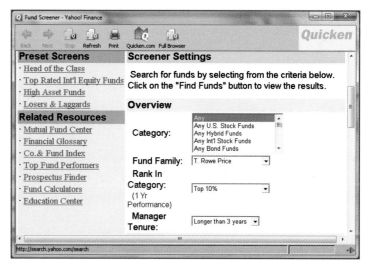

Figure 8-12: **Quicken helps you choose the best mutual fund for your needs with the Fund Screener.**

4. Click **Mutual Fund Finder** to open the Mutual Fund Screener to search for mutual funds that match criteria you determine, as seen in Figure 8-12.

5. Continue through the Overview screen, making relevant selections and leaving the others with the default selection of Any.

6. Click **Find Funds** to see a list of available funds that meet your criteria.

7. Click **Close** to return to the Portfolio tab.

WORK WITH THE ONE-CLICK SCORECARD

If you have registered with Quicken.com, you have yet another research tool available to you. After connecting to the Internet:

1. From the Tools Action Bar in the Investing tab, click **Investing Tools** and click **Online Research**.

2. Click **One-Click Scorecard**. The One-Click Scorecard window opens.

TIP

Make signing out of Quicken.com a habit even when using your home computer. This way, you won't forget to sign out when using a public computer.

CAUTION

If the ticker symbol you have entered for a specific security is not entered or entered incorrectly, you will see a warning dialog box that lets you know securities without ticker symbols will not be updated. Click **Edit Securities** to add or change a ticker symbol.

3. Click in the **Quote** text box, and enter the ticker symbol of the security you want to research.

4. Click **Go** to see the report. Quicken creates a report showing the opinions of three different industry experts about this security.

5. From the report window, you can:

   - Click **Add To Your Watchlist** to include this security in your Quicken Watch List.
   - Read comments from at least two financial analysts about this security.
   - Scroll down to view graphs reporting how the security has performed and a grade for each of seven different categories.

6. Click **Sign Out** to return to the Quicken registration page.

7. Click **Close** to return to Quicken.

8. Click **OK** to close the dialog box.

Manage Your Security List

Once you have entered your investment accounts, you may want to work with the individual securities in your accounts. When you created your investment accounts and told Quicken which securities were included in them, Quicken created a list of these accounts in its data file. To access your Security List:

1. Click **CTRL+Y** to open your Security List.

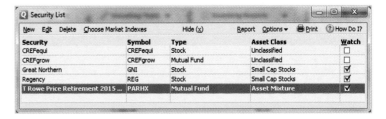

The Security List dialog box appears. From this list, you can add, edit, hide, and delete specific securities or add securities to your *Watch List*. (The Watch List is a special snapshot that allows you to track on a daily basis the performance of securities you own or may purchase. See the QuickSteps "Working with Your Watch List" later in this chapter.)

2. To add a new security to your Security List, click **New**. The Add Security To Quicken dialog box appears.

Click in the **Ticker Symbol** field, and type the ticker symbol for this security. If you don't know the symbol and have Internet access, enter the company name, and click **Look Up**.

b. Click **Include This Security On My Watch List** if you want to monitor its daily performance.

c. Click **Next** to continue. The Quicken One Step Update window opens briefly, and information about this security is downloaded into Quicken.

d. A summary window displays the name of your security, its ticker symbol, security type, asset class, and whether you have chosen to include this security on your Watch List. If the information is correct, click **Done**. The new security is displayed on your Security List in alphabetical order by name.

3. To edit an existing security, click the security name to select it, and then click **Edit**. The Edit Security Details dialog box appears. Click in and edit the fields you want to change.

4. To permanently delete a security, click the security and click **Delete**. A warning dialog box appears, telling you that you are about to permanently delete a security. Click **OK** if you want to continue.

5. To hide a security so that its information is available but not included in totals or reports, click its name and then click **Hide**. To include hidden securities in the Security List, click **Options** and then click **View Hidden Securities**. To restore a hidden security, select it and click **Hide** again.

Use the Look Up button to change the symbol of a security rather than typing it yourself in the Symbol field to ensure you have correctly entered the new symbol.

CAUTION

It is usually better to hide a security than to delete it. Before you delete a security, you must first find and delete all transactions related to it.

WORKING WITH YOUR WATCH LIST

The Watch List in the View Action Bar's Account Overview subtab of the Investing tab provides a convenient way to see the short-term performance of securities you may want to purchase in the future. From the Watch List you can add a new security to your Security List, edit the Watch List, download quotes, see your entire portfolio, research a stock or mutual fund with your Quicken.com account, set up a price alert, and display ticker symbols

Continued . . .

WORKING WITH YOUR WATCH LIST

(Continued)

rather than names in the Watch List. To work with the Watch List:

1. From the Investing tab's View Action Bar, click **Account Overview**.

2. Scroll to the Watch List, click **Options**, and click **Add Security To Watch List** to open the Add Security To Quicken dialog box.

3. Enter a ticker symbol or a company name for the new security, click **Look Up** for the security you want to track, and then click **Next**.

4. Confirm that the information that appears is for the correct company, and then click **Next**. A dialog box appears, notifying you that the new security has been added to Quicken.

5. If you want to add another security, click **Yes**, click **Next**, and repeat steps 3–5. When you are finished, click **Done** to return to the Account Overview subtab.

6. Scroll to the Watch List, click **Options**, and click **Edit Watch List** to display the Security List. Click the security you want to work with, click **Edit** on the Menu bar, make any desired changes, and click **OK**; or click the **Watch** check box to include or exclude the security or market index in the Watch List. Click **Close** to close the Security List.

7. Click **Download Quotes** to download the latest quotes for your holdings. The last date and time you downloaded appears as a note at the bottom of the Watch List.

---

6. Click **Choose Market Indexes** to display a list of market indexes, which you can include as part of your Security List and your Watch List. By including these indicators, you can compare their short-term performance to those of your securities.

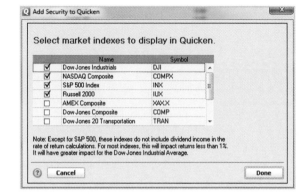

a. Click in the check box of each index you want to include. A small check mark is displayed.

b. Click **Done** to close the dialog box.

7. To create a report about a security, click the name of the security, and click **Report**.

8. Click **Print** to print the Security List.

9. Click **Close** to close the Security List.

How to...

- *Understand How to Plan with Quicken*
- *Enter Information About Yourself*
- *Understanding Your Social Security Retirement Age*
- *Enter Income Information and Your Tax Rate*
- *Estimating Inflation for Your Plan*
- *Include Checking and Savings Accounts*
- *Entering Your Expected Rate of Return*
- *Include Investment Accounts*
- *Work with Homes and Other Assets*
- *Associating Income with an Asset in Your Plan*
- *Use the Loans and Debt Planner*
- *Figure Your Living Expenses*
- *Planning to Pay for College*
- *Understand the Plan Results*
- *Use the Debt Reduction Planner*
- *Using What If's*
- *Work with the Spending Planner*
- *Get Quick Answers with Calculators*
- *Create a Budget*
- *Work with Your Budget*

Chapter 9

Making Plans for Your Future

Why should you plan for your financial future? It has been said that anyone who fails to plan, plans to fail. Gaining control over your finances, a debt-free lifestyle, college for your children, a house of your own, a once-in-a-lifetime cruise, retirement, or a vacation cabin are all major financial events. Will you have the money to fund them? By using the planners in Quicken, you can create a road map that will help you achieve your goals. In this chapter you will learn how to create plans in Quicken using assumptions. You will learn how to use the various planners and how to create a budget or spending plan that will help you reach your goals. In addition, you will see the various professional planning tools available in Quicken.

9

Work with Assumptions

All of the planners in Quicken are based on a set of assumptions that you create. You can change or add to these assumptions at any time. Quicken uses the data you have already entered to help you with your long-term plans, but if you have not yet entered all your data, you can enter it while you are creating your plans.

Understand How to Plan with Quicken

You begin by telling Quicken some information about yourself. Then you continue by including information about your income, tax rate, savings, investments, other assets, any debt, and living expenses. Quicken uses this information—along with the financial data you have already entered and a large database of financial resources—to help you create a plan. Within the Planning tab are several sections. This chapter discusses the Spending and Lifetime Planners and covers the Cash Flow subtab (see Figure 9-1). Taxes deserve a chapter of their own, and are covered in Chapter 10.

Figure 9-1: The Cash Flow tab in the Planning tab's View Action Bar displays details about your income and expenditures.

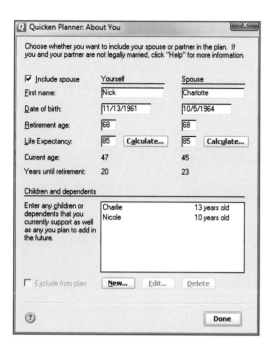

Figure 9-2: *The Quicken Planner: About You dialog box is used to enter age-related information about you, your spouse, and your children.*

TIP

You can include or exclude a dependent or a spouse at any time when making your assumptions.

CAUTION

If you support a parent or other family member who was born before 1930, you must enter all four digits in the year, for example, 1929. Otherwise, Quicken will use 2029 as the date of birth.

Enter Information About Yourself

All good plans start with information. This one is no exception. To begin your plan:

1. Click the **Planning** tab, and from the View Action Bar, click **Lifetime Planner**. In the Plan Assumptions section, click **About You** to begin entering information in the Quicken Planner, as seen in Figure 9-2.

2. Click **Include Spouse** if you want to include your spouse in the assumptions.

3. Under Yourself, click in the **First Name** field, and type your first name. If you are including your spouse, under Spouse, click in the **First Name** field, and type your spouse's first name.

4. Continue through the dialog box, entering all relevant information.

5. If you want to include information about children and other dependents, click **New** at the bottom of the dialog box. The Add Child/Dependent dialog box appears. This information can include children you plan to have that are not yet born.

6. Click in the **First Name** field, and enter the first name of your child.

7. Click in the **Date Of Birth** field, and enter the child's date of birth. You can use the format MM/DD/YY. Quicken will change the year to four digits.

8. Click **OK** to close the Add Child/Dependent dialog box and return to the Quicken Planner: About You dialog box.

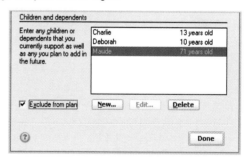

9. Click the name of a dependent, and click **Exclude From Plan** if you don't want Quicken to include dependents in the financial assumptions.

10. Click **Done** when you have entered all of your information and are ready to return to the Plan Assumptions section of the Lifetime Planner subtab.

The Plan Assumptions section now displays your name, your spouse's name if you included one, and the number of dependents you chose to include in your plan. If you want to change any of the assumptions that display, click the **Change Assumptions** button at the bottom of the Plan Assumptions section to open the Planning Assumptions dialog box. From that dialog box, click **Edit** to change any of the information.

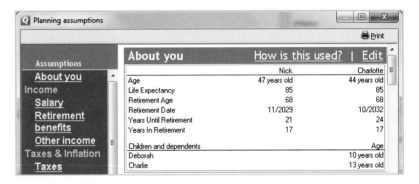

Enter Income Information and Your Tax Rate

The next item in the Plan Assumptions section pertains to information about your income. This includes regular salaries, self-employment income, retirement benefits, and other income, such as child support or alimony.

ENTER SALARIES AND SELF-EMPLOYMENT INCOME

1. Click the **Planning** tab, and from the View Action Bar, click **Lifetime Planner**. In the Plan Assumptions section, click **Income** to begin entering salary and other information in the Quicken Planner.

2. In the Plan Assumptions section, click **Income**. The Quicken Planner opens.

3. Click the **Salary** tab to enter salary information for yourself and your spouse, if you are including a spouse in your planning assumptions.

4. Click **New** in the middle of the dialog box under Salary. The Add Salary dialog box appears.

   a. Click **You** or **Spouse** in response to "Who Earns This Salary?"

   b. Click in the **Name Or Description Of The Salary** field, and type the relevant information.

c. Click in the **Gross Annual Salary** field, and type the amount in U.S. dollars.

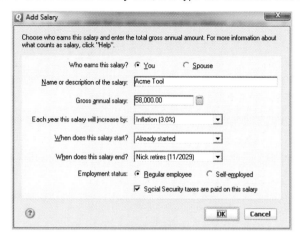

CAUTION

Gross annual salary should include all bonuses, commission, and salary. It should not include any real estate income, investment income, pension benefits, or Social Security income.

d. Continue through the questions, entering all relevant information.

e. Click **OK** when you are finished. You are returned to the Quicken Planner: Income dialog box. The information you entered for the starting and ending dates for this salary appear in the Adjustments To Salary section.

5. If you have other adjustments to your salary, such as a promotion or an expected bonus, click **New** under Adjustments. The Add Salary Adjustment dialog box appears. Enter any relevant information in the appropriate fields.

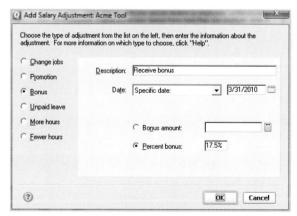

6. Click **Done** when you have entered all the information that pertains to your situation.

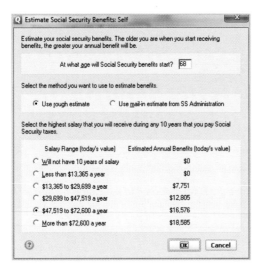

USE THE RETIREMENT BENEFITS TAB

If you have a retirement plan through your employer or want to include Social Security benefit information in your plan, use the Retirement Benefits tab in the Quicken Planner: Income dialog box (see "Enter Salaries and Self-Employment Income" to open this dialog box).

1. Click the **Retirement Benefits** tab to enter information about retirement income.

2. Click **Social Security Starting Age** to enter the age at which you expect to start collecting Social Security benefits. If you don't know, click the **Estimate** button. The Estimate Social Security Benefits dialog box appears.

3. Continue through the fields, entering information that pertains to your situation.

4. In the Pension Benefit section, click **New** to add information about any pension that you or your spouse may receive. The Add Pension dialog box appears. Enter all of the information that pertains to the pension, and click **OK** when you are finished.

5. If you want to change a pension that you have already entered, select that pension benefit, and click **Edit** to change that benefit, or click **Delete** to remove it from your list. If you want to exclude a specific pension benefit from your plan, select it from the list, and click **Exclude From Plan**.

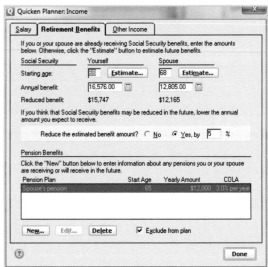

6. When you are done, click either the **Other Income** tab to enter additional, noninvestment income or **Done** to return to the Plan Assumptions section of the Lifetime Planner subtab.

TIP

Use the Reduced Benefit Amount text box, and type 100% if you don't want your plan to rely on Social Security benefits at all.

CAUTION

Do not include real estate income, pension benefits, investment income, Social Security benefits, or income from a small business as Other Income.

ENTER OTHER INCOME

The Other Income Tab in the Quicken Planner: Income dialog box is for gifts, inheritances, royalties, and other miscellaneous income you expect to receive. (See "Enter Salaries and Self-Employment Income" to open the Quicken Planner: Income dialog box.)

1. Click the **Other Income** tab, and then click **New**. The Add Other Income dialog box appears.

2. Click the option from the list on the left that corresponds to the type of income you want to include, as shown in Figure 9-3.

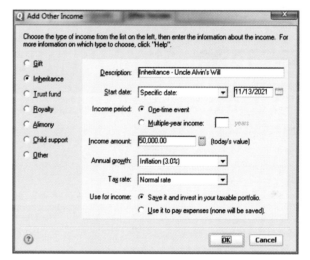

Figure 9-3: *Other income can be a one-time event or it can span several years.*

3. Continue through the planner, entering the relevant information. If you have chosen one of the specific types of income from the list on the left, this name appears in the field.

4. Click **OK** to close the Add Other Income dialog box and return to the Quicken Planner: Income dialog box.

5. Click **Done** to close the Quicken Planner: Income dialog box and return to the Planning tab's Action Bar Lifetime Planner.

DETERMINE YOUR TAX RATE

Quicken takes your tax liability into account when helping you create your plan. To tell Quicken what rate to use:

1. Click the **Planning** tab, and from the View Action Bar, click **Lifetime Planner**. In the Plan Assumptions section, click **Tax Rate**. The Quicken Planner: Average Tax Rate dialog box appears.

2. Click **Demographic Average** if you want Quicken to calculate your average tax rate based on the average rate of people in your income category in your state.

   a. Click the **What State Do You Live In?** down arrow, and click the name of your state.

   b. Click the **Approximate Combined Annual** down arrow, and click the approximate annual income for you and your spouse.

3. Alternatively, click **Tax Returns** if you want to enter information from your most recent tax return. A different set of questions appears.

   a. Enter the total income from Form 1040.

   b. Enter the total federal taxes from Form 1040.

   c. If your state has a state income tax, enter the total state taxes from your state tax form.

4. The average tax rate for your income bracket in your state appears in the Adjust The Rate If You Want It To Be Higher Or Lower Than The Estimate field. Enter any change in the estimated tax rate you want Quicken to use.

5. This same rate appears in the What Is Your Estimated After-Retirement Tax Rate? field. Enter any change you want Quicken to use.

6. Click **Done** when you have entered all of the information to return to the Planning tab's Action Bar Lifetime Planner.

NOTE

You can always enter a higher tax rate for Quicken to use in its planning calculations.

QUICKSTEPS

ESTIMATING INFLATION FOR YOUR PLAN

Quicken uses an average inflation rate of 3 percent. *Inflation* is a rise in the price of goods or services when consumer spending increases and supplies or services decrease. For the last 50 years, inflation in the United States has ranged from 0 to 23 percent, with an average of 2 to 3 percent per year. As you make your assumptions in Quicken, you may choose to be conservative and increase the default inflation rate of 3 percent, or be more optimistic and decrease the rate. To change the rate of inflation used by Quicken:

1. Click the **Planning** tab, and from the View Action Bar, click **Lifetime Planner**. In the Plan Assumptions section, click **Inflation**. The Quicken Planner: Estimated Inflation dialog box appears.

2. Click in the **What Inflation Rate Do You Want To Use In Your Plan?** field, and type the number you want to use.

3. Click **Done** to close the dialog box.

Consider Savings, Investments, and Rate of Return

Quicken can use the information you entered for your checking, savings, and investment accounts in its assumptions for planning. You can choose to have Quicken include or exclude any account from its computations, designate the use for each account, and indicate what contributions will be made to these accounts in the future.

Include Checking and Savings Accounts

To tell Quicken how to use your checking and savings accounts:

1. Click the **Planning** tab, and from the View Action Bar, click **Lifetime Planner**. In the Plan Assumptions section, click **Savings & Investments**. The Quicken Planner: Savings And Investments dialog box appears.

2. Click the **Savings** tab to display a list of your checking and savings accounts. If you have not yet entered all of your accounts, now is a good time. Click the **New** button to add a new account, and follow the directions in Chapter 3.

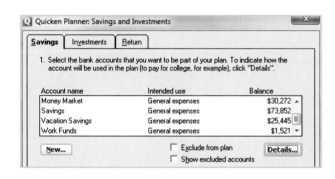

3. Click an account and click **Exclude From Plan** to exclude that account from the plan. Click **Show Excluded Accounts** if you want them to be displayed in the list even if they are not included in the plan.

4. Click **Details** to open the Account Details: Savings dialog box.

   a. Click the **Account Will Be Used For** down arrow, and select the purpose for this account. If you have used any of the specific planners, such as the Home Purchase Planner or the Retirement Planner, you will have that choice included; otherwise, your only choice is the default: General Expenses.

   b. Click **OK** to return to the Quicken Planner: Savings And Investments dialog box.

5. If either you or your spouse regularly puts money in any of these bank accounts, click **New** underneath Contributions To *nnn,* where *nnn* is the name of the account you have selected. The Add Contribution: *nnn* dialog box appears.

QUICKSTEPS

ENTERING YOUR EXPECTED RATE OF RETURN

The *rate of return* is how much you get back each year on your investments expressed as a percentage. For example, if you make $200 on a $2,000 investment, your rate of return is 10 percent ($2,000 divided by $200). You can use different rates for taxable and tax-deferred investments. Before retirement, your investments must grow enough to ensure that you have funds available to you even when you are not earning a salary. After retirement, your funds must grow to keep pace with inflation and fund your living expenses. To enter your estimated rate of return on your investments:

1. Click the **Planning** tab, and from the View Action Bar, click **Lifetime Planner**. In the Plan Assumptions section, click **Savings & Investments**. The Quicken Planner: Savings and Investments dialog box appears.

2. Click the **Return** tab.

3. Click **Use Separate Rates Of Return For Taxable And Tax-Deferred Accounts**, if applicable.

   - Enter the information in taxable accounts before retirement and after retirement.
   - Enter your tax-deferred rates both before retirement and after retirement.
   - Enter your spouse's tax-deferred rates both before retirement and after retirement.

4. If you did *not* choose Use Separate Rates Of Return For Taxable And Tax-Deferred Accounts in step 3, click in the **Rate Of Return** field under Before Retirement, and enter the return you expect on your investments before you retire.

Continued . . .

6. Enter the relevant information for your situation.

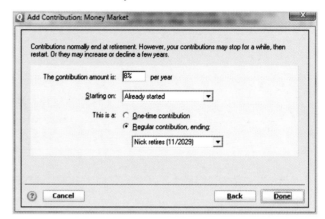

7. Click **Done** to return to the Quicken Planner: Savings and Investments dialog box.

Include Investment Accounts

The Investments tab shows all of the investment accounts you have entered. You can include or exclude any of these accounts from your plan and tell Quicken about any regular contributions you make to any of them.

Click the **Investments** tab, and follow the procedure in "Include Checking and Savings Accounts" earlier in this chapter.

Work with Homes and Other Assets

You can include your home and other assets in your plan, both those you currently own and those you plan on purchasing.

INCLUDE CURRENT ASSETS

To work with the Homes And Assets Planner:

1. Click the **Planning** tab, and from the View Action Bar, click **Lifetime Planner**. In the Plan Assumptions section, click **Homes And Assets**. The Quicken Planner: Homes And Assets dialog box appears.

2. Click the **Asset Accounts** tab to display a list of the accounts you have created so far in Quicken, including homes, vehicles, real estate, and so on. The list shows a

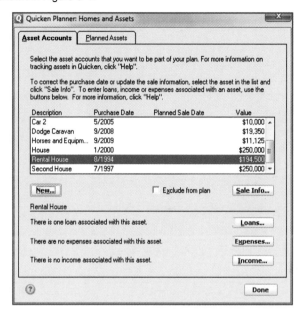

ENTERING YOUR EXPECTED RATE OF RETURN *(Continued)*

5. Click in the **Rate Of Return** field under After Retirement, and enter your expected after-retirement return.

6. In the **How Much Of Your Taxable Return Will Be Subject To Taxes Each Year?** field, enter an appropriate percentage. In most cases, all of the return may be taxable. Check with your financial professional to learn what you should enter.

Savings | Investments | **Return**

Enter the average rate of return that you and your spouse expect to achieve before and after retirement. For more information, click "Help".

☑ Use separate rates of return for taxable and tax-deferred accounts

	Before retirement	After retirement
Taxable accounts:	17%	8%
Your tax-deferred:	8%	4%
Spouse's tax-deferred:	15%	8%

If you are invested mostly in stocks that do not pay dividends or interest, less than 100% of your gain may be taxed each year. To be conservative enter 100% or click "Help" for more information.

How much of your taxable return will be subject to taxes each year? 100%

7. Click **Done** to return to the Planning tab.

description of the asset, its purchase date, a planned sale date (if any), and its current value, as shown in Figure 9-4.

Figure 9-4: *The Asset Accounts tab lists each asset you have entered, its purchase date, and its current recorded value.*

3. Click **New** to add a new account, follow the directions in Chapter 3, and return to the Quicken Planner: Homes And Assets dialog box.

4. Select an asset and click **Exclude From Plan** if you want Quicken to ignore this asset in your plan.

5. Click **Sale Info** to open the Asset Account Sale Information dialog box. Click in each of the fields, and select or type the requested information, clicking **Next** as needed.

6. Click **Done** to return to the Quicken Planner: Homes And Assets dialog box.

7. Click the **Planned Assets** tab to enter any large assets you plan to purchase in the future. Click **New** to open the Add Planned Asset dialog, and type the requested information, clicking **Next** as needed.

8. Click **Done** when you have finished entering the information to return to the Quicken Planner: Home And Assets dialog box.

CONSIDER LOANS ON ASSETS

If you intend to add, pay off, or change a loan using one of your assets as collateral:

1. Click the name of the asset, and then click the **Loans** button to open the Quicken Planner: Loans dialog box.

2. Click the **Loan Accounts** tab to display the current loans associated with this asset.

3. To enter early payoff information about a loan associated with an asset, select the loan and click **Payoff** to open the Loan Payoff dialog. Enter the appropriate information, and click **OK** when you are done.

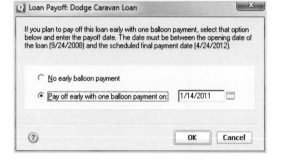

4. Select a loan and click **Exclude From Plan** if you want to exclude that loan from your plan.

5. To enter loans you plan for the future, click the **Planned Loans** tab, and click **New**. The Planned Loans dialog box appears. Click in each of the fields, and select or type the information that is correct for your loan.

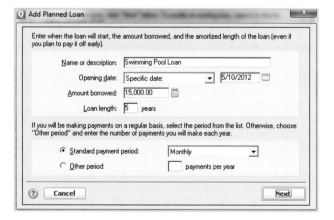

6. Click **Done** to return to the Quicken Planner: Loans dialog box. The details of this planned loan are displayed at the bottom of the dialog box. Click **Done** again to return to the Quicken Planner: Homes And Assets dialog box.

ENTER EXPENSES ASSOCIATED WITH AN ASSET

Many assets have expenses associated with them that must be included in the plan. You can include them here with their associated asset or include them later in the "Figure Your Living Expenses" section of this chapter. To include expenses with their associated asset:

1. Click **Homes And Assets** to open the Quicken Planner: Homes And Assets dialog box. Click the asset with which you want to work.

2. Click the **Expenses** button toward the bottom of the dialog box. The Quicken Planner: Asset Expenses dialog box appears.

3. Click in the **How Much Tax Do You Pay On This Asset?** field, and enter the tax amount, if any, that you pay.

4. If there are other expenses, such as homeowner association fees, moorage fees, maintenance fees, or gardening expenses, click **New**. The Add Asset Expense dialog box appears.

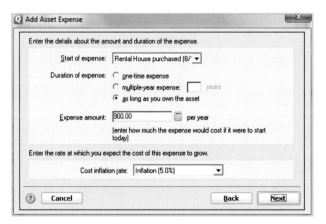

5. Click in the **Name Or Description** field, and type a name for this expense if you want a name different from the default Quicken supplies. Click **Next** to continue. Click in each of the fields, and select or type the information that is appropriate for this expense, clicking **Next** as needed and clicking **OK** to return from any subsidiary dialog box you open.

6. Click **Done** to return to the Quicken Planner: Asset Expenses dialog box. Click **Done** again to return to the Quicken Planner: Homes And Assets dialog box.

QUICKSTEPS

ASSOCIATING INCOME WITH AN ASSET IN YOUR PLAN

Part of your future retirement may come from income you earn by renting an asset you own, such as a motor home, boat, cabin, or real property. You can include this information in your Quicken Planner: Homes And Assets dialog box.

1. Click the **Planning** tab, and from the View Action Bar, click **Lifetime Planner**. In the Plan Assumptions section, click **Homes And Assets**. The Quicken Planner: Homes And Assets dialog box appears.

2. Click the name of the asset from which you earn income, and click **Income** at the bottom of the dialog box.

Continued . . .

ASSOCIATING INCOME WITH AN ASSET IN YOUR PLAN (Continued)

3. Click **New** to open the Add Other Income dialog box. Click in each of the fields, and select or type the information that is requested.

4. Click **OK** to return to the Other Income dialog box.

5. Click **Done** to return to the Quicken Planner: Home And Assets dialog box.

CAUTION

Ensure that any loans are included in the Loan Accounts section of the Plan Assumptions and that all credit cards or other consumer debt is included in the Expenses section.

INCLUDE PLANNED ASSETS

You can include in your planning the acquisition of additional assets, such as a new home, a new weekend property, a new business or income property, and so on.

1. From the Quicken Planner: Homes And Assets dialog box (see "Include Current Assets"), click the **Planned Assets** tab.

2. Click **New** to open the Add Planned Asset dialog box, click in each of the fields, and select or type the information that is requested, clicking **Next** as needed.

3. Click **Done** to return to the Quicken Planner: Homes And Assets dialog box. See the sections, "Include Current Assets," "Consider Loans on Assets," and "Enter Expenses Associated with an Asset" earlier in this chapter, as well as the QuickSteps "Associating Income with an Asset in Your Plan," to perform the same functions with planned assets as with current assets.

Use the Loans and Debt Planner

To have a comprehensive plan, you need to include your liabilities (loans and debts), as well as your assets.

1. Click the **Planning** tab, and from the View Action Bar, click **Lifetime Planner**. In the Plan Assumptions section, click **Loans And Debt**. The Quicken Planner: Loans And Debt dialog box appears.

2. Click the **Loan Accounts** tab to display a list of all the loans you have entered. You can select loans and exclude them from your plan, change the payoff date, and add new loans.

3. Click the **Planned Loans** tab to display a list of any loans you plan to take out in the future. You may have entered these loans in the Quicken Planner: Homes And Assets section. You can edit, delete, and exclude these loans from the plan, as well as add new ones.

4. Click the **Debt** tab. If you have not yet used Quicken's Debt Reduction Planner, a dialog box appears with a message to that effect. See "Use the Debt Reduction Planner" later in this chapter.

5. Click **Done** to close this dialog box.

Figure Your Living Expenses

Expenses are a critical part of your plan. To figure what your expenses will be:

1. Click the **Planning** tab, and from the View Action Bar, click **Lifetime Planner**. In the Plan Assumptions section, click **Expenses**. The Quicken Planner: Expenses dialog box appears.

2. Click the **Living Expenses** tab. You are prompted to enter your regular living expenses, such as food, transportation, rent, medical insurance payments, and utility bills. Quicken offers you two methods of entering these items: by rough estimate or by category detail.

3. Click **Rough Estimate** to let Quicken base an annual estimate of your expenses based on the transactions in your registers.

   - Click **Yearly Living Expenses**, and, if needed, modify the amount.

   - Click in the **What Percent Of Surplus Cash Do You Want To Sweep To Savings?** field, and enter a percentage if you feel you will be spending less than your income. The most conservative amount to select is 0 percent.

4. Click **Category Detail** if you want to track your expenses by category. See "Create a Budget" later in this chapter for further information on entering expenses by category.

CAUTION

Do not include amounts in your living expenses that are entered elsewhere, such as regular mortgage payments. Conversely, do not forget to include credit card and loan payments you make regularly.

CAUTION

Each time you enter the Category Detail dialog, you must check/uncheck and/or change the expense amounts. These changes are saved when you exit the dialog, but are reset to zero if you re-enter. Sometimes it is much easier to simply use the "rough estimate" option at this point.

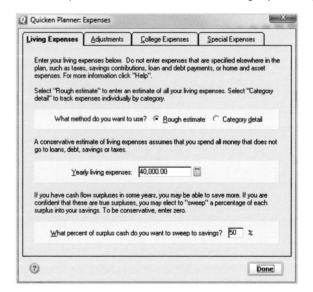

ENTER ADJUSTMENTS

The Adjustments tab is used to enter major changes to your living expenses. This could be due to a layoff from work, a new baby, or an illness.

1. Click the **Adjustments** tab, and click **New**. The Add Living Expense Adjustment dialog box appears.

2. Click **No Specific Person** if this is a general adjustment, such as rent from an extra room in your garage. Click **A Plan Member**, and choose the member from the drop-down list, if the change affects one of the persons in your plan. The members are you, your spouse, and any dependents you listed as being included in the plan.

3. Click in the remaining fields that are applicable, and select or type the appropriate information.

4. Click **OK** to close the dialog box.

ENTER COLLEGE EXPENSES

The College Expenses tab helps you enter information about the costs of college. See "Use the Calculators, Budgets, and Other Tools" section later in this chapter for information about calculating the costs you will enter here.

1. Click the **College Expenses** tab, and click **New**. The Add College Expense dialog box appears.

2. Click **This Expense Is For**, and choose a name from the drop-down list.

3. Make any necessary changes in the remaining fields, and click **Next**.

4. Enter an amount in the **Tuition & Fees** field, and continue through the dialog, adding fees as necessary.

5. Click **Next** to enter any anticipated financial aid and other help the student will receive. Click in each field to enter the applicable information.

6. Click **Next** to display a dialog that describes how you will fund these college costs. Make any changes that are necessary.

7. Click **Done** to return to the College Expenses tab. Click **New** to add another person's expenses.

8. To change information about a person's expenses, select the name from the list, and click **Edit** to open the Edit College Expense dialog. To remove a person's name from the list (and your plan), select the name and click **Delete**.

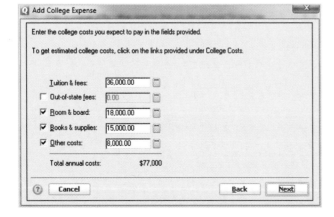

PLANNING TO PAY FOR COLLEGE

When you are planning for your children's college education, consider the following:

- How old is the child, and when will he or she actually start college? For most students, it is the fall after they graduate from high school.

- What are their options as to the type of school?

- Consider community or junior college so that the child can complete any lower-level requirements. Some community college programs guarantee entry into a four-year state school if the student graduates with an associate's degree.

- Community college tuition is usually much less expensive than a four-year institution.

- State colleges and universities usually charge less tuition to residents of that state than to out-of-state students.

- Many schools are now offering a large number of classes online. This saves room and board as well as transportation costs.

- How can the student receive grants or scholarships?

- Look for scholarships or grants early. Use the Internet to search on the Web, and contact friends or family members in organizations that offer scholarships.

- Check to see if your state offers a guaranteed education account. Many universities and colleges, both state and private, now offer a prepayment plan for parents that allows you to pay over a longer period at a reduced cost and ensure a four-year education at the state or private school offering such a plan.

Continued . . .

ENTER SPECIAL EXPENSES

Special expenses are those expenses that are not part of regular living expenses, but should be included in your plan. An example of a special expense might be an extended vacation, a 50th wedding anniversary party, or some other elaborate event.

1. Click the **Special Expenses** tab to open the dialog box.

2. Click **New** to open the Add Special Expense dialog box.

3. Enter all the applicable information, and click **Done** when you are through to return to the Quicken Planner: Expenses dialog box.

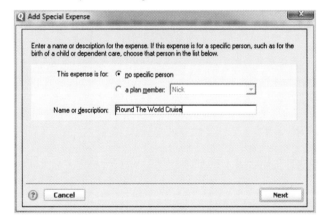

4. Click **Done** to close the dialog box. You are returned to the Lifetime Planner subtab of the Planning tab with a graphic displaying the results of your plan, as seen in Figure 9-5.

Understand the Plan Results

After you have entered all of your assumptions, the result of your hard work is displayed in graphical format in the Plan: Results section of the Planning tab. The graph shows if your plan is working and how much money you will have in retirement. A list of major events is displayed under the graph, as shown in Figure 9-5.

1. Click **Options** in the upper-right corner of the Plan: Results section of the Planning tab's Action Bar's Lifetime Planner subtab to see how you can change the graph.

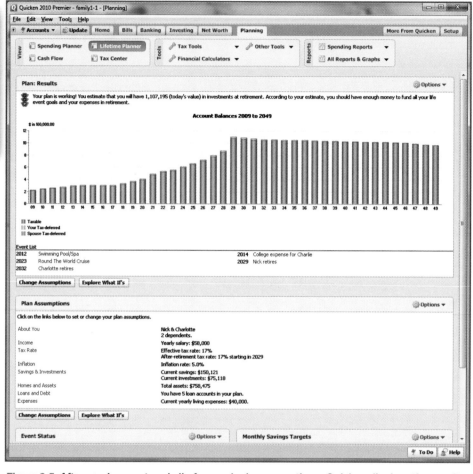

Figure 9-5: *After you have entered all of your plan's assumptions, Quicken displays the results.*

2. Click **Show Amounts In Future Value** to display the graph in future (inflated) dollars. Click **Options** and click **Show Amounts In Today's Value** to change it back.

3. Click **Options** and click **Review Or Change Plan Assumptions** to open the Plan Assumptions dialog box. Each assumption you entered is displayed with its result. Scroll through the dialog box, or click an area on the left to ensure that you entered everything correctly. If you did not, click **Edit** in the title of each section to open the

relevant dialog box, and change the information. You can also access this dialog box by clicking the **Change Assumptions** button underneath the Event List in the Plan: Results section of the Planning tab. Click **Close** to return to the Planning tab.

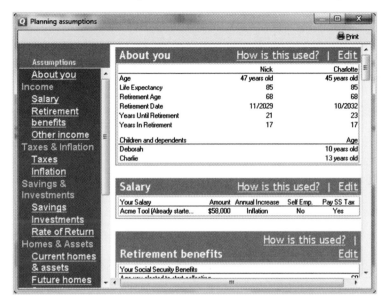

4. Again, click **Options** on the Plan: Results title bar, and click **What If I Did Something Different** to open the What If dialog box. This allows you to temporarily change any assumption by clicking the assumption area on the left and seeing the result. If you like the change, keep it; if not, close the dialog box without saving your changes. You can also open this dialog box by clicking the **Explore What If's** button to the right of the Change Assumptions button at the bottom of the Plan: Results section. Click **Close** to return to the Planning tab.

Use the Planners

In addition to the Lifetime Planner, Quicken offers other planners for specific goals designed for Quicken by the Financial Planning Association. Each link displays a thorough interview that enables you to take a comprehensive look at each goal. Using the information you entered in the Plan Assumptions section, these planners provide additional questions for you to think about, links to resources on the Internet, and a complete list of your information in an easy-to-understand format, and then reviews each part of your plan for potential problems.

You can use these planners to enter information rather than use the Plan Assumptions dialog boxes or to make changes to the data you entered in those assumptions. Perhaps the most important planner in this group is the Debt Reduction Planner. It is difficult to create financial stability when you owe a large amount of debt.

Use the Debt Reduction Planner

With more credit card debt per person in the United States than ever in history, many people's debt load is overwhelming. Quicken's Debt Reduction Planner can help you pay less interest and take control of your debt before you are snowed under. To use the Debt Reduction Planner:

1. From the Action Bar in the Planning tab, click **Tools** and click the **Other Tools** subtab. Click **Debt Reduction Planner**. The Debt Reduction Planner is displayed, as seen in Figure 9-6.

2. If you have entered information into the Lifetime Planner, as described in "Work with Assumptions" earlier in this chapter, your current debt reduction plan is displayed.

3. Click **Update Debt Balances** on the Menu bar of the Debt Reduction dialog box to update any balances not being tracked in Quicken. A dialog box appears telling you that all current Quicken debt account balances will be updated. Click **Yes** to confirm that you want to do this.

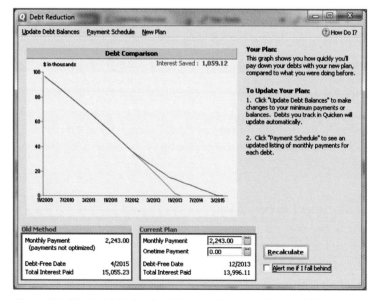

Figure 9-6: *The Debt Reduction Planner shows you how quickly your debts will be paid.*

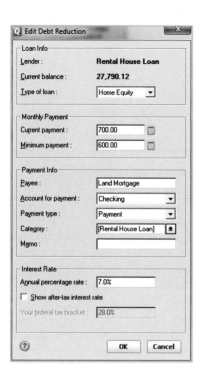

4. The Update Debt Balances dialog box appears showing all debt (other than credit cards) you have currently entered into Quicken. To edit a loan, select it and click **Edit**. The Edit Debt Reduction dialog box appears.

5. Click **Type Of Loan**, and select a type from the drop-down box.

6. Continue through the dialog box, entering any other changes. Click **OK** when you are through to return to the Update Debt Balances dialog box.

7. Select another debt if necessary, or click **Done** to return to the Debt Reduction Planner dialog box.

8. Click **Payment Schedule** to open a detailed list of your payments. Use the scrollbar to go to future years and see how the balances are reduced after each month.

9. Click **Help** to open the Help dialog discussing payment schedules. Click **Print** to open the Windows Print dialog box. You may print a specific date range or the entire schedule. The dialog warns that if you choose to print the entire schedule, it could be as much as 100 pages.

10. Click **OK** or **Cancel** to return to the Debt Reduction Payment Schedule dialog box.

11. Click **Done** to return to the Debt Reduction dialog box.

CREATE A NEW DEBT REDUCTION PLAN

If you want to create a plan to replace your current one:

1. Click **New Plan**. A dialog box appears telling you this new plan will replace your current plan. If you want to keep your current plan, click **No** to return to the Debt Reduction Planner. If you want to create a new plan, click **Yes** to continue. The Debt Reduction wizard appears.

2. Click **Next** to begin using the wizard.

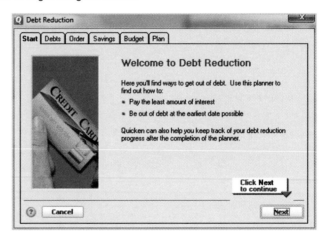

WORK WITH THE DEBTS TAB

The Debts tab lists all of the loans and credit card debt you have entered into Quicken, the interest rate for each liability, and the current balance. You may be prompted to enter additional information for one or more of your debts so that Quicken has all of the necessary information to assist you.

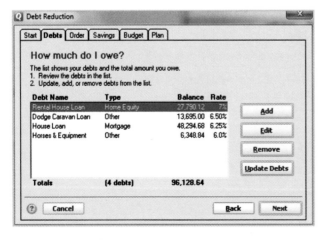

1. Click **Add** to add any debt you have not yet entered into Quicken. The Edit Debt Reduction dialog box appears. Click in each of the fields, and select or type the information that is requested.

2. Click **OK**. If there is no Quicken account associated with this loan, a dialog box appears and asks if you would like Quicken to set up an account for the debt. Click **Yes** to set up an account. Follow the procedure outlined in Chapter 3.

3. If you need to change or remove any of your listed loans, click the loan and click **Edit** or **Remove**. If you are editing a loan, repeat steps 1 and 2. If you are removing a loan, click **Yes** to confirm that you want to permanently remove the debt from the plan.

4. After you have entered any new loans or changed any existing loans, click **Next**. The subsequent Debt Reduction Planner page shows how much you owe and your total monthly payment. At the bottom of the page, Quicken displays when you will be debt-free and how much interest you will have paid for your total outstanding debts.

REVIEW THE ORDER TAB

The Order tab displays the optimum plan to get you debt-free in the shortest amount of time and paying the least amount of interest.

1. Click **Next** to display the Order tab.

2. Click **Next** to display the order in which Quicken suggests you pay off your debt. At the bottom of the page, the Optimized Payment Plan Results are displayed, showing the new debt-free date, the total interest that would be paid, and the total savings in interest if this new plan is followed. If you have only one debt, you do not need to display the pay-off order.

3. If you do not agree with Quicken, click **Change Payment Order**, and then click **Next** to manually change the order in which the debts are paid. Select a debt and click either the **Move Up** or **Move Down** button to change the order. As you make the changes, the results are displayed on the left side of the page.

4. Click **Reset To Optimized Order** to return to Quicken's order.

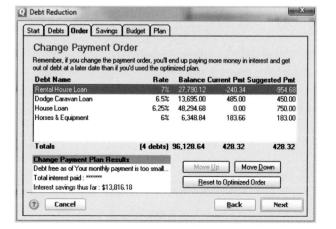

USING WHAT IF'S

As you spend time creating plans for your financial future, Quicken provides a utility that allows you to quickly see the result of a possibility or a different path. The What If scenarios allow you to change assumptions or make changes in each of the four different goal types: College, Home Purchase, Retirement, and Special Expense. You can save the new scenario or close the What If dialog box without saving your changes. To use the What If dialog box:

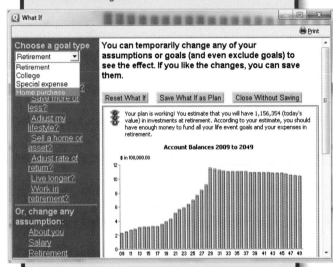

1. In the Lifetime Planner subtab of the Action Bar View of the Planning tab, click **Explore What If's** below the Plan: Results graph.

   –Or–

2. Click **Options** from the Plan: Results section, and choose **What If I Did Something Different?**.

Continued . . .

USE THE SAVINGS TAB

In the Savings tab, you are given the opportunity to see how making a one-time payment from your savings or investment accounts or both could reduce both your interest payments and the length of time it would take to become debt-free.

1. Click **Next** to open the Savings tab.

2. Click in the **Onetime Amount You Would Like To Apply To Reduce Your Debt** field, and enter a dollar amount to apply towards your debt.

3. Click **Recalculate** to see what result this payment would have. The results are displayed in the lower-left area of the page.

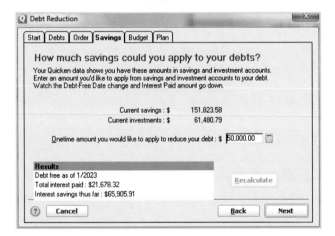

CUT EXPENSES IN THE BUDGET TAB AND SEE YOUR PLAN

The Budget tab displays how much you spend monthly in the top four discretionary categories. Each category displays the average amount you spend each month and allows you to enter an amount you can cut back.

1. Click **Next**. The Budget tab is displayed.

2. Click the first **Quicken Category** drop-down arrow, and select a category to cut. Observe the average monthly spending, and then, in the **Amount To Cut Back** text box, type how much you can decrease your spending in this category. The total amount that you will have available to apply to your debt each month is displayed at the bottom of the four categories.

USING WHAT IF'S *(Continued)*

3. Click the **Choose A Goal Type** down arrow, and select one of the four options. Each option has a different set of What If scenarios with which you can work.

4. Click a **What If I** option. A Quicken Planner dialog box will appear.

5. Click the area that might change, and click **Edit** in the appropriate area. Make any needed adjustments, and click **OK**.

6. Repeat step 4 for other What If scenarios or changes in assumptions. When you are ready, click **Done** to close the Quicken Planner dialog box. The result of this change is displayed in the Plan Results graph in the What If dialog box.

7. Click **Reset What If** to revert to your original settings or assumptions.

8. If you want, click **Save What If As Plan** to keep the change you entered and return to the Lifetime Planner subtab of the Planning tab. Otherwise, click **Close Without Saving**.

NOTE

You may only go to previous months if you set up a spending plan for that month.

---

3. Click in each of the fields, and select or type the information that is appropriate for this expense, clicking **Next** as needed and clicking **OK** to return from any subsidiary dialog box you open.

4. Click **Next** to see your plan. Click **Print This Action Plan** to print your new plan. Click **Help** to open a context-sensitive Help window. Click **Cancel** to cancel this new plan.

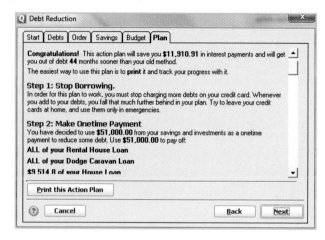

5. Click **Back** to return to other tabs in the wizard.

6. Click **Next** and click **Done** to close the wizard and return to the Debt Reduction dialog box.

7. If you are through working with the Debt Reduction dialog box, click **Close**.

Work with the Spending Planner

The Spending Planner helps you review your expected income, scheduled bills, and categorize your spending, as seen in Figure 9-7. You can tell Quicken how to handle any leftover cash, set allocations for spending categories, and create a spending report. To view the Spending Planner:

1. Click the **Planning** tab, and in the View Action Bar, click the **Spending Planner** subtab.

2. Click the left and right arrows by the month to see previous and future month's plans, respectively.

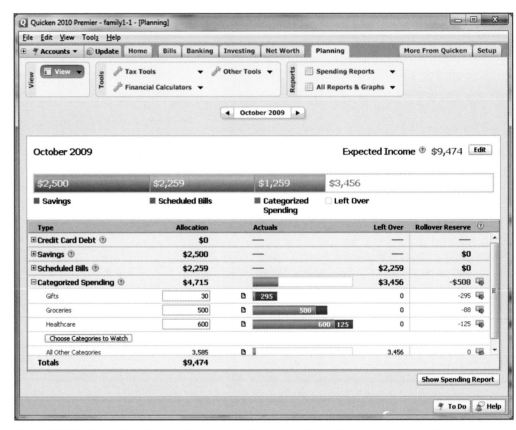

Figure 9-7: *The Spending Planner shows a monthly comparison of income and spending.*

3. Click **Edit** to open the Set Expected Income dialog box. Enter the amount of expected income in the **Set Income** field to change the amount of income that is expected for the month. Click **OK** to return to the Spending Planner. The Set Expected Income title will change to "Total Monthly Allocation."

4. Type an amount in the Allocation field for each item to change the amount currently showing. Click **Apply** to set the amount.

5. Click **Choose Categories To Watch** to add or remove categories from the Categorized Spending List.

6. Click **Show Spending Report** to display a Spending By Category report for the month.

Use the Calculators, Budgets, and Other Tools

Quicken provides several additional sets of tools to help you plan and achieve your financial goals. The calculators provide a quick look at your financial situation for a particular event without having to enter all the data in plan assumptions. The Budget tool helps you create a budget manually or helps you guide Quicken to set it up automatically. The Cash Flow Forecast helps you chart your cash flow, and you can identify and fund your dreams using the Savings Goals tool.

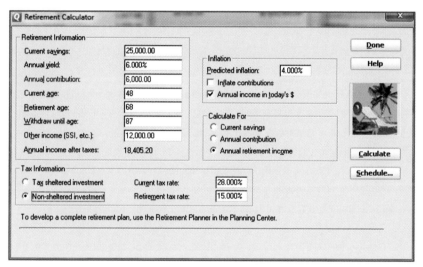

Figure 9-8: *The Retirement Calculator helps you see how you will fare in retirement.*

Get Quick Answers with Calculators

The five Quicken calculators—Retirement, College, Refinance, Savings, and Loan—help you to quickly calculate your current position without having to enter all of your assumptions. Each calculator has different questions but performs in the same manner. This section uses the Retirement Calculator as an example.

The Retirement Calculator lets you quickly see where you stand in your retirement preparations, as shown in Figure 9-8. To use it:

1. Click the **Planning** tab, and from the Tools Action Bar, click **Financial Calculators** and click **Retirement Calculator**.

2. Click in each of the fields, and select or type the information that is requested.

3. Click **Done** when you have finished with your calculations.

Create a Budget

A budget is simply a formal spending plan. Whether you scribble it on the back of an envelope or create color-coded charts and graphs, a budget helps you understand where your money comes from and where it goes. Quicken provides a tool you can use to create a budget simply and quickly using the data you have already entered. There are two steps in budgeting: setting it up and then fine-tuning the income, expense, and savings information.

SET UP A BUDGET

To set up your budget in Quicken:

1. From the Planning tab's Tools Action Bar, click **Other Tools** and then click **Budget**. The Budget window opens. If it is not already displayed, click the **Setup** tab to begin.

2. If you want Quicken to use your data to create an initial budget you can modify, click **Automatic**. If you want a blank budget template into which you can enter information, click **Manual**. Then click **Create Budget**.

3. If you chose Automatic, click **Create Budget** to open the Create Budget: Automatic dialog box.

4. In the Choose Date Range To Scan area, enter a date range from which Quicken will create your budget.

5. In the Select Budget Method area, click the **Average Amounts** option, click the corresponding down arrow, and choose from a list of time periods for computing averages.

6. Click **Monthly Detail** or **Quarterly Detail** to have Quicken use these amounts rather than the averages.

7. In the Options area, click the **Round Values To Nearest** check box, click the corresponding down arrow, and choose the detail for rounding averages.

8. Click **Exclude One-Time Transactions** to eliminate these transactions from the calculation.

9. Click the **Categories** button to include or exclude accounts or categories from the calculations. Click **OK** to close the Choose Categories dialog box.

10. Click **OK** to create the budget. A dialog box appears stating that the budget has been created and that you are to use the tabs at the top of the Budget window to proceed.

11. Click **OK** to close the dialog box. The Budget window opens with the income and expense categories displayed along the left side.

CREATE ADDITIONAL BUDGETS

After you have created your original budget, you can add, replace, edit, or delete other budgets.

1. From the Planning tab's Tools Action Bar, click **Other Tools** and click **Budget**.

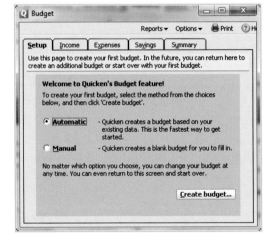

2. Click the **Setup** tab. If you have created a budget before, the dialog says "Create Another Budget," as seen in Figure 9-9.

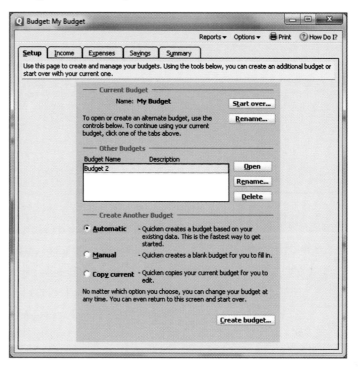

Figure 9-9: ***You can create more than one budget with the Quicken Budget dialog box.***

3. Click **Start Over** to open the Create Budget dialog as described previously.

4. Click **Rename** to rename your current budget.

5. If you have created additional budgets, select that budget in the Other Budgets section. Click **Open** to open the selected budget.

6. Click **Rename** to rename the selected budget, and click **Delete** to delete the selected budget.

7. If you choose to create another budget, click **Automatic** to create a new budget based on existing data. Click **Manual** to open a new, blank budget template.

8. Click **Open** to open a budget you have already created.

9. Click **Copy Current** to copy the current budget so that you can edit it.

10. Follow the steps outlined in "Set Up a Budget" earlier in this chapter.

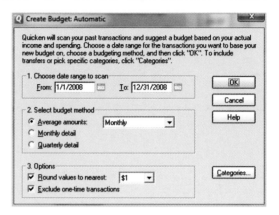

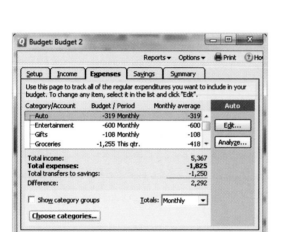

FINE-TUNE THE BUDGET

The Income, Expense, and Savings categories in the Budget window display details pertaining to your budget based on the assumptions you chose in the previous procedure. If you want to make changes:

1. Click one of the categories and/or accounts, and then click one of the options on the right—**Average Amount**, **Monthly Detail**, or **Quarterly Detail**—to change the original method. Click in each of the fields, and select or type the information that is appropriate for this expense, clicking **Next** as needed and clicking **OK** to return from any subsidiary dialog box you open.

2. Click **Close** to close the Budget window.

Work with Your Budget

After you have taken the time to create your budget, you may change its focus to create reports, print the reports, and create graphs from the results.

1. From the Planning tab's Tools Action Bar, click **Other Tools** and click **Budget**. The Budget dialog box appears with the Summary tab displayed.

2. Click **Reports** on the Budget Menu bar, and select one of the three report options, each of which can be customized to meet your requirements.

   - **Budget Report** creates a standard report based on parameters you set.
   - **Monthly Budget Report** creates a report by month rather than by annual amounts.
   - **Monthly Budget Graph** graphically portrays how much over or under each item is compared to the budget for the time period you stipulate.

3. Click **Options** to open the Options menu.

   - Click **Save Budget** or **Restore Budget**, if they are available, to save the current budget or restore it to the original settings.
   - Click **Show Cents** to display the cents in all the totals. By default, Quicken will round to the nearest dollar.

4. Select one of the three available budget views.

   - **Separate View** shows each set of categories—Income, Expense, and Savings—as separate tabs so that you can focus on one budget area at a time.
   - **Income/Expense View** includes income transfers and categories as part of the Income tab and expense transfers as part of the Expense tab.
   - **Combined View** includes all categories and transfers on one tab, the Budget tab, so that you can see all categories in one list.

5. Click **Set Up Alerts** to open the Alerts center. See Chapter 5 for information on setting alerts in Quicken.

6. Click **Go To Category List** to open the Quicken Category List.

7. Click **Print** to open the Windows Print dialog box and print your budget.

8. Click **How Do I** for budget-specific help.

9. At the bottom of the Summary tab, click the **Run A Budget Report** link to create a year-to-date budget report.

10. Click the **Scheduled Savings Transfer** link to open the Bills And Income Reminders dialog to enter a regularly scheduled savings transfer.

11. Click the **Savings Goal** link to open the Savings Goal dialog box.

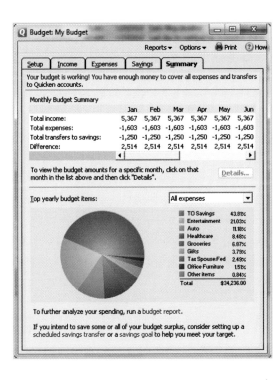

To further analyze your spending, run a budget report.

If you intend to save some or all of your budget surplus, consider setting up a scheduled savings transfer or a savings goal to help you meet your target.

SET A SAVINGS GOAL

Writing down a goal is often the best way to achieve it. The Savings Goal dialog box lets you plan for some future event, such as a world cruise or a vacation home, and save for it systematically. This is *not* a real bank account—it is just a way to track your savings (and hide it from yourself). To start from scratch to set a savings goal:

1. From the Planning tab's Tools Action Bar, click **Other Tools** and click **Savings Goals**.
2. When the Savings Goals dialog box appears, click **New**. The Create New Savings Goal dialog appears.
3. Click in the **Goal Name** text box, and type the name of your goal. Press **TAB** to continue.
4. Type what you want to save toward the goal in the Goal Amount text box.
5. Type the date by which you want to achieve this goal in the Finish Date text box.
6. Click **OK** to create the goal. At the bottom of the Savings Goals dialog is a progress bar, which you can use to track your savings. Quicken computes the projected monthly contribution you must make to achieve the goal by the finish date you entered.

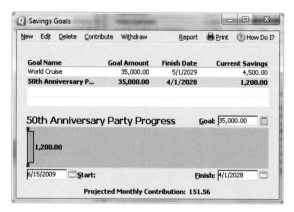

How to...

- *Enter the Tax Planner Options*
- *Enter Income into the Tax Planner*
- *Using the Tax Line in Categories*
- *Enter Interest, Dividend, and Business Income*
- *Enter Capital Gains*
- *Work with Other Income or Losses*
- *Determining the Type of Capital Gain*
- *Work with Income Adjustments and Deductions*
- *Deducting State Sales Tax*
- *Update Your Federal Withholdings*
- *Assign Tax-Related Expenses*
- *See Your Taxable Income*
- *Use Tax Tools*
- *Creating Tax Reports*
- *Use the Tax Category Audit*
- *Use the Deduction Finder*
- *Use the Itemized Deduction Estimator*
- *Use the Tax Withholding Estimator*

Chapter 10

Getting Ready for Tax Time

Tax preparation can be stressful and frustrating. You have to locate and organize your financial records, read complex publications, and fill out forms that are difficult to read, much less understand. In many cases, it means writing a check to the federal and/or state government taxing authority and worrying about how much more you will owe next year. Quicken can lessen the burden. With its organizational features, it can help you be ready well before the tax due date. Quicken also has a Tax Planner, a tool that helps you determine which deductions you can take, and another tool to help you decide how much withholdings you should claim. You can access additional tools online through the links provided in the Tax tab of the Planning tab. With Quicken, April 15 can be just another day in your smooth financial life.

Use the Tax Planner

The basis for all of your tax information can be entered into the Tax Planner. The Planner helps you evaluate your income tax position. It bases its estimates on numbers you give it, on the data you've entered into Quicken, or on last year's TurboTax return. It covers such areas as your employment income, interest, and dividends you earn; deductions and exemptions; withholding; and other taxes or credits for which you may be liable. Figure 10-1 shows an example of the Tax

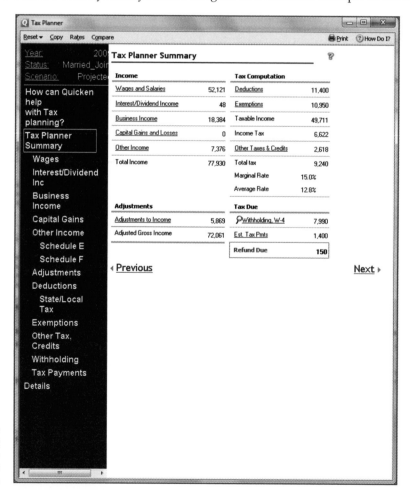

Figure 10-1: *The Tax Planner Summary worksheet displays information from Quicken or TurboTax, or that you enter yourself.*

Planner Summary worksheet. If you entered information earlier, the Tax Planner starts with that information; however, you can change it at any time.

Enter the Tax Planner Options

If you did not use the Setup tab to enter the information about yourself, the Tax Planner uses the Quicken default settings. These settings appear in the upper-left area of the Tax Planner.

To access the Tax Planner:

1. If the Planning tab is not present, click **View | Tabs To Show**, and choose Planning.

2. If needed, click the **Planning** tab to display it. From the Action Bar's View, click the **Tax Center** subtab. Click **Show Tax Planner** at the bottom of the Projected Tax section, as seen in Figure 10-2. A message box appears asking if you want to import your TurboTax data. If you do, click **Yes** and answer the TurboTax Data Import questions that are asked. If you do not have TurboTax data to import, or if you want to do it at another time, click **No**. If you choose to import Turbo Tax data at a later time, the Tax Planner appears.

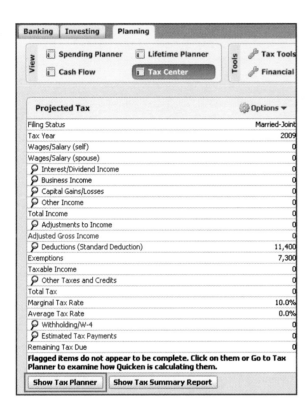

Figure 10-2: Open the Tax Planner from the Tax Center in the Planning tab.

3. Click **Year** in the upper-left area of the Tax Planner to open the Tax Planner Options in the right pane, and select the year you want to use. While you can click the **Year** down arrow to choose another year for which to plan, there is only one instance in which you want and can do it—the first quarter of a year in which you may still be working with the previous year. The default is the current year. If you try to change to a future year,

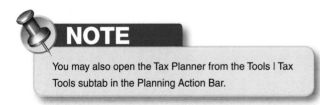

NOTE

You may also open the Tax Planner from the Tools | Tax Tools subtab in the Planning Action Bar.

a message box appears telling you that Quicken cannot display tax values for a future year. Click **OK** to return to Tax Planner Options.

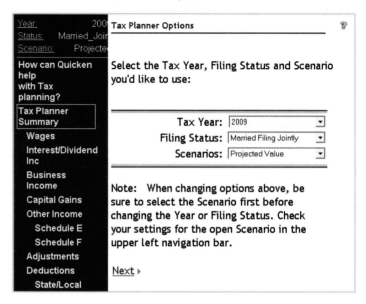

CAUTION

If you have entered information in the Planner before this session, change your scenario before you make changes to either the Status or Year fields.

TIP

If you create more than one scenario, you can compare them. Click **Compare** in the Tool Bar in the Tax Planner after you have entered data into two different scenarios.

TIP

From the left pane of the Tax Planner, click **Details** to learn more about the Planner. This opens a Help window displaying information about using the Tax Planner. When you are finished, click **Close** to return to the Tax Planner Summary.

NOTE

Items that Quicken does not consider complete are flagged with a small magnifying glass icon.

4. Click the **Filing Status** down arrow to change your income tax filing status from the default, Married Filing Jointly, if necessary. If you are not sure of your status, consult your tax professional.

5. Click the **Scenario** down arrow to create a new scenario. You can create up to three additional scenarios in the Tax Planner. For example, if you are thinking of starting a small business, you could enter information about your projected income in a second scenario to see how it would affect your tax situation.

6. Click **Next**. The How Can Quicken Help With Tax Planning page is displayed. If you see the Tax Planner Summary instead, which means that the Tax Planner has been used in the past, click **How Can Quicken Help With Tax Planning** in the left pane. If you have a previous scenario, that scenario will open in the place of How Can Quicken Help With Tax Planning.

Figure 10-3: The first step in tax planning is entering information into the Wages worksheet.

NOTE

If you are entering a projected-values scenario, you have the option of showing the details about where the information came from. To show the detail information, click one of the underlined text entries, or click **Show Details**. If you are using an alternate scenario, you do not have this option.

---

7. If you are not already at the Tax Planning Summary, when you are finished with the How Can Quicken Help With Tax Planning page, click **Let's Get Started**. The Tax Planner Summary appears. Unless you have an existing scenario that either you built or Quicken built out of your current year's data, the Tax Planner Summary should be mainly blank and you need to begin by filling it in.

8. From the Tax Planner Summary, click **Next** to continue to the Wages worksheet, as shown in Figure 10-3.

Enter Income into the Tax Planner

Start the Planner by entering your income information.

1. If the Tax Planner isn't already displayed, click the **Planning** tab, click **Tax Center** in the View subtab, click **Show Tax Planner** at the bottom of the Projected Tax area, and click **Wages** on the left, or click **Wages And Salaries** in the Tax Planner Summary. The Wages worksheet is displayed as seen in Figure 10-3.

2. Click in the **Wages And Salaries – Self** text box. Enter the amount of wages or salary you expect to earn for the year. After you enter the information, your projected tax due or refund due is computed and displayed.

3. Click in the **Wages and Salaries – Self (Other)** text box, and enter the taxable amounts from other income sources. Check with your tax professional to find out if this option applies to you.

4. Click in the **Wages And Salaries – Spouse** text box, and enter your spouse's wages.

5. Click in the **Wages And Salaries – Spouse (Other)** text box, and enter any other income amounts. The total wages for the both of you is displayed in the Total Wages field.

6. Click **Next** to continue to the Interest And Dividend Income worksheet.

USING THE TAX LINE IN CATEGORIES

You have the option to include tax information when entering a new category.

1. Click the **Tools** menu, and click **Category List**.

2. Click **New** in the upper-right area of the window to enter a new category, or select an existing category and click **Edit**.

3. Click the **Tax Line Item** down arrow to display a list of possible tax-line items. These items are arranged by IRS form number and schedule letter. Check with your tax professional if you have questions about the meaning of each tax line. Click the name of the tax item.

4. Click **Extended Line Item List** if the item you need does not appear on the standard line-item list, and then click the **Tax Line Item** down arrow and click the item you want you use.

5. Click the **Tax-Related** check box.

6. Click **OK** to close the Edit Category dialog.

7. Close the Category List.

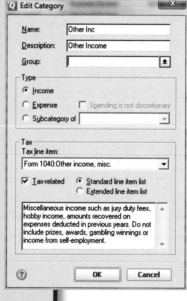

NOTE

On a profit-and-loss statement outside of Quicken, what is called gross margin by Quicken might be called *gross profit* or *gross income*.

Enter Interest, Dividend, and Business Income

If you have received forms from your financial institutions, such as 1099-INTs or partnership K-1s, use the information shown on these forms. Otherwise, enter estimates in this area.

1. If the Tax Planner isn't already displayed, click the **Planning** tab, click the **Tax Center** subtab in the View Action Bar, click **Show Tax Planner** at the bottom of the Projected Tax area, and click **Interest/Dividend Inc** in the left pane.

2. Click in the **Taxable Interest Income** text box, and enter the amount of taxable interest you will receive for the year from savings, money market accounts, or other loans you have made.

3. Click in the **Dividends** text box, and enter all the amounts reported on K-1 forms from mutual funds, stocks, partnerships, estates, trusts, or S corporations. If you have not yet received a K-1 form, estimate the amount that you received.

4. Click **Next** to display the Business Income worksheet.

5. If you have a small business, use this worksheet to enter the information from your Schedule C (see Figure 10-4) or from a profit-and-loss statement.

6. Click in the **Revenue-Self** text box, and enter the total revenue for your business. Click in the **Revenue Spouse** text box, and enter the revenue for your spouse's business, if applicable.

7. Click in the **Cost Of Goods Sold** text box, and enter the costs of the items you sold for each business. After you have entered the cost of goods sold, the gross margin appears. The gross margin is the total revenue minus the total cost of goods sold.

8. If you have associated any expense category with a Tax Schedule C line, that amount will appear in the appropriate fields. Click in the **Other Allowable Expenses** and the **Unspecified Business Expenses** text boxes to enter any additional amounts. After you have entered the amount for these expenses, Quicken calculates your total expenses.

CAUTION

There are some specific rules about using your home or part of it for your business. Consult your tax professional for more information.

9. Click in the **Exp. For Business Use Of Home** text box, and enter the amount you allot for the business use of your home. The total business income or loss amount is displayed for each business, as well as the total remaining tax due.

10. Click **Next** to display the Capital Gains And Losses worksheet.

Enter Capital Gains

Before you can enter information into the Capital Gains And Losses worksheet, you must know whether a gain is a short-term or a long-term gain. See the QuickFacts "Determining the Type of Capital Gain" later in this chapter. A capital gain is the difference between the price for which you have sold an asset and the price you paid for it. You *realize*, or achieve, a capital gain when you sell an investment for more than you paid for it. (You may receive information from your broker that some of your investments have *unrealized* capital gains. That means an investment hasn't been sold yet, but would give you a profit if you did sell it.) You may owe federal income tax (and in some cases, state income tax) on that capital gain. Capital gains are earned on many types of investments, including mutual funds, bonds, stocks, homes, and businesses. If you sell an investment for less than you paid for it, you have a *capital loss*.

When you use the Capital Gains And Losses worksheet, make sure you understand which type of gain or loss, short-term or long-term, you are entering. In this, as in all areas, it is important that you consult with your tax professional.

1. If the Tax Planner isn't already displayed, click the **Planning** tab, click **Tax Center** in the View subtab, click **Show Tax Planner** at the bottom of the Projected Tax area, and click **Capital Gains** in the left pane.

Figure 10-4: If you operate a small business, enter the data from a financial statement.

NOTE

Unrecaptured depreciation is a special type of gain that may apply when you sell real property you have previously depreciated, as you might with a home office or a daycare center in your home. Consult your tax professional if you feel this might apply to you.

NOTE

Long-term 28% property is taxed at a special rate. Check with your tax professional to determine if any of your property falls under this classification.

QUICKFACTS

DETERMINING THE TYPE OF CAPITAL GAIN

A capital gain can be either long-term or short-term, depending on the length of time you have owned an asset. Generally speaking:

- Any asset you have owned for less than 12 months and one day is considered a short-term asset.

- Normally, a gain on a short-term asset is taxed at your regular income tax rate.

- Any asset you have owned for more than 12 months and one day is deemed to be a long-term asset and is taxed at a special rate, depending on your tax bracket.

- Additional information about how to determine whether an asset is short-term or long-term can be found in IRS publications or from your tax professional.

2. Click in the **Short-Term Gains And Losses** text box, and enter the result you get when you subtract your short-term losses from any short-term gains.

3. Click in the **Unrecaptured Depreciation Gains** text box, and enter any unrecaptured depreciation you have.

4. Click in the **Long-Term 28% Gains And Losses** text box, and enter the gains or losses you have that fall into this tax category.

5. Click in the **Long-Term Gains And Losses** text box, and enter the amount of your long-term gains or losses.

6. Click in the **Loss Carryovers From Prior Years Short Term** and **Long Term** text boxes, and enter any losses from previous years that you had to carry over to this year.

7. Click **Next** to display the Other Income Or Losses worksheet.

Work with Other Income or Losses

The Other Income Or Losses worksheet allows you to enter information that affects your tax situation but that is not covered in other areas of the Tax Planner. These items include taxable state income tax refunds, alimony, taxable Social Security benefits, and so on. As with all items in the Tax Planner, review your entries and discuss them with your tax professional.

1. If the Tax Planner isn't already displayed, click the **Planning** tab, click the **Tax Center** subtab in the View Action Bar, click **Show Tax Planner** at the bottom of the Projected Tax area, and click **Other Income** in the left pane. Figure 10-5 displays a typical Other Income Or Losses worksheet.

2. If needed, click in the **Taxable Refund Of State/Local Income Tax** text box, and enter any refund of taxes that you deducted as an itemized deduction on your federal tax return in earlier years.

3. If needed, click in the **Alimony Received** text box, and enter the total amount of alimony received by either you or your spouse for the year.

4. If needed, click in the **Taxable IRA/Pension Distributions** text box, and enter any amounts shown on a Form 1099-R. These items can be complex. Check with your tax professional or consult IRS Publications 575 and 590.

Figure 10-5: Enter other income, such as unemployment benefits, into the Other Income Or Losses worksheet in your Tax Planner.

NOTE

The Tax Planner does not determine which, if any, of your Social Security or Railroad Retirement income is taxable. The instruction booklet that comes with your 1040 form has a worksheet to help you determine this. You can also consult your tax professional.

5. If needed, click the **Sched E Income-Rents, Royalties, And Partnerships** link. A corresponding worksheet is displayed. For each of the following categories where you have receipts:

   a. Click in the **Rents** text box, and enter any rental income you have received.

   b. Click in the **Royalties** or **Partnership Income/Loss** text box, and enter the relevant amounts. Quicken will calculate your total income from these items.

   c. Click in the **Depreciation** text box, and enter the total depreciation you claim on these items. Click in the **Expenses** text box, and enter any expenses relating to your rent income. Quicken calculates your net income or loss and displays it at the bottom of the worksheet.

   d. Click **Previous** to return to the Other Income Or Losses worksheet.

6. If needed, click the **Sched F Income-Farm** link. The Farm Income worksheet is displayed. Use the following categories as needed:

   a. Click in the **Sales** text box, and enter the total sales from farming.

   b. Click in the **Supplemental Payments** text box, and enter the total you have received in supplemental payments.

   c. Click in the **Other Income** text box, and enter the relevant amount. Quicken calculates the total income and displays it.

   d. Click in the **Expenses** text box, and enter the total expenses that pertain to farming. Quicken calculates the net income or loss from farming.

   e. Click **Previous** twice to return to the Other Income Or Losses worksheet.

7. If needed, click in the **Unemployment Compensation** text box, and enter the amount of unemployment benefits you received (or will receive) for this year.

8. If needed, click in the **Taxable Social Security Benefits** and **Social Security RRA Income** text boxes, and enter the relevant amount.

9. If needed, click in the **Other Income, Gains, Or Losses** text box, and enter money you won as a prize or award, jury duty stipends, or other such one-time income. You may receive a 1099 or other documentation showing the total taxable amount.

10. Click **Next** three times or click **Adjustments** in the left pane to display the Adjustments To Income worksheet.

Work with Income Adjustments and Deductions

After entering all your income, you need to consider those items that reduce your income before taxes. These are primarily income adjustments, deductions, exemptions, and tax credits.

ENTER ADJUSTMENT TO INCOME

Adjustments to income are those items that, while not deductible, reduce your income. They include Individual Retirement Account (IRA) contributions, health insurance paid by self-employed persons, Keogh or Simplified Employee Pension (SEP) contributions, alimony you have paid, moving expenses, and other adjustments.

1. If the Tax Planner isn't already displayed, click the **Planning** tab, click **Tax Center** in the View subtab, click **Show Tax Planner** at the bottom of the Projected Tax area, and click **Adjustments** in the left pane.

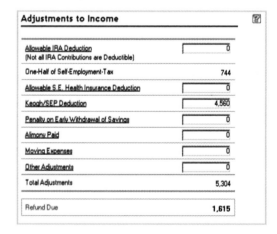

2. Click in each text box, and enter the relevant amounts if any of these items pertain to you.

3. Click **Next** to display the Standard And Itemized Deductions worksheet.

ENTER STANDARD AND ITEMIZED DEDUCTIONS

According to the IRS, most people take the standard deduction to reduce their income tax bill. However, if you pay high mortgage interest payments or have

State and Local Income Tax

Projected Withholdings	SELF	SPOUSE
Withholdings	1,230	56
Next Pay Date	10/01/09	10/09/09
Pay Period	Every 2 weeks	Every 2 weeks
Withholding per Pay Period	Project: Included	Sched: Included
Projected Future Withholding	1,230	0
Projected Total Withholding	1,230	56
Projected Total Withholdings for Self and Spouse		1,286
Estimated Taxes Paid to Date plus Projected Payments Through Year-End		0
Tax Payments this Year for Last Year's State Tax		0
Total Tax Payments to Date plus Projected Withholding Through Year-End		1,286
Refund Due		**1,615**

large medical bills, itemizing your deductions might reduce your tax liability even more. Quicken provides a Deduction Finder to help you with this. See "Use the Deduction Finder" later in this chapter.

1. If the Tax Planner isn't already displayed, click the **Planning** tab, click **Tax Center** in the View subtab, click **Show Tax Planner** at the bottom of the Projected Tax area, and click **Deductions** in the left pane.

2. Click in the **Medical And Dental Expense** field to enter all of your medical and dental expenses for the year. Quicken will compute the amount of your deduction, if you can take one, and display it in the Allowable Medical Deduction area. If you cannot take a deduction, the Allowable Medical Deduction area shows zero.

3. If your state or locality has an income tax, click **State & Local Income Tax** to display the State And Local Income Tax worksheet. If figures are already filled in from the paycheck detail you entered and you believe that it is correct, you can skip to step 4. Otherwise:

   a. Click in the **Withholdings To Date** text box, and enter the state or local withholding amounts for you and your spouse through your last paychecks. This information should appear on your paystubs.

   b. Click in the **Next Pay Date** text box, and enter the date on which you will receive your next paychecks.

   c. Click the **Pay Period** down arrow, and choose how often each of you is paid.

   d. Click in the **Withholding Per Pay Period** text box, and enter the amount of state or local taxes withheld from your paychecks.

   e. Click in the **Estimated Taxes Paid To Date Plus Projected Payments Through Year End** text box, and enter how much estimated tax you have paid to the state and local taxing authorities.

   f. Click in the **Tax Payments This Year For Last Year's State Tax** text box, and enter any amounts you have paid in state income tax during this calendar year.

   g. Quicken calculates what your total payments for state and local income taxes will be.

   h. Click **Previous** to return to the Standard And Itemized Deductions worksheet.

4. Click in the **Real Estate And Other Taxes** text box, and enter the amount of real estate taxes you have paid or will pay for the current year.

5. Click in the **Deductible Investment Interest** text box, and enter the relevant amount.

6. Click in the **Mortgage & Other Deductible Interest** text box, and enter your mortgage interest, as shown on the Form 1098 you received from your mortgage company.

7. Click in the **Charitable Contributions** text box, and enter the amount of money you have given to charity for the current year. The Tax Planner will adjust your deduction to comply with IRS regulations.

8. Click in the **Deductible Casualty Losses** text box, and enter any losses in this category. To understand what you can deduct, consult your tax professional.

9. Click in the **Misc. Deductions** and **Misc. Deductions (No Limit)** text boxes, and enter any qualifying deductions. Quicken will calculate your total itemized deductions.

10. In the Standard Deduction column, click any check box that pertains to your situation. The amount of your standard deduction appears in the Deduction field. If your itemized deductions are larger than your standard deduction, the larger amount appears in the Larger Of Itemized Or Standard Deduction field.

Itemized Deductions (Schedule A)		Standard Deduction	
Medical and Dental Expense	890	☐ Taxpayer can be claimed as a dependent on another return.	
Allowable Medical Deduction	0		
State & Local Income Tax	1,286	SELF ☐ Blind ☐ 65 or Older	
Real Estate and Other Taxes	0	SPOUSE	
Deductible Investment Interest	0	☐ Blind ☐ 65 or Older	
Mortgage & Other Deductible Interest	4,500	Deduction 11,400	
Charitable Contributions	325	**Deduction**	
Deductible Casualty Losses	0	Larger of Itemized or Standard Deduction	
Misc. Deductions	0	11,400	
Less: Income-Related and Misc. Deduction Limitations	0		
Misc. Deductions (No Limit)	0	**Refund Due**	
Total Itemized Deductions	6,111	1,615	

Exemptions

Number of Exemptions	
Self and Spouse	2
Dependents	1
Total Exemptions	3
Exemption deduction	10,950
Refund Due	**1,615**

11. Click **Next** twice to display the Exemptions worksheet.

12. If you have entered information about your family in the Setup tab, some of the information about your situation is already displayed. If the information is not complete, enter the relevant information and click **Next** to display the Other Taxes And Credits worksheet. The information you entered earlier regarding your self-employment income is already included on this worksheet. If your tax professional tells you that you are subject to the alternative minimum tax, enter any relevant information; otherwise, click **Next** to display the Federal Withholdings worksheet.

DEDUCTING STATE SALES TAX

Under current law, taxpayers may deduct state and local sales tax from their tax returns if they itemize their deductions. However, you should consider the following:

- To take the deduction, you must itemize deductions.

- If you live in a state that collects income tax, you must choose to deduct either the state (or local) income tax you paid or the sales tax deduction—you cannot deduct both.

- You can add up the sales tax you paid from your cash register and credit card receipts to determine your deduction. This requires that you keep these receipts with your income tax records for the year.

- Alternatively, you can use the appropriate amount from the sales tax tables created by the IRS. These tables are included in your Form 1040 packet and are also available online at the IRS website: www.irs.gov.

- The American Recovery and Reinvestment Act of 2009 provides a deduction for state and local sales and excise taxes paid on the purchase of qualified new vehicles through 2009.

- You may want to consult your tax professional to see if you qualify for any of these deductions.

Update Your Federal Withholdings

The Withholdings worksheet may already display information you have entered, either from your paycheck setup or on earlier worksheets of the Tax Planner. If not, enter the information as needed.

In the center of the worksheet, the Tax Payment Summary displays your projected tax as well as your projected withholdings from the Total Withholdings To Date amount. Your estimated tax due or refund due has been calculated by Quicken, as shown in Figure 10-6.

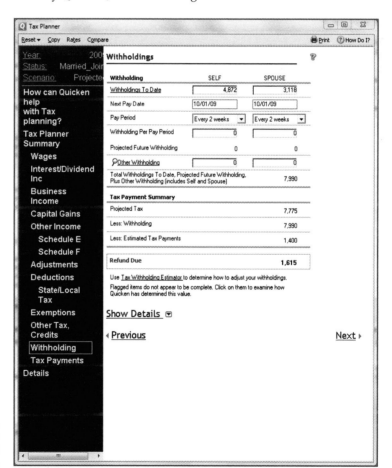

Figure 10-6: The Withholdings worksheet displays your projected withholdings as well as your current tax or refund due.

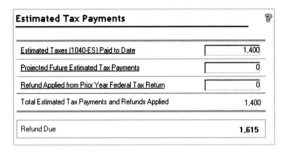

ESTIMATED TAX PAYMENTS

You may enter your total estimated tax payments for the year in the Estimated Tax Payments worksheet.

1. If the Tax Planner isn't already displayed, click the **Planning** tab, click **Tax Center** in the View subtab, click **Show Tax Planner** at the bottom of the Projected Tax area, and click **Tax Payments** in the left pane.

2. Click the **Estimated Taxes (1040-ES) Paid To Date** to enter the amount you have paid this year to date.

3. Click **Projected Future Estimated Tax Payments** to enter any amounts you plan on paying for this year.

4. Enter the amount of refund from prior years.

5. Quicken will total your estimated payments.

TAX PLANNER DETAILS

If you are using the Projected scenario (it's not available with the other scenarios), you can review the details and make any changes to your Tax Planner information from the Tax Planner Details worksheet.

1. If the Tax Planner isn't already displayed, click the **Planning** tab, click **Tax Center** in the View subtab, and click **Show Tax Planner** at the bottom of the Projected Tax area.

2. Click **Details** in the left pane, and click the **Form** down arrow to choose the form you want to change.

3. Click the **Item** down arrow to select the specific item with which you want to work.

4. Click **Return To Tax Planner Summary** when you have entered all the information you wish to change and you want to see the result of your entries into the Tax Planner. A sample Tax Planner Summary is shown in Figure 10-1.

5. Click **Close** to close the Tax Planner when you're ready.

NOTE

The Tax Withholding Estimator helps you determine how much to withhold from your paycheck. See "Use the Tax Withholding Estimator" later in this chapter for more information.

NOTE

The Tax Calendar, which appears in the Tax Center, displays the important tax dates for the current taxing period.

TIP

The Projected Tax section of the Tax tab displays the information you entered into Quicken or the Tax Planner. You can click any of the links to go to the relevant Tax Planner.

Work with the Tax Center

The Tax Center subtab in the Planning tab provides an overview of your tax standing at any time during the year. It shows your projected tax, the tax calendar, any tax-related expenses, and all of your taxable income for the year. From the Tax Tools subtab, the Tax Center offers a variety of tools to help you plan. All of this information is based on data you have entered. You can adjust this data, add to it, and create reports based on it. While ultimately all tax questions should be reviewed with your tax professional, Quicken provides a host of useful tools and reports to help you. To see what information is currently available in the Tax Center:

- Click the **Planning** tab, click the View Action Bar, click **Tax Center** to display your tax information, as shown in Figure 10-7.

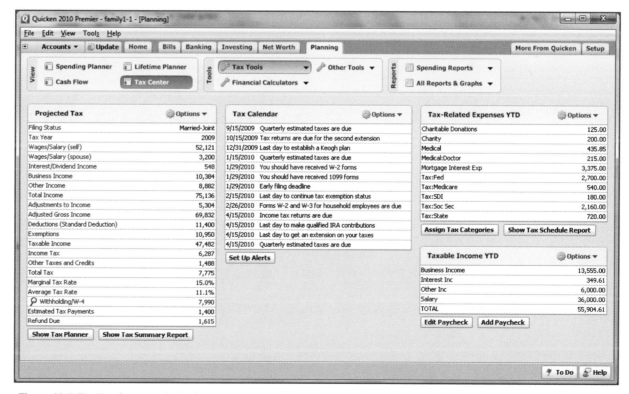

Figure 10-7: The Tax Center subtab gives an overview of your tax information and provides you with links to several tax tools.

Tax-Related Expenses YTD   ⚙ Options ▾

Charitable Donations	125.00
Charity	200.00
Medical	435.85
Medical:Doctor	215.00
Mortgage Interest Exp	3,375.00
Tax:Fed	2,700.00
Tax:Medicare	540.00
Tax:SDI	180.00
Tax:Soc Sec	2,160.00
Tax:State	720.00

| Assign Tax Categories | Show Tax Schedule Report |

Assign Tax-Related Expenses

The Tax-Related Expenses YTD section of the Tax Center helps you track any tax-related expenses. To assign a tax line to an expense category:

1. Click **Assign Tax Categories** at the bottom of the Tax-Related Expenses YTD section to open the Category List.

2. Select the category to which you want to assign a tax line, scroll to the right, and click **Edit** on the right of that category.

3. From the Edit Category dialog, click **Standard List** under the Tax Line Item Assignments section on the right of the window.

4. Click the **Tax Line Item** down arrow, and click the tax line that is relevant for the category. If the tax item you want to assign does not appear on the Standard List, click **Extended List** to include more tax items, and click the appropriate tax line.

5. Click **OK** to return to the Category List, and click **Done** to close the Category List and return to the Tax Center.

6. Click **Show Tax Schedule Report** to display an itemized report of the information that relates to income tax schedules, as seen in Figure 10-8.

7. Close the Tax Schedule report. Back in the Tax Center, click **Options** in the title bar of the Tax Related Expenses YTD section to open a menu from which you can:

   - Find other deductions by using the Deduction Finder, as discussed later in this chapter.

   - Learn how your deductions will change your income tax liability.

   - Create a tax schedule report.

   - Link categories to tax forms.

   - Audit your tax categories (see "Use the Tax Category Audit" later in this chapter).

   - Go to the Category List to make any tax or other changes.

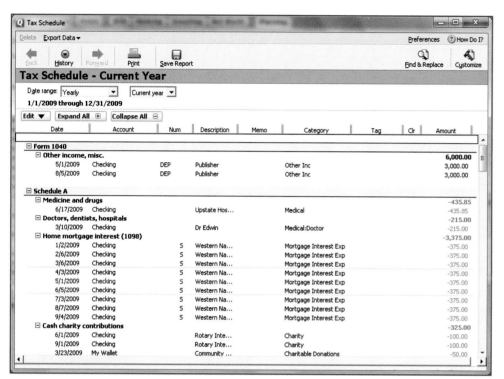

Figure 10-8: *As you enter information into Quicken, you can run a report that shows the detail for each income tax schedule.*

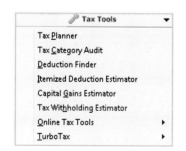

See Your Taxable Income

The Taxable Income YTD section offers links to edit an existing paycheck or add a new paycheck, which are discussed in Chapter 1. From the Options menu in the Taxable Income YTD section, you can:

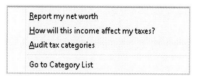

- Click **Report My Net Worth** to create a net worth report for any time period.

- Click **How Will This Income Affect My Taxes?** to open the Tax Planner.

- Click **Audit Tax Categories** to open the Tax Category Audit, discussed later in this chapter.

- Click **Go To Category List** to open the list if you want to make any changes.

Use Tax Tools

In the Planning tab, click Tools in the Action Bar, and click **Tax Tools** to see tools you can use to help with your tax planning.

- The **Tax Planner**, which is covered earlier in this chapter, helps you determine how much you will owe in taxes.

- Click **Tax Category Audit** to open the Tax Category Audit dialog, discussed later in this chapter.

- Click **Deduction Finder** to open the Deduction Finder, discussed later in this chapter.

- The **Itemized Deduction Finder** opens a worksheet that helps you find additional itemized deductions, as discussed in "Use the Itemized Deduction Estimator" later in this chapter.

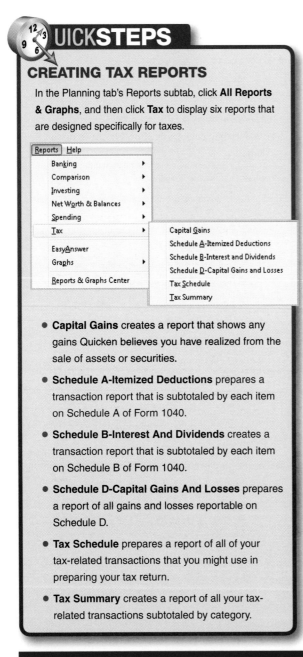

CREATING TAX REPORTS

In the Planning tab's Reports subtab, click **All Reports & Graphs**, and then click **Tax** to display six reports that are designed specifically for taxes.

- **Capital Gains** creates a report that shows any gains Quicken believes you have realized from the sale of assets or securities.

- **Schedule A-Itemized Deductions** prepares a transaction report that is subtotaled by each item on Schedule A of Form 1040.

- **Schedule B-Interest And Dividends** creates a transaction report that is subtotaled by each item on Schedule B of Form 1040.

- **Schedule D-Capital Gains And Losses** prepares a report of all gains and losses reportable on Schedule D.

- **Tax Schedule** prepares a report of all of your tax-related transactions that you might use in preparing your tax return.

- **Tax Summary** creates a report of all your tax-related transactions subtotaled by category.

- The **Capital Gains Estimator** helps you determine the tax implications of selling assets and investments. This wizard gives you general information about potential sales, but does not substitute for a financial or tax advisor. You can create up to three scenarios that combine with the information you entered into the Tax Planner. This utility is discussed in Chapter 8.

- The **Tax Withholding Estimator**, which is covered at the end of this chapter, helps you determine whether you are having the appropriate amount withheld from your earnings.

- Click **Online Tax Tools** to work with tax calculators and state and federal income tax forms, get answers to common tax questions, and access federal tax publications. You must have an Internet connection to use this feature.

- Click **Turbo Tax** to go online and use Turbo Tax, to order either a CD or downloaded version, or to import a current Turbo Tax file.

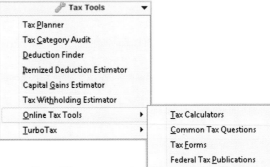

Use the Tax Category Audit

From the Planning tab's Action Bar, select **Tools**, click **Tax Tools**, and then click **Tax Category Audit** to open the worksheet.

1. The Tax Category Audit window opens, as shown in Figure 10-9. This utility checks two types of categories:

    - Standard categories that are not linked to the correct tax line

    - Categories you created that may need to be linked to a tax-line item or categories that are linked to an incorrect tax-line item:

        a. From the Proposed Tax Line Item Action section, click **Change** to make changes. The Edit Selected Tax Audit Category dialog will appear. When you are done using it, click **OK**.

        b. Click **Ignore** if you feel the tax-line assignment is correct, and the category is removed from the problem list.

        c. Click **Done** at the lower-left corner of the window to close it.

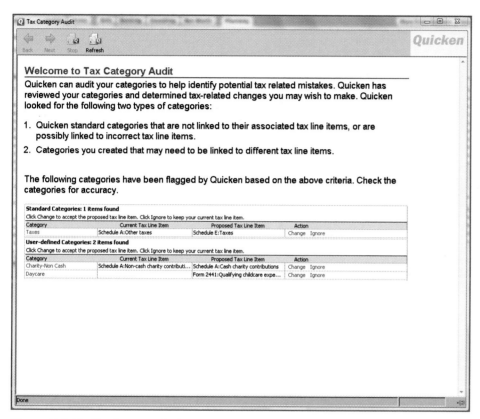

Figure 10-9: The Tax Category Audit dialog warns you of potentially incorrect tax-line assignments.

Use the Deduction Finder

If you are not sure you have assigned tax-line items for all of your categories, or if you would just like to identify other potential deductions, you can use the Deduction Finder.

1. From the Planning tab's Tools subtab, click **Tax Tools** and then click **Deduction Finder** to open the worksheet.

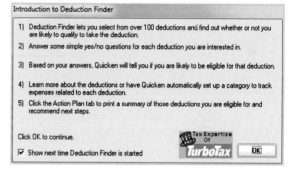

2. The Introduction To Deduction Finder dialog box appears, explaining how it works. Click **OK** to continue.

3. Click the **Choose A Deduction Type** down arrow, and click one of the six types of deductions from the drop-down list. A list of deductions appears on the left side of the window.

4. Click any item on the list to display questions about that possible deduction on the right side of the window. Click either **Yes** or **No** to answer each question, as shown in Figure 10-10.

5. After you have answered all the questions, a green check mark appears to the left of any deduction for which you may be eligible and a red X appears if you are not eligible. The result also is displayed at the bottom of the section.

6. Click **More Information** at the bottom of the window if you want to learn more about this deduction. Click **Create A Category** to display an explanation about a potential new category for this deduction, and then click **OK** to create it.

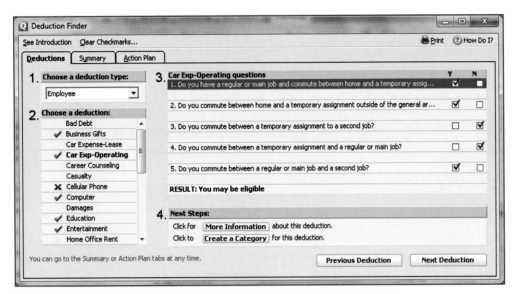

7. Click **Next Deduction** to go to the next deduction on the list, or select one that may pertain to your situation, and follow the same steps.

8. Click the **Summary** tab to see how many deductions are available for each deduction type, how many you have viewed and answered, and how many for which you are eligible.

9. Click the **Action Plan** tab to see the steps to take to use the deductions you have found.

10. Click **Clear Checkmarks** in the Menu bar to clear all of your answers and start over.

11. Click **Close** to close the Deduction Finder.

Figure 10-10: The Deduction Finder helps you find additional deductions for which you may be eligible.

Use the Itemized Deduction Estimator

You can take a wide variety of tax deductions, some of which are more common than others. Quicken provides the Itemized Deduction Estimator to ensure that you are deducting all to which you are entitled. It uses information from the Tax Planner and lets you create what-if scenarios. To use the Itemized Deduction Estimator:

1. From the Action Bar in the Planning tab, click **Tools**, click **Tax Tools**, and then click **Itemized Deduction Estimator** to open the worksheet.

2. A welcome message appears, shown in Figure 10-11. The Itemized Deduction Estimator displays your projected data as you entered it in the Tax Planner.

3. Click **Let's Get Started** to begin the process.

4. The Medical Deductions worksheet is displayed. Each worksheet in this wizard displays the tax projection data on the right side so you can see any changes. As you make entries into the scenario, your projected tax bill changes if your scenario information decreases your liability.

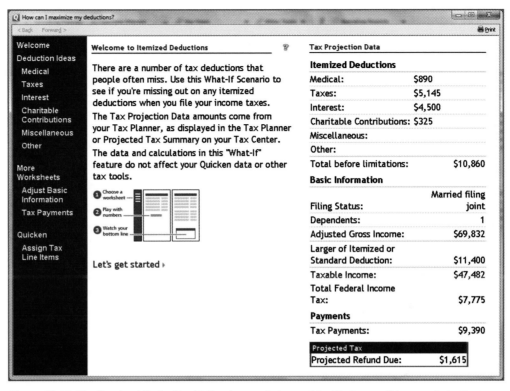

Figure 10-11: The Itemized Deduction Estimator can help you identify less well-known deductions.

5. Click in the **Miles Driven To And From Appointments** text box, and enter the number of miles you drove. Quicken will calculate the dollar value that is deductible, as shown in Figure 10-12.

6. Click in any of the remaining text boxes that are applicable to you, and enter any costs you incurred.

7. Enter any other relevant items in this worksheet. Your total additional medical expenses appear in the Total area.

8. Click **Next** to display the Taxes worksheet.

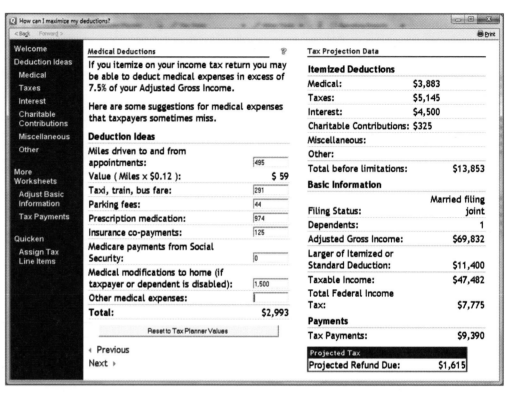

Figure 10-12: *The Medical Deductions worksheet helps you identify medical expenses you may not have remembered otherwise.*

ENTER REMAINING DEDUCTION WORKSHEETS

The remaining deduction worksheets follow a similar pattern to the Medical Deductions worksheet. Open the sheet by either clicking in the left column or clicking **Next** in the previous sheet. Then click in the text boxes that are applicable to you and type the amount. Close the Estimator when you are finished.

Use the Tax Withholding Estimator

The Tax Withholding Estimator Wizard allows you to determine how much you should have taken out of each paycheck. You can create a what-if scenario to ensure that you are not withholding too much or too little.

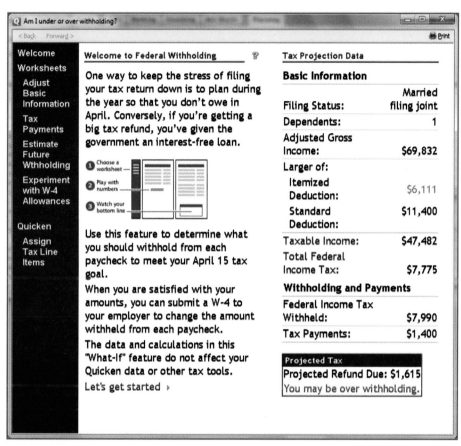

1. From the Planning tab's Action Bar, click **Tools**, click **Tax Tools**, and then click **Tax Withholding Estimator** to display the Tax Withholding Estimator, as shown in Figure 10-13. Each worksheet has two parts. The left section allows you to enter possible changes. The right side displays the tax-projection data reflecting the current information you have entered into Quicken or into your Tax Planner. As you make changes on the left side, the right side displays the result of those changes.

2. Click **Let's Get Started** to display the Adjust Basic Information worksheet. Select each of the fields you want to change, and either select or type the information that is correct for you, clicking **Next** as needed.

3. When you have completed all of the worksheets, click **W-4 Information** to create a printed worksheet you can take to work and use to complete a new W-4.

Figure 10-13: *Use the Tax Withholder Estimator to make sure you are not withholding too much or too little from your paycheck.*

NOTE

You should provide your employer with a new W-4 each January.

Numbers

401(k) accounts, 70
 adding, 84–86
 how Quicken works with, 195
 updating, 193–196
 See also retirement
403(b) accounts, 70
 adding, 84–86
 how Quicken works with, 195
 updating, 193–196
 See also retirement
529 Plan accounts, 70

A

Account Bar, changing, 34–35
Account Details dialog, 41–42
Account List dialog, 37–41
account registers, 35–36
 cash accounts, 124
 changing transactions, 113
 creating scheduled transactions, 139–141
 defined, 27, 99
 deleting transactions, 114
 differences between checking and credit card
  registers, 122
 entering a credit card charge, finance charge,
  or credit, 122–123
 entering checks into the register, 107–108
 entering credit card payments, 124
 entering deposits, 112
 filtering transactions, 117
 locating transactions, 116–117
 opening a register, 106
 printing, 121
 printing checks, 108–111

restoring deleted transactions, 113
 setting preferences, 100–103
 sorting transactions, 118
 splitting transactions, 113–115
 transferring funds from one account to another,
  115–116
 voiding transactions, 113–114
accounts
 adding investment accounts, 20–22
 adding manually, 18–20
 adding property and debt accounts, 22–23
 cash flow accounts, 47–50
 defined, 26
 deleting, 93
 editing, 41–42
 hiding, 94
 managing, 37–41
 online account access, 52
 types of, 27
 See also individual account types
Address Book, 23–24
adware, 53
 See also security
alerts, 165–166
 deleting, 166
amortization schedules, printing, 96–97
asset accounts, 87
Asset Allocation Guide, 210–214
assets, 70
 adjusting the value of, 156–157
 linking multiple liability accounts to one
  asset account, 156
 linking to a liability account, 155
 updating, 197
Automatic Categorization, 108
Average Annual Return tool, 208–210

B

backing up data, 67–68
bank accounts
 setting up a bank account manually, 9–10
 setting up a bank account with online services,
  7–9
banking alerts, 165
 setting up, 166
Banking menu, 41
Bill Pay, 51, 52, 61
 See also online services
bills
 adding recurring bills, 10–12
 scheduling, 134–137
Bills menu, 40–41
brokerage, 70
brokerage accounts, 70
 setting up, 72–76
budgets
 changing, 254
 creating, 251–254
 creating reports and graphs from, 254–255
 printing, 255
Buy/Sell Preview tool, 217

C

calculators
 Loan Calculator, 174–175
 Refinance Calculator, 174
 Retirement Calculator, 251
calendar, 43–45, 143–144
 color-coding information, 147
 options, 147
 showing transactions, 147
 working with specific dates, 145–146

capital gains
  determining the type of, 264
  entering in Tax Planner, 263–264
Capital Gains Estimator, 217–219
capital improvements, recording, 156–157
capital losses, 263–264
cash accounts, 124
cash flow accounts, 47–50
categories, 61
  adding, 63, 64–65
  assigning category groups, 65
  Automatic Categorization, 108
  Category List, 62–64
  creating, 112
  defined, 27
  deleting, 67
  inserting an expense category with
    subcategories, 66–67
  removing, 63
  renaming, 66
  Tax Category Audit, 274
  using the tax line, 262
check boxes, 30
checking accounts, 99
  entering a check, 107–108
  entering a deposit, 112
  entering credit card payments, 124
  including in planning, 233–234
  opening a register, 106
  preferences for writing checks, 104–105
  printing checks, 108–111
  registers, 122
checks
  entering into the register, 107–108
  printing, 108–111
Classic menus, 40–42
Clipboard, 121

Close button, 18
college expenses, 240
  529 Plan accounts, 70
  planning to pay for college, 241–242
command buttons, 30
connection methods, 52, 55
credit card accounts, 99
  entering a credit card charge, finance charge,
    or credit, 122–123
  finding and resolving errors, 189–190
  making adjustments, 188–189
  reconciling a credit card account online, 188
  reconciling a paper credit card statement,
    186–187
  registers, 122

D

data files, defined, 26
dates, 50
debt accounts, adding, 93–94
Debt Reduction Planner, 244–249
Deduction Finder, 275–276
default, 70
deleting accounts, 93
Deluxe Edition, 2
deposits
  entering into the register, 112
  scheduling, 137–138
depreciation, 70, 157
dialog boxes, 30
Direct Connect, 52, 55
downloading quotes, 203
downloading transactions, 18, 19, 52
  renaming rules, 128–130
  setting preferences, 105
drop-down list boxes, 30

E

EasyStep Loan Setup Wizard, 89–92, 94–97
equity, 70
escrow, watching for discrepancies, 199–200
exiting Quicken, 25–26
Express Web Connect, 52, 55

F

filtering transactions, 117
Find and Replace dialog box, 197–198
folders, defined, 26
follow-up flags, 120
fonts, in the register, 102

G

general alerts, 165
  setting up, 166
goals, setting, 14–15, 256
graphs
  creating, 151–152
  creating from budgets, 254–255
  Portfolio Value Vs. Cost Basis, 209
  viewing payment graphs, 164
  See also reports
Growth Of $10,000 utility, 206–208

H

Help, 23–25
hiding accounts, 94
Home & Business Edition, 2
home equity loans, 154
  including tax and insurance payments, 160
  See also loans

Home menu, 40
Home page
amending views, 35–37
changing the Account Bar, 34–35
customizing, 32
managing accounts, 37–41
modifying the main view, 33
setting preferences, 44–46
Home tab, 16–18
home valuation, 157
house accounts, 86
setting up a house account with a mortgage,
87–92

I

importing, from Microsoft Money, 25–26
improvements, recording, 156–157
income
adding, 12–13
adding paycheck information, 13–14
inflation, estimating, 232
installing Quicken, 3–5
InstallShield Wizard, 3
interest, 70
interest rate, 70
adjusting, 158–159
interest-only loans, 161–163
See also loans
Internet service providers (ISPs), 53–54
Internet window, 27
investing alerts, 165
setting up, 166
Investing center. *See* Investing tab
Investing menu, 41
Investing tab
Asset Allocation subtab, 210–214
Average Annual Return tool, 208–210
Buy/Sell Preview tool, 217

Capital Gains Estimator, 217–219
customizing, 203
customizing the portfolio view, 214–216
displaying, 73
Growth Of $10,000 utility, 206–208
Online Portfolio subtab, 216
online research tools, 220–222
opening the Account Overview subtab, 202
Performance subtab, 206–210
Portfolio Analyzer, 219–220
Portfolio subtab, 214–224
Portfolio Value Vs. Cost Basis graph, 209
reviewing investing activity, 210
tracking investments, 71
types of investment accounts, 70–71
investment accounts
adding, 20–22
entering holdings, 76–81
including in planning, 234
placeholders, 76, 80
preference settings, 100
reconciling to a paper statement, 189–190
Security List, 222–224
setting up, 72–76
types of, 70–71
updating prices manually from a paper
statement, 192
See also 401(k) accounts; 403(b) accounts;
Quicken.com; single mutual fund accounts
investments, 70
IRA accounts, 70
setting up, 72–76
Itemized Deduction Estimator, 276–278

K

Keogh accounts, 70
keyboard shortcuts, 28–29
alternative mappings of shortcut keys, 46

L

liability accounts, 87
Debt Reduction Planner, 244–249
linking an asset to, 155
linking multiple liability accounts to one asset
account, 156
updating, 197
Lifetime Planner. *See* Planning tab
list boxes, 30
list windows, 28
living expenses, 239–241
Loan Calculator, 174–175
loans
adjusting the interest rate, 158–159
balloon payments, 161–163
changing loan balances, 159–160
Debt Reduction Planner, 244–249
EasyStep Loan Setup Wizard, 89–92, 94–97
including tax and insurance payments, 160
interest-only loans, 161–163
making additional principal payments, 161–162
printing a loan summary, 163–164
types of loans you can track in Quicken, 154
Update Balance dialog, 157
viewing payment graphs, 164
See also liability accounts
Loans and Debt Planner, 238
See also loans
locking, memorized payees, 131

M

market value, 70
Maximize button, 18
memorized payees
adding renaming rules from the Memorized
Payee List, 129
changing, 127–128

memorized payees *(cont.)*
  creating, 126–127
  creating and memorizing a split transaction
      using percentages, 130–131
  locking, 131
  merging and renaming payees, 130
Menu bar, 16, 28
menus
  Classic menus, 40–42
  defined, 28
Microsoft Money, importing from, 25–26
Minimize button, 16
minus sign (–) key, 107
mortgages, 154
  including tax and insurance payments, 160
  setting up a house account with a mortgage, 87–92
  watching for escrow discrepancies, 199–200
  See also loans; reverse mortgages
Multiple Security Charting, 220–221
mutual funds, 70
  See also single mutual fund accounts

N

net worth, creating a net worth report, 173
Net Worth menu, 41
Net Worth tab, 86–87
  adding vehicle accounts, 92–93
  displaying, 87
  setting up a house account with a mortgage,
      87–92
notes, 120
Notify, setting preferences, 104

O

One Step Update
  activating, 57
  Connection tab, 83

Portfolio tab, 83
Quotes tab, 82
scheduling, 214–215
setting up, 81–82
One-Click Scorecard, 221–222
online research tools, 220–222
online services
  connection methods, 55
  deciding to use online services, 53
  reconciling an online account to a paper
      statement, 178–180
  reconciling an online account to the online
      balance, 181
  scheduling repeating online payments,
      148–149
  setting up a bank account with, 7–9
  setting up online banking, 53–57
  using Quicken online, 50–52
  See also Bill Pay; security
option buttons, 30

P

passwords, 10
  changing your master password, 60
  managing, 57–61
  Password Vault, 51, 61
  strong passwords, 61
paychecks
  adding income, 12–13
  adding paycheck information, 13–14
  scheduling, 140–141
payments
  balloon payments, 161–163
  estimated tax payments, 270
  scheduling, 134–137
  scheduling repeating online payments,
      148–149
  viewing payment graphs, 164

performance, 70
personal loans, 154
  See also loans
placeholders, 76, 80
Planning menu, 42
Planning tab, 226
  associating income with an asset,
      237–238
  budgets, 251–255
  considering loans on assets, 236
  Debt Reduction Planner, 244–249
  determining your tax rate, 232
  entering expected rate of return,
      234–235
  entering expenses associated with
      assets, 237
  entering information about yourself,
      227–228
  entering other income, 231
  entering salaries and self-employment income,
      228–229
  estimating inflation, 232
  figuring living expenses, 239–241
  including checking and savings accounts,
      233–234
  including current assets, 234–236
  including investment accounts, 234
  including planned assets, 238
  Loans and Debt Planner, 238
  planning to pay for college, 241–242
  Retirement Benefits tab, 230
  savings goals, 256
  Spending Planner, 249–250
  Tax Center subtab, 271–279
  understanding the plan results, 241–243
plus sign (+) key, 107
pop-up registers, 35–36
Portfolio Analyzer, 219–220
Portfolio Value Vs. Cost Basis graph, 209

portfolios, 70
  customizing the portfolio view, 214–216
  terminology, 214
preferences
  for downloading transactions, 105
  Notify, 104
  QuickFill, 103–104
  renaming rules, 129
  setting, 44–46
  setting for registers, 100–103
  setting for reports, 148–150
  for writing checks, 104–105
Premier Edition, 2
principal, 70
printing
  amortization schedules, 96–97
  budgets, 255
  checks, 108–111
  loan summaries, 163–164
  printer setup, 120–121
  registers, 121
  scheduled transactions, 143
privacy, 10
  See also security
Property & Debt center
  adding property and debt accounts, 22–23
  See also assets; liability accounts; loans

Q

Quicken Backup, 67–68
Quicken Bill Pay, 51, 52, 61
  See also online services
Quicken Calendar, 43–45, 143–144
  color-coding information, 147
  options, 147
  showing transactions, 147
  working with specific dates, 145–146

Quicken Planner. *See* Planning tab
Quicken toolbar
  adding a report to, 172
  customizing, 204–205
Quicken.com
  setting up, 203–204
  signing out, 206
  tools, 206–207
  using, 204–206
QuickFill, setting preferences, 103–104
QuickZoom, 150

R

rate of return, 234–235
real property, 70
reconciling accounts
  activating automatic reconciliation, 188
  dealing with unrecorded items, 185–186
  finding statement discrepancies, 185–186
  for the first time, 184
  making corrections in the Statement Summary
    window, 183–184
  reconciling a manual account to a paper
    statement, 182–183
  reconciling an online account to a paper
    statement, 178–180
  reconciling an online account to the online
    balance, 181
  reconciling credit card statements, 186–189
  reconciling investment accounts, 189–196
  using a Quicken adjustment, 186–187
recurring bills, adding, 10–12
Refinance Calculator, 174
registers, 35–36
  cash accounts, 124
  changing transactions, 113
  creating scheduled transactions, 139–141

defined, 27, 99
deleting transactions, 114
differences between checking and credit card
  registers, 122
entering a credit card charge, finance charge,
  or credit, 122–123
entering checks into the register, 107–108
entering credit card payments, 124
entering deposits, 112
filtering transactions, 117
locating transactions, 116–117
opening a register, 106
printing, 121
printing checks, 108–111
restoring deleted transactions, 113
setting preferences, 100–103
sorting transactions, 118
splitting transactions, 113–115
transferring funds from one account to another,
  115–116
voiding transactions, 113–114
renaming rules, 128–130
report windows, 28
reports
  adding to the Quicken toolbar, 172
  creating, 150–151
  creating a net worth report, 173
  creating folders for saved reports, 171
  creating from budgets, 254–255
  customizing an existing report, 166–170
  deleting and moving folders and reports, 171
  mini-reports, 151–152
  recalling a saved report, 172
  renaming a folder or report, 171
  saving a customized report, 170–171
  setting preferences, 148–150
  tax reports, 274
  See also graphs

Reports menu, 42
research, online tools, 220–222
retirement
  Retirement Benefits tab, 230
  Social Security retirement age, 228
  See also 401(k) accounts; 403(b) accounts;
    Planning tab
Retirement Calculator, 251
reverse mortgages, 154
  See also loans; mortgages

S

sales tax, 269
savings accounts, 99
  including in planning, 233–234
savings goals, 256
scheduled transactions, 132
  creating from a register, 139–141
  frequency, 136
  incoming transactions, 140
  outgoing transactions, 139
  printing, 143
  repeating online payments, 148–149
  scheduling a transaction, 133–139
  scheduling One Step Update, 214–215
  working with, 142–143
searching
  Find and Replace dialog box,
    197–198
  for transactions, 116–117
securities, 70
  entering costs for, 79–81
  Security List, 222–224
  Watch List, 222, 223–224
security, 10, 52–53
Services menu, 42

Setup tab, 15–16
shortcut keys, 28–29
  alternative mappings of, 46
single mutual fund accounts
  creating, 85–86
  reconciling accounts, 190–193
sizing handles, 18
sliders, 30
Social Security, retirement age, 228
sorting
  bill and income reminders, 143
  transactions, 118
Spending Planner, 249–250
spinners, 30
split transactions
  creating, 113–115
  creating and memorizing using percentages,
    130–131
spyware, 53
  See also security
Starter Edition, 2
starting Quicken, 5
  adding income, 12–13
  adding paycheck information, 13–14
  adding recurring bills, 10–12
  creating a quick start shortcut, 6–7
  setting goals, 14–15
  setting up a bank account manually, 9–10
  setting up a bank account with online
    services, 7–9
  setting up Quicken for the first time, 6
Statement Summary window
  entering items from, 185
  making corrections in, 183–184
stocks, 70
sweep accounts, 76

T

tabs, 30
tax alerts, 165
  setting up, 166
Tax Category Audit, 274, 275
Tax Center, 271
  assigning tax-related expenses, 272, 273
  taxable income, 273
  See also Deduction Finder; Itemized Deduction
    Estimator; Tax Withholding Estimator
Tax Planner, 258–259
  deducting state sales tax, 269
  Details worksheet, 270
  entering adjustments to income, 266
  entering capital gains, 263–264
  entering income, 261
  entering interest, dividend, and business
    income, 262–263
  entering options, 259–261
  entering standard and itemized deductions,
    266–268
  estimated tax payments, 270
  updating federal withholdings, 269–270
  working with other income or losses,
    264–265
  See also Deduction Finder; Itemized Deduction
    Estimator; Tax Withholding Estimator
tax rate, 232
tax reports, 274
tax tools, 273–274
Tax Withholding Estimator, 278–279
tax-line assignments, 66
  in categories, 262
terminology, 26–28, 70, 99–100, 214
text boxes, 30
Ticker Symbol Lookup, 22–23, 76–77

title bar, 16, 30
toolbars
  defined, 28
  See also Quicken toolbar
transaction lists, defined, 27
transactions
  adding a follow-up flag or note, 120
  attaching digital images to, 118–119
  changing, 113
  defined, 27
  deleting, 114, 128
  filtering, 117
  locating, 116–117
  restoring deleted transactions, 113
  scheduled transactions, 132–143
  showing on your calendar, 147
  sorting, 118
  terminology, 99–100
  voiding, 113–114
  See also downloading transactions

transfers, 115–116
  scheduling, 138–139
Trojan horses, 53
  See also security

U

Update Balance dialog, 157
upgrading Quicken, 2–3
usernames, 10

V

vehicle accounts, 86, 154
  adding, 92–93
  See also loans
versions, 2, 4
views
  adding, 33
  amending, 35–37

deleting, 33
  modifying, 33
viruses, 53
  See also security

W

Watch List, 222, 223–224
Web Connect, 52
What If dialog box, 248–249
window border, 18
windows, 27, 30
Windows Clipboard, 121
worms, 53
  See also security